A Daily Devotional of

God's Unending Love

through the Psalms, Proverbs and New Testament

Mindi Colchico

Copyright © 2013 by Mindi Colchico

*A Daily Devotional of God's Unending Love
through the Psalms, Proverbs and New Testament*
by Mindi Colchico

Printed in the United States of America

ISBN 9781628394573

All rights reserved solely by the author. The author guarantees all contents are original and do not infringe upon the legal rights of any other person or work. No part of this book may be reproduced in any form without the permission of the author. The views expressed in this book are not necessarily those of the publisher.

Unless otherwise indicated, Bible quotations are taken from The New International Version of the Bible. Copyright © 1973, 1978, 1984 by International Bible Society.

www.xulonpress.com

INTRODUCTION

Scholars say the Psalms were written over the course of approximately 1,000 years by various authors. Many of the Psalms were written during the time of King David, a majority by David himself. The word "psalm" literally means "twang" or "pluck," referring to the instruments used to accompany singing of the psalms. There are psalms of praise, sorrow, wonder and questions. They were written with passion and emotion and are intended for those who choose to believe in God and walk according to His precepts. To appreciate and receive the full meaning of each psalm, it is beneficial to read them aloud. The atmosphere becomes filled with the presence of God when we do this. He loves to hear our praises and worship. If it says shout, then we should shout; raise our hands, then we should raise our hands. We are so blessed by the words of praise when we speak them to the Lord.

A critical part of this spiritual exercise includes prayer because it brings us into His presence where He reveals Himself to us. It is a time to be open and honest, for there is no pretense with Him. When we acknowledge our sin and ask forgiveness, it brings freedom of thought and releases us from guilt; clears our minds and opens a path of communication with our Creator. It is my hope that this devotional makes the Psalms, Proverbs and New Testament come alive in a way that brings greater understanding of their relevance to our lives today.

My journey for this devotional began in 2008 when the pastor at my church suggested we read one chapter of Proverbs every day and choose a verse to memorize. Scripture memorization is something that has eluded me in my Christian walk and so I decided to give it a try. As I did this, I wrote what the verse meant to me and how Christians overall could apply it to their daily lives. After a few days, I emailed a friend about what I was doing and she asked me to share my writing with several young people she was mentoring at the time. So I began writing a Verse of the Day. After Proverbs, I went through the entire New Testament*. Then the journey ended, or so I thought. In 2011, I felt the Holy Spirit urge me to read through the Psalms with the goal of writing a yearly devotional. It has been a labor of love which has brought me to the very throne of God and given me the realization that His love knows no boundaries and His mercies endure forever. The purpose of this book is not to isolate anyone or pit believers in Christ against non-believers, for we are all sinners saved by the grace of our Lord Jesus Christ. This is a culmination of a lifelong journey of prayer and study of God's word. My only desire is that everyone who reads the pages of this book experiences a closer walk with the Father, Son, and Holy Spirit.

PREFACE

I have known Mindi for almost five years now, and am still in awe of how the Lord brought us together as friends and sisters. She is an amazing woman of God, who has a passion for life and is talented and knowledgeable in many areas. She loves Jesus, and shows it with her compassion and generosity to so many people. It has been an honor and a privilege to share a small part with her in writing this book. As we worked together editing the book, we spent many hours in the Word, reading scriptures out loud from Genesis to Revelation. My heart was so full of God – His love, His grace, and His mercy for us – His love letter from beginning to end. As we were reading through the Book of Revelation about the river that flows out from the throne of God, I felt as if I was running to the river, jumping in and splashing in the clear, crystal, bubbling waters; totally submersed in His presence. What a joy! What refreshment! What cleansing! What healing! What freedom! The everlasting River of Life! This water is free to all who are thirsty. The Spirit and the bride say, "Come! Whoever is thirsty, let him come; and whoever wishes, let him take the free gift of the water of life."

I hope you will be blessed as you read this daily devotional; that your heart and soul will find the comfort, rest and renewal that this precious gift, the Word of God, gives to us. He loves each of us so very much. This is His love letter to you.

Noni Burak

DEDICATION

This book is dedicated to all those who call God their Father and have the privilege of being His sons and daughters!

ACKNOWLEDGEMENTS

Special thanks and appreciation to Noni Burak, Mireyah Burak, and Lucy Louis for their help in making this book possible. Without their input and suggestions, it never would have happened. Thanks also to Donna Briley for her generous spirit in supplying the picture for the cover of this book from her vast repertoire of photos!

JANUARY 1
HIS PRESENCE

Psalm 1:2-3: But his delight is in the law of the Lord, and on His law he meditates day and night. He is like a tree planted by streams of water, which yields its fruit in season and whose leaf does not wither. Whatever he does prospers.

The sky begins to brighten as the sun rises on the horizon. A new day has dawned. The air is fresh with the dew that has settled on the leaves of the trees, the flowers, and the grass, quenching their thirst and adding nutrients to the soil. As we begin our journey into the psalms, let the presence of God overtake us and fill us with His love and compassion. Let the power of the Holy Spirit guide our thoughts into the heavenly realms and teach us the spiritual truths of God. Taking time to meditate and hold fast to Him, to serve Him with all of our hearts and souls, we become like a river that receives its sustenance from a waterfall pouring over the high mountain cliff. His peace and presence flow into us, and out of His rich abundance we are filled to overflowing and discover who we are meant to be in Him.

Read Psalm 1
Joshua 22:5, Psalm 36:8-9, Isaiah 66:12-14

Heavenly Father, help us to slow down and live in the present moment with You by our side. Each day that goes by without contemplating You takes us down a lonely path of self-centeredness. Teach us to trust in You; to meditate on who You are and draw strength from Your presence in our lives. Amen.

JANUARY 2
OUR GOD REIGNS

Psalm 2:10-11: Therefore, you kings, be wise; be warned you rulers of the earth. Serve the Lord with fear and rejoice with trembling.

Today's psalm instructs us to be in reverent and humble fear of the God who creates all things. Rulers and kings often get puffed up with themselves when they are in powerful positions and they forget that their life is but a twinkle in all eternity. God's Word always comes to pass, and He tells us that the kings of the earth will come against His Anointed One. In the end, the Lord will install His King in Zion, make the nations His inheritance and the ends of the earth His possession. When that time comes, there will be true peace on earth, for Jesus, the Wonderful

Counselor, the Mighty God, the Prince of Peace, will be the King of kings and Lord of lords. He will establish and uphold His kingdom with justice and righteousness forever.

Read Psalm 2
Isaiah 9:6-7, Revelation 17:14

Heavenly Father, continually humble us and help us realize that we are like the grass that is here today and withers and is gone tomorrow. Help us to remember that life on this earth is very short and we should look to the eternal where there will be true peace and You will reign with complete love. Amen.

JANUARY 3
PROTECTOR AND DELIVERER

Psalm 3:3: But You are a shield around me, O Lord; You bestow glory on me and lift up my head.

Jesus has been called a crutch to lean on because Christians are too weak to stand on their own. Well, yes, that is the whole point. In our weakness, He is made strong. We need His strength and should desire it above our own. The Lord is near to all who call on Him, to all who call on Him in truth. He is God Almighty, the great I Am, the Alpha and the Omega, the beginning and the end, and only He controls and knows everything. We are unable to control the very air we breathe. We cannot stop the aging process and say, I want to remain the age that I am and never grow older! This is impossible. He is the only true Redeemer of mankind, and He protects and delivers those who call upon His name.

Read Psalm 3
Psalm 145:18, 1 John 3:19-20, Revelation 22:13

Gracious and Heavenly Father, may we never lose sight of who You are in our lives. Open our eyes to Your presence. Protect us from the temptations we face in this world and deliver us. Help us to live for You so that others may see Your light in us and they too will come to know You as their Redeemer. Amen.

JANUARY 4
QUIET TIME

Psalm 4:4: In your anger do not sin; when you are on your beds, search your hearts and be silent.

Every day we make decisions on issues and circumstances that come our way. There are times we respond in anger to situations that arise in our lives, but this accomplishes nothing except angering others. Before speaking, we should stop and consider what is happening; be quiet and say a silent prayer, for the Lord hears when we call upon Him and gives us the appropriate response. When we make a decision to follow Jesus Christ, our lives take on a different purpose. We are no longer living to satisfy ourselves. We want to please our Lord, seek His wisdom and serve others. We draw closer to our Lord as we spend time alone with Him. The end of each day is a good time to think about what the day has brought and consider whether we have been pleasing to Him. It can be a time of meditation and reflection, searching our hearts, seeking and asking Him to show us how we can do better the next day. The Lord has set the Godly apart for Himself and He hears when they call upon Him.

Read Psalm 4
Proverbs 15:1, Habakkuk 2:20, James 1:19-20

Precious Lord, we are Your creation. You made us for Your pleasure. Help us to take time out of our busy lives to come into Your presence. It is in the calm after the storm, when we are silent before You, that we hear You as You call to us. Help us to be kind, patient and loving towards others and not respond in anger, even if we feel justified in doing so. Give us the strength to look to You for answers so that we will respond appropriately in all circumstances. We thank You for this day and praise Your Holy Name. Amen.

JANUARY 5
SONS AND DAUGHTERS

Psalm 5:12: For surely, O Lord, You bless the righteous; You surround them with Your favor as with a shield.

Today's Psalm speaks of the vast distinction between good and evil. It tells us that the Lord hates all who do wrong. That is such a strong statement – that He hates – and so counter to who we know our God to be. But He is holy and He cannot look upon sin. It is against His very nature. This is why He sent His Son, Jesus Christ, who is the high priest able to save completely those who come to God through Him because He always lives to intercede for them. The world did not recognize Him, but to those who believed on His name He gave the right to become children of God. Because we are His sons and daughters, God sent the spirit of His Son into our hearts, the Spirit who calls out, "Abba, Father." So we are no longer slaves but sons and daughters; and since we are sons and daughters, God has made us also heirs. Those who do not know Him mock and revile Him and take His name in vain. The evil they do He abhors, but He looks upon them with pity and would be merciful to them immediately if they repented.

Read Psalm 5
Psalm 28:7, John 1:10-12, Acts 17:28, Galatians 4:4-7, Hebrews 7:24-25

Merciful and Holy Judge of all, bless those who do not know You that by Your blessing they will seek and find You and learn of your love for them and Your promise of eternal life. Keep and protect those who call upon Your Name. Amen.

JANUARY 6
HEAR MY CRY, LORD

Psalm 6:9: The Lord has heard my cry for mercy; the Lord accepts my prayer.

Just as the psalmist cries out to the Lord, we too have times in our lives when we feel forsaken and cry out. We may wonder if the Lord really listens to our pleas or do we have to go this journey alone. We can rest easy when we have a relationship with Him because no matter our circumstances in life, He is faithful. He is always, always there to lift us up, to walk the walk with us. Especially in our darkest hour, we have no reason to fear because He is by our side. If we make the Most High our dwelling place, then no harm will befall us; no disaster will come near our tent. He asks us to keep ourselves in His love as we wait for the mercy of our Lord Jesus Christ to bring us to eternal life.

Read Psalm 6
Psalm 3:3, Psalm 91:9-11, Jude 21

Merciful Father, thank You that You are always with us. We have no cause for fear or doubt because You are the one true God who never changes. You assure us that You are always with us, and it is so! Give us trusting hearts so we never doubt this. Amen.

JANUARY 7
OUR RIGHTEOUS GOD

Psalm 7:17: I will give thanks to the Lord because of His righteousness and will sing praise to the name of the Lord Most High.

After Adam and Eve disobeyed the Lord's command, they were banished from the Garden of Eden. The ground was cursed and by the sweat of their brow they ate food until they returned to the ground from where they had come. The snake, Satan, was cursed above all livestock and wild animals, crawled on his belly and ate dust all the days of his life. The woman was told that there would be enmity between her and the devil and that her offspring would crush his head; that in childbearing her pains would increase. The battle between good and evil began. The Lord chose a people through Abraham to be His servants and proclaim the wondrous works of their God, but they also chose to go their own way without Him. The Old Testament is filled with the Lord calling His people, instructing them in His way, giving His law and telling them the blessings they would receive if they followed Him and the curses they would endure if they forsook Him. For many years, the Lord did not speak to His people because they had gone their own way, and then the prophecies of the Old Testament were fulfilled when Jesus, the Messiah, was born. He was conceived of a virgin by the power of the Holy Spirit and was the only person ever born without sin. He is worthy of our praises for He is the Lord Most High. He has called us to serve Him, to know Him and to live with Him forever in eternity. Why some men choose to do evil and others good is a mystery we will only know when Our Lord's fullness is revealed at His coming. Until that time, the Lord answers the cry of those who believe in Him.

Read Psalm 7
Genesis 3:14-19, 2 Chronicles 24:19, Psalm 40:1, Matthew 1:20-23, Acts 10:43

Lord, have mercy on Your creation. Bless those who curse You, who say You are not the God You proclaim to be, that by Your blessings they will repent and be drawn to You who loves them as much as You love those who serve You. You are not willing that any should perish but that all should come to You and receive the gift of eternal life, where death reigns no more and You will be our Holy God for all eternity. Praise Your Holy Name. Amen.

JANUARY 8
CREATOR OF ALL THINGS

Psalm 8:3-4: When I consider Your heavens, the work of Your fingers, the moon and the stars which You have set in place, what is man that You are mindful of him, the son of man that You care for Him?

In our natural bodies we cannot fully comprehend the Creator. We must have faith that He is who He says He is and that He has created us in His image to reflect His glory. He has entrusted us with all His other creations and in return we should love and respect Him, and behold His majesty in all we see about us. No one can say that they created the sky, the moon, the fruit of the field, the animal that produces milk, the trees. We can't even stare at the sun but a few seconds without causing permanent damage to our vision, it is so powerful. Mankind did not create the vast oceans and all that they contain. Only He measured the waters in the hollow of His hand and with the breadth of His hand marked off the heavens. He held the dust of the earth in a basket and weighed the mountains on the scales and the hills in a balance. No one has understood the mind of our Lord and instructed Him as His counselor. No one among us has taught Him knowledge or showed Him the path of understanding. We are His most treasured creation. He gave us breath and life and He loves us with an everlasting love. We honor Him by taking care of all He has entrusted us with.

Read Psalm 8
Genesis 1:27, Job 6:26, Isaiah 40:12-14, Jeremiah 31:35

Lord, so often we forget that we are not our own. Help us consider our beginnings and where we come from. You have made us a little lower than the angels and entrusted us with all Your creation. Give us Your grace to live to the fullest in You and help us to be ever mindful that we were bought with a price, the blood of Jesus Christ, and in Him we have the fullness of life, both now and in the world to come. Amen.

JANUARY 9
THE LORD IS OUR REFUGE

Psalm 9:10: Those who know Your name will trust in You, for You, Lord, have never forsaken those who seek you.

Those who seek the Lord, find Him. He is a place of refuge that refreshes the weary and satisfies the faint. He knows the plans He has for us; plans to prosper and not harm us; plans to give us hope and a future.

When we call upon Him in prayer, He listens. He is the vine of life. If we remain in Him, He remains in us and we bring forth much fruit. Without Him we become like a branch broken off from the tree. We wither and die. When we remain in Him, we glorify the Father and we show ourselves to be His disciples.

Read Psalm 9:1-10
Jeremiah 29:11-13 & 31:25, John 15:5-8

Father, have mercy on all Your creation. Those who seek You and know You do not always understand why others reject You. Fill us to overflowing with Your compassion and love that we may lead others to Christ by our example, so they too may share in Your goodness and grace. Help us preach the gospel by our actions, by the way we live and serve You, and use words when necessary. Amen.

JANUARY 10
LET NOT MAN TRIUMPH

Psalm 9:19: Arise, O Lord, let not man triumph; let the nations be judged in Your presence.

We want to have control over our lives and often over the lives of others, but we forget that we are not really the ones in control; He is. There is no one holy like the Lord, no Rock like our God. When we entered this world, we brought nothing with us. When we leave this earth, we take nothing with us. Only He chose our time of birth, who we were born to, and where we were born. He is the One who appoints the time of our death. He did this so that we would seek Him and perhaps reach out for Him and find Him, though He is not far from each one of us. Unbelief causes people to curse Him. It causes nations to fall, because without an anchor there is no stability. To think that there is not a God who is just and who judges us all is arrogant, for we will all stand before God's judgment seat. One day every knee shall bow and every tongue confess that Jesus is the Lord of all, and we will each give account to God for our lives.

Read Psalm 9:11-20
1 Samuel 2:3, Acts 17:25-27, Romans 14:11-12, Philippians 2:10-11

O God of all creation, we pray for our nation. We have turned our backs on You by going our own way and seeking pleasure instead of You who provides all things. Have mercy on us, Lord, and bring us back to our beginnings when we trusted and worshiped only You. Amen.

JANUARY 11
WHERE ARE YOU, LORD?

Psalm 10:1: Why, O Lord, do You stand far off? Why do You hide Yourself in times of trouble?

When we look at the world, and even our own lives and circumstances, and those around us, the question we might ask is: How can there be a loving God when heartache and wickedness abound? If He is there, why doesn't He just take it all away and bring the peace and love that we all long for? Ever since the fall of mankind, there has been an enemy of our souls who wants nothing more than to destroy us and take us away from our Heavenly Father. He fights with all of his might to make God's creation doubt His existence. But the Lord laughs at the wicked for He knows their day is coming. We do not need to worry when evil abounds. Even though we are in the world, we are not of the world. Jesus has given us His Word and He brings us through the storms of life if we trust Him to do so.

Read Psalm 10:1-11
Psalm 37:13, Proverbs 3:5, John 17:14-16

Heavenly Father, who sees all things and knows the hearts and intentions of each of us, may we never doubt You. Even when all seems lost, give us insight into Your goodness and draw us closer to You. Amen.

JANUARY 12
THE LORD HEARS OUR CRIES

Psalm 10:17: You hear, O Lord, the desire of the afflicted; You encourage them, and You listen to their cry.

There is a song which begins with the words, "Our God is an awesome God. He reigns from heaven on high." As followers of the Lord Jesus Christ, we can be assured that no matter the circumstances in life, no matter what political party or persons run the nations of the world, we have a King in heaven who hears our cries. Once we come to know the God of Heaven and the One who sits at His right hand to intercede for us, we begin to pray with the help of the Holy Spirit, who is our Counselor, the Spirit of Truth, who will be with us forever. The world cannot accept Him because it neither sees Him nor knows Him but for those who do know Him, He lives with us and in us. He encourages us. We have no fear of rejection from Him. We never have to wonder if He's too busy to listen because He never is. Our frustration sometimes comes when we don't think He hears us. He knows what is best and when we wait upon Him, He answers according to what He knows we need.

Read Psalm 10:12-18
John 14:17, Revelation 20:12

Father, forgive us our sins and cleanse us continually that we might walk with You and boldly proclaim Your love and righteousness in all the earth, that all who hear will repent from their sin and turn to You, the true Giver of Life eternal. Amen.

JANUARY 13
WE WILL SEE HIS FACE

Psalm 11:7: For the Lord is righteous; He loves justice; upright men will see His face.

Scripture gives those who believe in God Almighty the knowledge that no matter how wicked men can be, there is a God in Heaven who sees all things and who one day will judge those things, both great and small. When we are hurt in some way, or perhaps a friend or family member has broken their trust with us, we should tell them, but more importantly we need to tell our Lord because He knows our thoughts and intents and He judges with true justice. Wickedness and death entered the world by the disobedience of one man, Adam. One day, wickedness and the curse of death will no longer exist because of one man, Jesus. The throne of God and of the Lamb will be in the city and His servants will serve Him. They will see His face and His name will be on their foreheads. They will not need the light of a lamp or the light of the sun, for the Lord God will give them light and they will reign forever and ever in His kingdom.

Read Psalm 11
Romans 5:17-19, Revelation 22:3-4

Heavenly Father, thank You for the assurance that no matter how much wickedness is about us, You love justice and when all is said and done upright men will see Your face. Help us to look to You for real justice and thank You for Your righteousness that overcomes all. Amen.

JANUARY 14
REFINED AND TESTED

Psalm 12:6: And the words of the Lord are flawless, like silver refined in a furnace of clay, purified seven times.

In order to get pure silver, it goes through a refining process that squeezes every other impurity out. Once the process is complete, the silver has many fine qualities. Many times, this is what happens to us. The Lord refines and tests us in the furnace of affliction. He never told us that serving Him was going to be easy. We are to be joyful in hope, patient in affliction and faithful in prayer. There are times we also harbor things in our hearts. God's word is flawless, and He searches and reveals those things to us so we can ask forgiveness and be purified from all unrighteousness. He puts our sins in the sea of forgetfulness and remembers them no more. This is a life-long process we go through until the One who died for all appears in the clouds. Then we will be changed in a moment, in the twinkling of an eye, from the perishable to the imperishable, from the mortal to the immortal.

Read Psalm 12
Isaiah 48:10, Romans 12:12, 1 Corinthians 15:50-54

Father, when we sometimes give up on life, enter in and lift us high above it all with Your mighty words that proclaim You and You alone are the true God and everything done in darkness will one day be revealed by the light of Your glorious presence. Amen.

JANUARY 15
UNFAILING LOVE

Psalm 13:5: But I trust in Your unfailing love; my heart rejoices in Your salvation.

There are times we have prayed until we were blue in the face with no apparent answer and have become distraught and filled with worry and unbelief. This is such a lie from the enemy of our souls because no matter the answer to our prayers, the Lord still sits upon His throne. He hears every prayer. He sees each tear that falls and collects them in a bottle. As believers in Christ, we can never doubt that He is with us in our trials and struggles. If we lack wisdom, we should ask God, who gives generously to all without finding fault. But when we ask, we must believe and not doubt because he who doubts is like a wave of the sea, blown and tossed by the wind. We will not receive anything then, for a double-minded man is unstable in all he does. When we delight greatly in the Lord, our souls rejoice for He clothes us with garments of salvation and arrays us in a robe of righteousness.

Read Psalm 13
Psalm 56:8, Isaiah 61:10, James 1:5-8

Merciful Father, as one man once cried out to You, Help thou my unbelief, we too cry out to You that You would increase our faith. In times of loneliness and tears, touch us by the power of Your presence and give us a renewed assurance that You are by our side. Amen.

JANUARY 16
THE FOOL'S HEART

Psalm 14:1: The fool says in his heart, there is no God. They are corrupt. Their deeds are vile; there is no one who does good.

What a sad state of affairs when men and women forsake the living God and believe He does not exist. What folly, indeed! We are then left to our own devices. Without God, we are self-centered. Even when we think our intentions are honorable, we often put ourselves first. We can say He does not exist; it is all a figment of our imagination; we don't need God; we can do life alone. If we fulfill all the goals we set, when we die it all goes with us to the grave. We are soon forgotten and all that we worked for goes to another. When we don't believe in God, we have no hope that there is more to life than setting goals and accomplishing them. Those who believe know what they hope for. It is by faith that we understand the universe was formed at God's command and that what is seen was not made out of what was visible. Without faith, it is impossible to please God because anyone who comes to Him must believe that He exists and that He rewards those who earnestly seek Him. We can only gain understanding of God when we are enlightened by His Holy Spirit, who was sent after Jesus rose from the dead and ascended into Heaven. Yes, there is a God. He is the living God and beside Him there is no other.

Read Psalm 14
Deuteronomy 4:39, Galatians 3:11-12, Hebrews 11:1-3 & 6

Merciful God of all creation, You have given us life. Help us to realize that without You we are truly nothing and that fullness of life comes from You. We pray that You give us revelation of Yourself, Almighty God, who was, who is and who is to come, world without end. Amen.

JANUARY 17
WHO MAY LIVE ON YOUR HOLY HILL?

Psalm 15:5b: He who does these things will never be shaken.

When Jesus died on the cross, He fulfilled His purpose for coming to earth. The sins of the world were thrust upon Him. He sacrificed His life for everyone so that we might become the righteousness of God. As He was hanging on the cross, He was in such agony, yet our Heavenly Father was pleased with Him. He did this because we can never be good enough to stand before the Lord. Jesus changed all of that and we now have full access to our Father, if we believe in His Son. Jesus did not come to change God's law but to fulfill it and in that fulfillment He expects, even commands, that we live righteously and treat others as we ourselves want to be treated. So who may stand on God's Holy Hill? He whose walk is blameless; who does what is righteous and speaks the truth from his heart and has no slander on his tongue; who does his neighbor no wrong and casts no slur on his fellowman; who despises a vile man but honors those who fear the Lord; who keeps his oath even when it hurts; who lends his money without interest and who does not accept a bribe against the innocent. We can do all of these things through Jesus Christ, and when we do we will live on His Holy Hill.

Read Psalm 15
Matthew 5:17-18, 2 Corinthians 5:21

Thank You, Father, for Your promises; for the truth of Your word. As we journey through the psalms, teach us how to live more fully for You. Amen.

JANUARY 18
SECURE IN THE LORD

Psalm 16:11: You have made known to me the path of life; You will fill me with joy in Your presence, with eternal pleasures at Your right hand.

Life is full of hope when we trust in the God of all creation. He promises to counsel us. He promises to hold us secure. Though good and bad happen to all of us, when we hold onto God, especially in the bad times – and we all experience those – He is the One constant we can be sure of. He never falters. He never fails. When doubts arise, we can cry out to Him to help our unbelief. He has given us the key that opens the door to eternal life. That key is Jesus Christ. He is the immovable anchor for our eternal souls, and we are firm and secure in Him.

Read Psalm 16
Mark 9:24, Hebrews 6:19

Our hope is in You, Heavenly Father. Sometimes our struggles seem so overwhelming and we think we need to take matters into our own hands but when we gaze up to Your throne and realize that it is You who gives us strength and help, we can have peace and joy knowing that You guide us through all adversity. We need You, Father. Help us. Amen.

JANUARY 19
HE ANSWERS

Psalm 17:6: I call on you, O God, for You will answer me; give ear to me and hear my prayer.

During the time when the Philistines ruled over Israel, there was a certain couple whom the Lord chose to have a son. He was a Nazirite, set apart to God, and no razor was to come upon his head. His name was Samson and the Lord chose him to begin the deliverance of Israel from the hands of the Philistines. He was a man of great strength. For seven days during their wedding feast, his wife sobbed and begged him to reveal the secret of a riddle he had told, which he did. He struck down 30 men from Ashkelon, stripped them of their belongings and gave their clothes to those who had solved the riddle. His wife was taken from him and given to another. He was so angry he caught 300 foxes and tied them tail to tail in pairs. He fastened a torch to every pair of tails, lit the torches and let the foxes loose in the standing grain of the Philistines, which burned up the shocks, together with the vineyards and olive groves. He was bound with ropes for what he had done but the ropes on his arms became like charred flax and the bindings dropped from his hands. Finding a fresh jawbone of a donkey, he grabbed it and struck down a thousand men. Sometime later he fell in love with a woman in the Valley of Sorek whose name was Delilah. The rulers of the Philistines went to her and she finally convinced Samson to tell her the secret of his great strength. Delilah put him to sleep on her lap and called a man to shave off the seven braids of his hair and his strength left him. The Philistines seized him and gouged out his eyes. They bound him with bronze shackles and set him to grind in the prison. But the hair on his head began to grow again. The rulers were offering a great sacrifice to Dagon their god and wanted to make sport of Samson. When they brought him to the temple, He asked to be put between the pillars that supported the temple so he could lean against them. He then prayed to the Lord, "O Sovereign Lord, remember me. Please strengthen me just once more and let me with one blow get revenge on the Philistines for my two eyes. Let me die with the Philistines." He then put his right hand on one pillar and his left on the other and pushed with all his might and down came the temple on the rulers and all the people in it. He killed many more that day when he died than while he lived. This all happened during a time when God destroyed His enemies, and He heard Samson's prayer and answered. Because of Jesus, He now extends His mercy to all who call upon Him. Prayer is what brings us into the presence of God. Even when we have strayed, He answers when we humble ourselves before Him.

Read Psalm 17
Judges 13:2-6; 14:16-17, 19-20; 15:4-5, 14-15; 16:4-5, 17-30; 1Timothy 1:15-16

Heavenly Father, you heard Samson's prayer and answered. We know that when Jesus came things changed and You extended Your grace to everyone. We also know that You judge by the heart and answer according to Your will. We pray for the power of Your Spirit to guide us. Help us to put our trust in You and be ever mindful of Your love and mercy. Amen.

JANUARY 20
NO OTHER GOD

Psalm 18:6: In my distress I called to the Lord; I cried to my God for help. From His temple He heard my voice; my cry came before Him, into His ears.

King David had just been delivered from the hands of his enemies. The God whom David cried out to is the same God we serve today. He loves all of His creation but He does not force Himself on anyone. He gives us free will to choose Him or not. He answers those who believe and call on His name. There is no God like the God of Abraham, Isaac and Jacob, who rides on the heavens to help us and on the clouds in His majesty. He is worthy of praise and trust. He is ever present in time of trouble. Love Him. Serve Him. Know Him. He is our great and mighty Father. Among the gods there is none like Him.

Read Psalm 18:1-15
Deuteronomy 33:26-27, 2 Samuel 7:22, Psalm 86:8

Father, You know the thoughts and intents of all who walk on this earth. You know those who love You and those who do not. Help us pray for those who do not know You that they might receive salvation and dwell eternally in Your presence. Amen.

JANUARY 21
HE PROVIDES

Psalm 18:21: For I have kept the ways of the Lord; I have not done evil by turning from my God.

One day God tested Abraham. He told him to take Isaac, the son whom he loved, and go to the region of Moriah. He asked Abraham to sacrifice Isaac as a burnt offering. We are not told what emotions Abraham had at this request, only that early the next morning he got up and saddled his donkey and took his son with him. After he had cut enough wood, he set out for the place God told him about. In their travels, his son said, "The fire and wood are here but where is the lamb for the burnt offering?" Abraham answered, "God Himself will provide the lamb for the burnt offering." When they reached the mountain, Abraham bound his son and laid him on the altar. He reached out his hand and took the knife to slay his son, but the angel of the Lord called out to him from heaven, "Do not lay a hand on the boy. Now I know that you fear God because you have not withheld from me your son, your only son." When Abraham looked up, there in a thicket he saw a ram caught by its horns, and he sacrificed it as a burnt offering instead of his son. Abraham knew that God does not require human sacrifice but he was still obedient and knew if he was faithful that God would be faithful in return. The lesson we can take away from this story is to trust the Lord when He tells us to do something, for He always provides.

Read Psalm 18:16-24
Genesis 22:1-14, Psalm 34:9

Lord, open the eyes of all Your creation to see the majesty of who You are and how much You love us. You are vast beyond our comprehension. You spoke the world into existence and You know everything about it and everyone who has ever lived in it. Keep us, protect us and watch over us. Help us to always trust You, even when we don't understand. Amen.

JANUARY 22
THE ONLY TRUE ONE

Psalm 18:30-31: As for God, His way is perfect; the word of the Lord is flawless. He is a shield for all who take refuge in Him. For who is God besides the Lord? And who is the Rock except our God?

The armor of God gives us strength and makes our way perfect. His shield gives us victory over all of our battles. He is trustworthy and His word is flawless. When we trust people, we take for granted that what they tell us is true. There are times, though, when the ones we trust most let us down. It is never this way with the Lord. He means what He says and He says what He means. He does not change like shifting shadows. We never have to doubt what He says is the truth. Our Lord prepares us throughout our lifetime to become perfect through Him, in order to show His glory. When we trust Him, He leads us down the perfect path. We should not hesitate to follow Him when we know He is directing us to an unfamiliar place. He will not lead us astray. In His hand is the life of every creature and the breath of all mankind. With His help, we can advance against a troop. With our God, we can scale a wall.

Read Psalm 18:25-42
Job 12:10, Jeremiah 9:5, James 1:17

Lord, when we doubt You, draw us nearer to You. We are but flesh and have many frailties and faults. Others let us down when we thought we could count on them, but You are always faithful. Help us to keep that knowledge in our hearts that we might trust You unconditionally. Amen.

JANUARY 23
DELIVERANCE

Psalm 18:46: The Lord lives! Praise be to my Rock! Exalted be God my Savior!

When David was delivered from the hands of his enemies and from King Saul, he was made ruler and king over the nation of Israel and Judah. His heart was so full of God's mercy and grace, all he could do was shout praises to Him. This same God also sustains us. He delivered us from death and the grave through the gift of His Son, Jesus Christ. The sting of death is sin and the power of sin is the law, but thanks be to God He gives us the victory through our Lord Jesus Christ. He knows our weaknesses, forgives us of all of our sins and has prepared a place for us in eternity with Him. Let's shout praises to our mighty God for His deliverance!

Read Psalm18:43-50
Joel 2:32, 1 Corinthians 15:54-56, 2 Corinthians 1:9-10

Almighty Father, who sits on Your throne in the heavenly realms, increase our faith daily as we walk with You. Be our rear guard and walk before us to make the way of deliverance from all the plans that the enemy of our souls makes for us. Thank You that You are our Deliverer and Protector. Amen.

JANUARY 24
THE GLORY OF GOD

Psalm 19:1: The heavens declare the glory of God; the skies proclaim the work of His hands.

Today's psalm gives us a glimpse of the glory and goodness of God. When we look into the sky and see billowing clouds that wrap up the water yet do not burst under its weight, the rising and the setting sun, the moon and stars, His presence is evident. He marks out the horizon on the face of the waters for a boundary between light and darkness. By His word, He spoke the world into existence; He spread out the northern skies over empty space and suspended the earth upon nothing. He is trustworthy. His ordinances are more precious than gold. This is an infinitesimal description of the God whom we serve. He forgives us of our sins. He calls us to Him and promises to always be by our side. He is the living God who endures forever. His kingdom will not be destroyed, nor will his dominion ever end.

Read Psalm 19
Leviticus 18:4-5, Job 26:7-14, Daniel 6:26-27

Heavenly Father, who reigns in heaven on high, lift us into Your presence and increase our faith that we may walk with blessed assurance that You are always with us no matter what the situation. Help us to take one day at a time, to live in the present and trust You with all of our hearts, minds, souls and spirits. Amen.

JANUARY 25
OUR PROTECTOR

Psalm 20:6: Now I know that the Lord saves His anointed. He answers him from His holy heaven with the saving power of His right hand.

Animals intuitively protect their young, such as a hen gathering her chicks under her wings or a mother bear keeping watch over her cubs. Parents go to great lengths to protect their children from harm. Walls are built around entire cities for protection. In days gone by, motes surrounded castles to keep the enemy from entering. We even build walls around our hearts to protect ourselves from being hurt because we cannot bear the thought of going through such pain again and again. But there is no protection on earth that rivals what we receive from our Heavenly Father. His love is patient and kind. It rejoices with the truth and always protects, always trusts, always hopes and always perseveres. As we journey through life, He is with us. He watches over us, never letting us wander far from His chosen path. Even when we forget Him, He waits patiently for us to return to His everlasting arms. Those who take refuge in Him sing for joy. He spreads His protection over them so that those who love His name may rejoice in Him.

Read Psalm 20
Psalm 5:11, 1 Corinthians 13:4-7

Heavenly Father, our strength and our salvation come from You alone. Help us to keep You uppermost in our thoughts as we journey through each day. In our weakness, protect us and spread your wings over us. When we fall, pick us up and guide us in all Your ways. Amen.

JANUARY 26
VICTORY

Psalm 21:6: Surely You have granted him eternal blessings and made him glad with the joy of Your presence.

King David was a man after God's own heart. Even though he stumbled, the Lord forgave him. David was victorious in the battles he fought because he sought and trusted the Lord. There are many examples of victory in the Old Testament. The Lord fed the children of Israel with manna after they fled from Egypt. He brought down the walls of Jericho at the sound of a trumpet. He gave Samson water in the hollow of his jaw when he was thirsty. We too can be victorious in our battles when we seek the One who lives in our heart, when we ask Him to enter in. The final victory comes in knowing the Almighty One who reigns forever and ever. He has swallowed up death and wipes away the tears from all faces, and He removes the disgrace of His people from all the earth.

Read Psalm 21
Exodus 16:31-32, Joshua 6:20, Judges 15:19 (KJV), Isaiah 25:8

There's a hymn with the words, "Victory in Jesus, our Savior forever; He sought me and He bought me with His redeeming blood." We thank You, Lord, for the ultimate victory over death because of Jesus. Give us strength and wisdom to overcome the battles of life until the day we enter your eternal glory. Amen.

JANUARY 27
DESPAIR

Psalm 22:1: My God, my God, why have you forsaken me? Why are You so far from saving me, so far from the words of my groaning?

Jesus' crucifixion was foretold in the verses of today's scripture. When He walked this earth as a man, He was continually in the presence of God the Father, but as He hung on the cross, battered, beaten and bruised, with a crown of thorns on His head, His blood dripping down to the ground for the sins of the world, the Father turned away from Him because He could not look upon sin. Jesus was not forsaken long, though, for the Father heard His cry. Jesus took His final breath and said, "It is finished," and God's eternal plan for salvation was complete. After His resurrection, He ascended into the clouds to be with the Father, where He intercedes for those who call upon His name.

Read Psalm 22:1-18
Matthew 27:45-46, Mark 16:19, Luke 24:44-47, Romans 8:34

Lord, help us to continually remember that You and You alone have brought salvation to a fallen world and that You love all of Your creation. When we are sad, give us Your joy. When everything around us is dark, be the light of our life, so that we might go forward each day in Your strength and find solace in the knowledge that You are with us even when we despair. Amen.

JANUARY 28
HOPE

Psalm 22:27-28: All the ends of the earth will remember and turn to the Lord, and all the families of the nations will bow down before Him, for dominion belongs to the Lord and He rules over the nations.

As Jesus hung on the cross and cried, "It is finished," those who followed Him felt hopeless and abandoned. The One they thought had come to set up His earthly kingdom and save them was now dead. But it was only Friday, and Sunday was acoming! It was a glorious day when Jesus rose from the dead. Hope was restored for they knew that all He told them was true. During His lifetime, Jesus revealed His Heavenly Father – our Heavenly Father – and we can trust that He rules from His throne on high. No matter the schemes that man devises, He is still in control, even of the nations. He has a perfect plan and He will fulfill it in His timing.

Read Psalm 22:19-31
Matthew 28:5-6, John 19:30

Father, thank You for Your precious word, the Bible. Give us a measure of faith to trust and believe that You order the footsteps of those who know You and that You will never lead us astray. Amen.

JANUARY 29
HE RESTORES MY SOUL

Psalm 23:3: He restores my soul. He guides me in paths of righteousness for His name's sake.

To restore something is to put back what has been taken away. Job was blameless and upright. He feared God and shunned evil. He had seven sons and three daughters and owned many sheep, camels, oxen, donkeys, and had a large number of servants. Early in the morning he sacrificed a burnt offering for each of his children in case they had sinned and cursed God in their hearts. Through no fault of his own, everything was taken away from him by tragic events, but not once did he blame or curse God. His three friends, who supposedly came to comfort him, accused him of doing something to cause these things to happen. Even his wife told him to curse God and die. He was afflicted with painful sores from the soles of his feet to the top of his head. He took a piece of broken pottery and scraped himself with it as he sat among the ashes. He cursed the day of his birth. After long discourses with his friends, he proclaimed that God understands for He views the ends of the earth and sees everything under the heavens. The Almighty was with Job this entire time, and though his first sons and daughters could not be replaced, the Lord blessed the latter part of Job's life more than the first. He restored his sheep, camels, oxen and donkeys and he had seven other sons and three daughters. After this, he lived 140 years and died old and full of years. This is a heart-rending story of a man who never lost faith in God and who, in the end, was given back more than he had lost. We may never have an experience as extreme as Job but we will have things and loved ones taken from us. During these times, may we remember that the Lord leads us beside quiet waters and He restores our souls.

Read Psalm 23
Job 1:1-3, 2:7-8, 3:1, 28:23-24, 42:12-13, 42:16-17

Lord, restore that which was been taken from us. Increase our faith so that we will never lose hope when tragedy comes our way. Fill our hearts to overflowing with Your presence and Your love. Give us clean hands and a pure heart so that we may receive a blessing and vindication from You, our Savior. Amen.

JANUARY 30
THE KING OF GLORY

Psalm 24:1-2: The earth is the Lord's and everything in it, the world and all who live in it, for He founded it upon the seas and established it upon the waters.

Our God is the Creator of everything. Imagine! We can have a real and personal relationship with the One who created and knows everything. He knows the sun, the moon, and calls the stars by name. He speaks every language. He knows the name of every animal and tree on earth, and every human being who has ever lived and ever will live. We are so finite, yet we think we know so much. When we believe in Jesus, our horizon expands. We come to know Him in His fullness and understand that there is more to life than what we see, hear and touch. Our God is so glorious, so majestic. It makes the heart rejoice that we can know the One who loves us with no strings attached, except to love Him in return and believe that He is the Lord God Almighty and the Everlasting Father, the King of Glory.

Read Psalm 24
Psalm 147:4, Romans 10:12

Lord, this psalm brings comfort and rejoicing to our souls. You, the King of Glory, want us to know You intimately. Take our thoughts and make them Your thoughts that we might know You and receive the unconditional love You have for us. Amen.

JANUARY 31
NEVER PUT TO SHAME

Psalm 25:3: No one whose hope is in You will ever be put to shame, but they will be put to shame who are treacherous without excuse.

Shame comes from doing things that are not pleasing to God. It's not something we see or touch but it is an emotion we experience. Others may never know the shame we feel because of a hidden secret in our lives that we have never told. Those are the things that keep us bound up, unable to live our lives in total freedom. We were once in darkness but now we live in the light of the Lord. We are to be children of light, which consists of all goodness, righteousness and truth. We are to have nothing to do with the fruitless deeds of darkness but rather expose them; for it is shameful even to mention what the disobedient do in secret. Because the Sovereign Lord helps us, we will not be disgraced for we have set our faces like flint and know we will not be put to shame. As the Scripture says, "Anyone who trusts in Him will never be put to shame." Jesus Christ is the chosen and precious cornerstone in Zion and the one who trusts in Him will never be put to shame. There is no shame in serving Jesus Christ, for in Him is the truth. When we give our lives to Him, we do not do things that bring shame on Him or ourselves. Nothing impure will ever enter into God's kingdom, nor will anyone who does what is shameful or deceitful, but only those whose names are written in the Lamb's Book of Life.

Read Psalm 25:1-11
Psalm 31:1, Isaiah 50:7, Romans 10:11, Ephesians 5:11-12, 1 Peter 2:6

Heavenly Father, thank You for the Book of Psalms. We gain such insight into who You are as we read these Holy Scriptures and meditate upon them. As we seek You, open our hearts and minds so we might have a greater understanding of You, the One we can trust with our very lives and never be ashamed of serving. Amen.

FEBRUARY 1
THE LORD CONFIDES

Psalm 25:14: The Lord confides in those who fear Him; He makes His covenant known to them.

Abraham was sitting at the entrance to his tent in the heat of the day. He looked up and saw three men standing nearby. When he saw them, he hurried to meet them and bowed low to the ground, for he knew it was the Lord. He prepared a feast for them, and while they ate he stood near them under a tree. When the men got up to leave, they looked toward Sodom where they were headed, and the Lord said, "Shall I hide from Abraham what I am about to do?" Because of Abraham's faithfulness, He confided in him and revealed His plan. It is required that those who have been given a trust must be faithful, and that is who we ought to be in Christ Jesus, faithful servants of the Most High God. He has revealed His plan of salvation to those who believe and confided in us the secrets of His kingdom. The plans of the Lord stand firm forever, the purposes of His heart through all generations. Once we have committed to serving Him, He leads us into His righteousness and rewards our faithfulness.

Read Psalm 25:12-22
Genesis 18:1-2, 7-8 & 16-17, Psalm 33:8-11, 1 Corinthians 4:4

How can we show our appreciation to You, Almighty Father, for all You do? Help us to keep our minds steadfast on You so that our relationship might grow more intimate every moment of everyday. You are our Deliverer, our Redeemer, and our strength in the day of trouble. May we live our lives in this confidence. Amen.

FEBRUARY 2
SET APART

Psalm 26:4-5: I do not sit with deceitful men, nor do I consort with hypocrites. I abhor the assembly of evildoers and refuse to sit with the wicked.

The choices we make affect the course our lives take. When we choose the Lord, we have a firm foundation on which to stand. There is no other way we can become blameless for we are all human and there is no one who can make us blameless except God Himself, by and through His Son. He is the One who is holy, blameless, pure, set apart from sinners, exalted above the heavens. King David did not have the blood of Jesus to wash away his sins and make him clean but he had unwavering faith in his Heavenly Father. Although wickedness surrounded him, he did not partake in it. He kept his eyes firmly fixed on God Almighty, the source of his strength. Now that Jesus has come to set us free from the grip of sin and death, we can become the people God intends us to be. Through Him, we are able to stay on the narrow path that leads to life eternal with Him.

Read Psalm 26
Matthew 7:13-14, Hebrews 7:26

Heavenly Father, in You alone are we made righteous. Help us to make choices in life that keep us headed down that path of righteousness so that we may proclaim, yes, no wickedness can be found in us and we can hold our heads high in the knowledge that You have found us innocent in Your sight. Amen.

FEBRUARY 3
NO FEAR IN TRUSTING GOD

Psalm 27:1: The Lord is my Light and my Salvation, whom shall I fear? The Lord is the Stronghold of my life, of whom shall I be afraid?

Trust is like holding onto a tree branch that is hanging over a cliff and about to break but we know that down below there is someone to catch us and keep us from harm. It's not necessary to put God to the test, though. While Jesus was in the desert fasting for 40 days, the devil led him to

Jerusalem and had him stand on the highest point of the temple. He told Jesus to throw himself down from there if He was truly the Son of God, for it is written that He will command His angels concerning You to guard You carefully, to which Jesus responded, "It says do not put the Lord your God to the test." Even Jesus would not tempt the Father by doing something stupid like throwing Himself over a cliff. But it is when adversity strikes that we must show how much we trust the Lord to take care of us. If we fret and worry or hold onto a problem and look elsewhere for answers, that is no different than what the world does. Christians should run to the throne of God. That's how King David responded. God was his refuge and strength in times of trouble. We don't have to wait until He comes in all His glory to trust Him. When we turn our hearts to walk in all His ways, we are able to keep His commands and decrees. No matter how bad circumstances appear to be, we don't have to test the Lord but only trust that He is in control and we can let go of that branch because He is there to catch us.

Read Psalm 27
1 Kings 8:58, Psalm 37:39, Luke 4:9-12

O Lord, help us to keep a song of rejoicing in our heart so when trials come we can praise You. You are the Lord God Almighty who sits on Your throne in Heaven, yet You know every detail of our lives. Help us to draw our strength from You that we may not grow weary. Amen.

FEBRUARY 4
OUR STRENGTH AND SHIELD

Psalm 28:7: The Lord is my Strength and my Shield. My heart trusts in Him and I am helped. My heart leaps for joy and I will give thanks to Him in song.

Songs of praise fill the atmosphere with God's glory. It's like a horse with side blinders on. We look straight ahead and see only the pathway to heaven, which should make our hearts leap with joy. When we are in a congregation of saints who join their voices in unison to praise the Lord, it gives us strength. It feeds our spirits with His presence and helps us to focus on Him. He becomes our shield and hiding place. He protects us from trouble and surrounds us with songs of deliverance. Shout for joy to the Lord all the earth. Worship Him with gladness and joyful songs, for it is He who made us. We are His people, the sheep of His pasture.

Read Psalm 28
Psalm 32:7 & 100:1-3, Isaiah 26:7, Jeremiah 17:7

Father, when we feel as though wickedness surrounds us and we cry out for your judgment and justice, help us remember that You alone know the hearts of man and are not willing that any should perish but that all should come to repentance and eternal life in You. Increase our faith that we may trust in You and have peace in our hearts and minds. Amen.

FEBRUARY 5
THE VOICE OF THE LORD

Psalm 29:4: The voice of the Lord is powerful; the voice of the Lord is majestic.

During the life of Moses, the Lord began to speak to His chosen people directly. Mount Sinai was covered with smoke because the Lord descended on it in fire. The smoke billowed up from it like smoke from a furnace and the whole mountain trembled violently. Such fear came upon the people that they said to Moses, "Speak to us yourself and we will listen but do not have God speak to us or we will die." The voice of God is so powerful that He gave the Sermon on the Mount with no microphones and thousands heard His message. He spoke the world into existence. When He speaks, His voice breaks the cedars, which are vast trees that all we can do is look up at them in wonder. The mountains quake before Him and the hills melt away. The earth trembles at His presence, the world and all who live in it. The majesty of God is so excellent that He is worthy of our praise, worship and solemn reverence. His voice can thunder with greatness or it can be that gentle whisper that calls to us to come and follow Him.

Read Psalm 29
Exodus 19:16-19 & 20:18-19, 1 Kings 19:12, Psalm 18:13, Nahum 1:5,
2 Corinthians 3:13, Hebrews 12:18-21

Heavenly Father, words are inadequate to describe Your greatness. We stand in awe of who You are, the One who spoke the world into existence. Help us to comprehend You and live our lives knowing that You, the Great King, the Almighty Creator, want us to know You and hear Your voice. Amen.

FEBRUARY 6
ANGER

Psalm 30:5: For His anger lasts only a moment but His favor lasts a lifetime; weeping may remain for a night but rejoicing comes in the morning.

In the days of revival there was a lot of preaching about an angry God and that if we did this and that or didn't do this and that we would come under His wrath and judgment. They were talking about the God of the Old Testament who became angry at Judah and Israel when they left Him and went their own way seeking after other gods. They were under the law that God had given Moses, but they never kept it and as a result they were subject to God's anger. This is not the God that Jesus Christ taught about. We are no longer subject to the law of the Old Testament, which is impossible to keep. Our Father is loving and merciful and He tells us that man's anger does not bring about the righteous life that He desires, for anger, when not dealt with, is an emotion that wells up within us like a volcano. The molten lava bubbles and gurgles deep within the belly of the earth and then without warning it explodes into the air and destroys everything it touches. We should never let the sun go down while we are still angry for in doing so we give the devil a foothold. With His love, we are not easily angered and keep no record of wrongs, for His love is patient and kind.

Read Psalm 30
Acts 13:39, Galatians 5:18, Ephesians 4:26, James 1:20

Lord, look upon us with favor, especially when we ask forgiveness for our sins. Search us and see if there be any sin hidden in our hearts. Help us to live our lives so we are pleasing to You and others might see the light of Your presence in us and desire to know You. Amen.

FEBRUARY 7
OUR REFUGE

Psalm 31:2: Turn Your ear to me; come quickly to my rescue; be my Rock of Refuge, a strong fortress to save me.

A mighty fortress is our God, a bulwark never failing; our helper He amid the flood of mortal ills prevailing. These are words of praise and worship from the hymn "A Mighty Fortress is Our God." The song goes on to proclaim the sovereignty of God and His power over the ancient foe, Satan, who seeks to work us woe. It ends with the words "God's truth abideth still; His kingdom is forever." This we can be certain of. The storms of life may take us adrift but the Lord is our rock and our refuge in times of trouble. He is referred to as our fortress and deliverer five times in the Book of Psalms. In the time of King Solomon, there is archeological evidence of 50 fortresses existing along the borders of his kingdom. These fortresses most likely had towers that were manned 24 hours a day to keep watch for an approaching enemy. The fortresses were a place of refuge to keep the people safe. This is why our Heavenly Father is referred to as a fortress. He keeps constant watch over us. He protects us. He is a mighty God whose vastness encompasses the entire universe and He loves us beyond measure. When we trust in Him, He is our solid rock, our refuge and our fortress.

Read Psalm 31:1-13
2 Samuel 22:2, Psalm 71:3, 91:2, 144:2, Jeremiah 16:19

Heavenly Father, our refuge, our source of strength, reveal Yourself to us in a way that we can receive what we need from You. At times, You seem so distant but in reality You dwell within us and are our Guiding Light. Help us realize that we are never alone and that You are truly our Place of Refuge. Amen.

FEBRUARY 8
ALWAYS PRESENT

Psalm 31:19: How great is Your goodness which You have stored up for those who fear You, which You bestow in the sight of men on those who take refuge in You.

The remainder of this psalm gives us insight into what we can expect from the Lord. King David had such a close walk with God that he shared with Him his very soul and innermost thoughts, whether good or bad, and knew that his Lord was near him. Prayer is such a powerful tool that draws us close to the Lord. He is present when we pray. Jesus said that where two or three come together in my Name, there am I with them. Our relationship with Him is like any other. It has to be nurtured to grow. The more time we spend together, the closer we become. We learn about each other. When we open up our hearts and share the most intimate details of our lives while in prayer, His presence surrounds us and we fall in love with the God whom we serve.

Read Psalm 31:14-24
Amos 3:3, Matthew 18:20, Luke 11:9

Father, when we pray and come into your presence, draw us closer to You. Jesus gave us the Lord's prayer: Our Father, which art in Heaven.

We ask that You help us to expound on that prayer so that each day we might discover more about You, the One who loves us unconditionally and is always present. Amen.

FEBRUARY 9
THE WEIGHT OF SIN

Psalm 32:4-5: For day and night, Your hand was heavy upon me; my strength was sapped as in the heat of summer. Then I acknowledged my sin to You and did not cover up my iniquity. I said, I will confess my transgressions to the Lord, and You forgave the guilt of my sin.

The day we ask Jesus to come into our lives, it is like a heavy weight lifted off of our chest. Instead of taking short, shallow breaths, we are at peace and take deep, long, lingering breaths that fill our bodies with nourishment and rest. We are free to live godly lives that give glory to our Savior. But unconfessed sin hinders our prayers. There are times we mull something over and over that we have done wrong and try to figure a way around it. By doing this, we are trying to find a way to hide from God. We cannot hide from His Spirit. We cannot flee from His presence. If we go into the heavens, He is there. If we make our bed in the depths, He is there. We cannot hide in the darkness, for even the darkness is not dark to Him; the night shines like the day, for darkness is as light to Him. When we allow sin to cloud our vision, it's like devoting ourselves to study and exploring all that is done under heaven; it is meaningless, like chasing after the wind. The Lord must laugh at times wondering how long we will try to get away with something, but He waits patiently. Let us throw off everything that hinders and the sin that so easily entangles us and let us run with perseverance the race marked out for us. Once we are humble and confess our sin, we are set completely free from its weight.

Read Psalm 32
Psalm 139:7-12, Ecclesiastes 1:13-14, Hebrews 12:1-2

Merciful Father, forgive us of our sins (name them specifically) that we might come into a closer relationship with You. Search our hearts and minds, and reveal to us any unconfessed sin before You that we might be set free from its weight and destruction. Help us to fix our eyes on the author and perfecter of our faith, Jesus Christ. Amen.

FEBRUARY 10
HIS PLAN STANDS FIRM

Psalm 33:11: But the plans of the Lord stand firm forever; the purposes of His heart through all generations.

It is impossible to accomplish a goal without a plan to implement it. Every great dancer does not become one by listening to music. A great swimmer does not stand by the edge of the pool and watch others do the backstroke and butterfly. No one becomes a great athlete by going to the ball games and sitting in the bleachers. It takes practice, endurance, and more practice before a plan to become the best can be achieved. It doesn't just happen because we want it to. From the beginning, God has had a plan and it has never been altered. When He spoke the world into existence and breathed life into mankind, His plan was for His creation to be in close communion with Him, and it still is. When sin entered the world, death was the result. His plan was to send His only begotten Son into the world to die for our sins and overcome death. From generation to generation his plan has stood firm. He calls each of us to fulfill His plan. He is not slow in keeping His promise, as some understand slowness. He is patient with us, not wanting anyone to perish but for everyone to come to repentance. He desires that we live for Him and that whatever we do, whether in word or deed, do it all in the name of the Lord Jesus, giving thanks to God the Father through Him. His plan includes an eternity with Him and what we do in this life determines whether we are a part of His plan or our own.

Read Psalm 33
Genesis 2:7, Isaiah 14:24 & 46:11, Colossians 3:17, 2 Peter 3:9

Our Father, You are worthy of all praise. Thank You that You have a plan for our lives. Help us to keep our minds upon You so we are sensitive to the leading of Your Holy Spirit and the plans You have for us are fulfilled. Amen.

FEBRUARY 11
EXALT THE LORD

Psalm 34:3: Glorify the Lord with me, let us exalt His name together.

The Lord made the heavens, even the highest heavens, and all their starry host, the earth and all that is on it, the seas and all that is in them. He has given life to everything and the multitudes of heaven worship Him. Wealth and honor come from the Lord. He is the ruler of all things. In His hands is strength and power to exalt and give strength to all. There is no one higher than the God of Heaven. He is worthy to be praised. Satan wanted to be worshiped. He said in his heart that he would ascend to heaven, that he would raise his throne above the stars of God but he was brought down to the grave, to the depths of the pit, for there is no one greater than God. Many people exalt themselves above God but the Lord Almighty has a day in store for all the proud and lofty; for all that are exalted will be humbled. The arrogance of man will be brought low and the Lord alone will be exalted in that day and the idols will totally disappear. He is the Alpha and the Omega, the beginning and the end. To him who is thirsty He gives to drink without cost from the spring of the water of life.

Read Psalm 34
Nehemiah 9:5-6, Isaiah 2:12-18, Micah 4:1-2, Revelation 21:6

Lord, we lift up Your mighty name and exalt You above all else. You are from the beginning and always will be. When we lift ourselves up, humble us. Help us not to exalt ourselves above You but with praise and thanksgiving make our petitions known to You. Amen.

FEBRUARY 12
THE AVENGER

Psalm 35:10: My whole being will exclaim, Who is like You, O Lord? You rescue the poor from those too strong for them, the poor and needy from those who rob them.

David was king of Judea and Israel but he had many enemies whose sole intention was to bring him down to the point of killing him. His son Absalom tried taking the kingdom away from him, to no avail. When David was close to death, Adonijah, another son, proclaimed himself king but David anointed Solomon to take his place on the throne, and it was so. David knew that the Lord was with him, for He fought not only the kingdom's battles but David's personal battles. He does the same for us today. When we have been wronged, we should not repay evil for evil. Do not take revenge but leave room for God's wrath, for it is written: "It is mine to avenge; I will repay," says the Lord. If our enemy is hungry, we should feed him; if he is thirsty, we should give him something to drink. In doing so, we heap burning coals on their head. Only the Lord knows the thoughts and intents of everyone as to why they do what they do. That is why it is His place to judge. In faithfulness He will bring forth justice.

Read Psalm 35:1-10
Deuteronomy 32:35, 1 Kings 1:5, Isaiah 42:3, Matthew 5:43-44,
Romans 12:17-20

Heavenly Father, when the storm clouds of life overtake and surround us, we pray for Your protection. Send a band of heavenly angels to watch over us. Help us to look heavenward and trust that You are righteous and just. Give us strength and wisdom to do what is right in Your eyes. Amen.

FEBRUARY 13
JUDGMENT BELONGS TO GOD

Psalm 35:14: I went about mourning as though for my friend or brother. I bowed my head in grief as though weeping for my mother.

King David continues to cry out to God for vindication from his enemies. He pours out his heart to the Lord because of the persecution surrounding him. At the same time, he humbles himself to pray for those who seek him harm. He also leaves any judgment in the hand of God by asking Him to take care of those who slander him. This is an example of trusting God implicitly. We all encounter adversity and at times there are those who devise schemes against us. This is when we must draw nearer to our Lord because our human nature is to take matters into our own hands when we feel we have been wronged. He asks us to look to Him and trust Him because He knows the thoughts and attitudes of every person on this earth. Those who trust in Him have assurance that He takes care of every situation.

Read Psalm 35:11-28
Isaiah 30:18, Hebrews 4:12

Heavenly Father, give us patience and peace, knowing that when the enemy comes in like a flood, You have everything under control. Help us to fall on our knees before You and seek You, for when we seek You with all of our hearts we find You. Amen.

FEBRUARY 14
FOUNTAIN OF LIFE

Psalm 36:9-10: For with You is the fountain of life; in Your light we see light. Continue Your love to those who know You, Your righteousness to the upright in heart.

Fountains and water go hand in hand, for a fountain without water serves no real purpose. It becomes a place where leaves and debris accumulate and over time it deteriorates and chips away. Before plumbing, fountains were connected to a main water source to provide drinking water and water for bathing and washing for those who lived in towns and villages. Today, fountains can be magnificent structures, spewing water high into the air. The sound of water flowing from a fountain brings peace and tranquility. Jesus Christ is like a fountain that provides the spiritual water for our souls. If anyone is thirsty, let him come to Jesus and drink for whoever believes in Him, as the Scripture has said, streams of living water will flow from within him. Everyone who drinks water will be thirsty again but whoever drinks the water that Jesus gives them will never thirst. Indeed, the water He gives will become a spring of water welling up to eternal life. This is possible when we are born into His kingdom by the Spirit of God. This comes through faith and not by works, lest any man should boast.

Read Psalm 36
John 3:7-8, John 4:13-14, John 7:37-38, Ephesians 2:8-9

Father, we rejoice in You and Your promises to never forsake us, giving us the hope of life eternal. Help us to draw from Your fountain of living water that we might be renewed spiritually. Guide us along life's path until that day when we will be face to face with You and live in Your kingdom forever. Amen.

FEBRUARY 15
DELIGHT IN THE LORD

Psalm 37:4: Delight yourself in the Lord and He will give you the desires of Your heart.

As we read our psalm today, let's meditate for a while on what it means in our lives. It may be necessary to read it several times in order to sink in. God is all-knowing, all-powerful, all-merciful and all-loving. He judges by what He sees in the heart, not by what is seen with human eyes. He delights in those who seek Him with all of their hearts. We are not to be jealous of those in the world who seem to have no cares and triumph in their endeavors. We need not fret when we see injustice. Yes, if we can help in some manner, we definitely should. Our Lord does not intend that we sit in a corner and not speak out when we know something is wrong or help when there is a need. The Lord's greatest desire for us is to delight in Him and He will give us the desire of our hearts.

Read Psalm 37:1-20
1 Chronicles 28:9, Psalm 1:1-3

Heavenly Father, it is an awesome thing to delight in You, to seek Your face and to draw close to You. There is no God like You, the Almighty King, the Creator, the all-knowing, all-loving God. We rejoice in who You are and thank You for all of Your promises. We pray for wisdom. We pray for Your love to flow through us that it might flow through to others. Amen.

FEBRUARY 16
NEVER FORSAKEN

Psalm 37:27-28: Turn from evil and do good; then you will dwell in the land forever. For the Lord loves the just and will not forsake His faithful ones.

God promised that the Messiah would come from the tribe of Judah, and He did. In the Old Testament, God bound Himself by a covenant to one people and one nation. He has never forsaken that covenant. He promised His people two things: that He would bless their obedience and curse their disobedience. Even though historically it seemed His people would be annihilated because of their disobedience, there was always a remnant remaining to go back to the Promised Land. After the second exile of Israel, Ezra, a priest and direct descendant of Aaron, returned to help rebuild the temple in Jerusalem. He was a man who studied, lived and taught the Scripture. He knew that despite the sins of the people, God had not forsaken them, and so he prayed: "Though we are slaves, our God has not deserted us in our bondage...He has granted us new life to rebuild the house of our God and repair its ruins..." Though they forsook Him many times, He never forsook His chosen people. He has now bound Himself to us with a new covenant and He will never forsake those who call upon His name.

Psalm 37:21-40
Ezra 9:8-9, Jeremiah 23:6, Micah 5:2, Matthew 2:6, Hebrews 8:7-8

Lord, although we do not see with our natural eyes the spiritual battle that takes place every moment of every day, we know we are in a battle for our souls, and it is difficult to realize the gravity of it. We pray You keep us focused on the things that have eternal value, for the things of this life quickly pass away. Guide us down the path You want for us, teach us of Your ways, that we might be a light in this world to those who are searching for answers. Thank You for this awesome responsibility as Your children. The true answers of eternal life lie in a relationship with Jesus Christ, the One who gave His life for the world so we can be reconciled to You. Amen.

FEBRUARY 17
WHEN WE SIN

Psalm 38:4: My guilt has overwhelmed me like a burden too heavy to bear.

King David was a man after God's own heart; yet he was still a man with human emotions and desires. When he took his eyes off the Lord he loved, he saw a woman and wanted her, even though she was married to another. He summoned her and slept with her and she conceived a child. David tried to cover his sin by bringing her husband from the battle he was engaged in so that he would be with his wife. Because of this man's dedication to the king and his soldiers, he would not go to his wife but slept on their doorway. King David sent him back to the battle with a note to instruct the captain of the army to put him on the front lines where the husband of this woman was killed. King David was guilty of murder and the Lord was not pleased. When David repented, the Lord was merciful to forgive, but there were grave consequences for his actions. The Lord spoke to David through His prophet and said, "Now, therefore, the sword will never depart from your house, because you despised me and took the wife of Uriah the Hittite to be your own." When we fail our Lord, which we are sure to do, we must come to Him immediately and confess our wrongdoing. We have to be honest with Him because He already knows anyway. He never holds our failures over our heads, but there are consequences. He is faithful and just to forgive our sins and to restore us to Himself.

Read Psalm 38
2 Samuel 11:2-17 & 12:10-14, Jeremiah 15:19

Lord, forgive us when we turn from You. Help us to acknowledge our wrongdoing and ask You for forgiveness. Remember that our sinful nature sometimes gets the better of us and we lose sight of who we are in You. Thank You for Your mercy and grace. Amen.

FEBRUARY 18
EACH MAN IS BUT A BREATH

Psalm 39:5: You have made my days a mere handbreath; the span of my years is as nothing before you. Each man's life is but a breath.

From the time we begin to form our own thoughts, we act as though we can control our own destiny. We think we are in control of ourselves, of situations in our lives, of those who surround us. Yet we are a mere breath away from eternity! Those who have come before us experienced similar thoughts and lives as we have, and those who come after us will do so as well. We all have different experiences but it all leads to the same thing. One day we will breathe no longer and our time on earth will be over. As we contemplate the meaning of our lives, let's look heavenward to the Giver of Life, the One who breathed life into the first man and breathes life into us today. Let us not be silent any longer but proclaim His great glory, for He is the light, hope and salvation of all mankind.

Read Psalm 39
Job 33:4, Psalm 8:3-9, Ecclesiastes 3:1-2 & 20, 1 Corinthians 15:21-22

All-powerful Father, who was and is and is to come, breathe new life into our very souls and spirits. Renew our minds afresh with Your Spirit and help us to never lose sight of You, the giver of life and breath. Amen.

FEBRUARY 19
COUNTLESS WONDERS

Psalm 40:5: Many, O Lord my God, are the wonders You have done. The things You planned for us no one can recount to You; were I to speak and tell of them, they would be too many to declare.

Renewed life, countless blessings, ability to speak to others about the salvation of God Almighty, a cry for mercy, these are all encompassed in this one psalm, ending with "You are my help and deliverer; O my God, do not delay." Unlike our Heavenly Father, who never changes, we change all the time. We believe, we trust, we praise but then we also stumble, fall, distrust and question. It is awesome to know that we have a Father who is always the same, who sees our every need, who even knows our every thought before we speak it. When we call out to Him, when we take time to pray and communicate our needs and desires, it draws us closer to Him because it builds our faith when we see the results of our prayers.

Read Psalm 40
Psalm 102:27, Malachi 3:6

Thank You, Lord, for being a solid rock that can never be moved. You have revealed Yourself to us by Your precious Word. Give us a burning desire to consume Your Word so we might come to know You more fully and know that You are who You say You are and we can trust You in all things. Amen.

FEBRUARY 20
UNRELIABIITY OF MAN

Psalm 41:6: Whenever one comes to see me, he speaks falsely, while his heart gathers slander, then he goes out and spreads it abroad.

As we continue our journey through the psalms, we should be able to discern how feeble man is and how great our Lord is. Just because a person says one thing, we cannot always know that what they say is really what they are thinking or what they will do. In contrast, when God speaks we can know, without any question, it will come to pass. God reveals Himself to us. He hides nothing. We can come to know Him intimately. He never forsakes us. He never says anything to us that is not the absolute truth. He is not a man that He should lie, nor the son of man that He should change His mind. He speaks and then acts. He promises and then fulfills. This is why, no matter what someone else says, no matter our circumstances, we can always, always trust the Lord to be with us and to bring us through every situation.

Read Psalm 41
Numbers 23:19, Psalm 12:1-2 & 7, Isaiah 32:6-8

Father, forgive us that we so often put our trust in others. We are all sinners. We all fail each other, whether intentional or not. Help us to realize how much we need to depend on You. For the closer we are to You, the more we become like You. Take us into Your everlasting arms that we might draw strength from You. Amen.

FEBRUARY 21
WHERE IS OUR GOD?

Psalm 42:9-10: I say to God my Rock, why have You forgotten me? Why must I go about mourning, oppressed by the enemy? My bones suffer mortal agony as my foes taunt me, saying to me all day long, where is Your God?

At times, we suffer turmoil because we lose sight of the Mighty One. We begin to doubt that He hears us. We might even feel abandoned and wonder: Where is our God? Even Jesus, at the time of His most desperate need, cried out, "My God, my God, why have You forsaken me?" But He was and is always there; always! We can count on it. At the time of Jesus' death, He took on the sins of the entire world. God, who is holy, could not look upon sin. Jesus felt forsaken because for the only time in His life His Father could not look upon Him. He was there, though, right at His side, waiting to receive Him. No matter our struggle, no matter the hardships we may have, God is by our side. He waits for us to cry out to Him so that He can bring us through.

Read Psalm 42
Deuteronomy 32:36-39, Psalm 37:40, Mark 15:33-34

Almighty God, through life's trials help us realize You are there. In our times of disillusionment, bring us through to the glorious light of Jesus Christ. Help us to remember that life is short but eternity is forever. Amen.

FEBRUARY 22
PUT YOUR HOPE IN GOD

Psalm 43:5: Why are you downcast, O my soul? Why so disturbed within me? Put Your hope in God, for I will yet praise Him, my Savior and my God.

When we take our eyes off the Lord and begin to look at the world, we are pulled down to its level and at times can feel weak and all alone. It's not that we live in a place of despair, but without belief in the Almighty to guide our way through life, we have no hope beyond this life. That is truly a sad state of affairs. The Scriptures tell us that everything written in the past was written to teach us so that through endurance and encouragement we might have hope. We are made in the image of God to commune with Him, to seek Him, to praise Him. When we keep our focus on Him, we are not carried away with the trials of this world because we know there is coming a time when we will see the Lord face to face and be with Him forever.

Read Psalm 43
Deuteronomy 1:21, Isaiah 40:31, Romans 15:4

Lord, You are the One who dwells in Heaven above. Let us never lose sight of You. Take our hand and guide us in our lives. We thank You for the hope that we have in You. Amen.

FEBRUARY 23
THE LORD VICTORIOUS

Psalm 44:6-7: I do not trust in my bow, my sword does not bring me victory; but You give us victory over our enemies; You put our adversaries to shame.

In the Old Testament, God chose Abraham to bring forth a nation that would serve Him and that would show the world why it should choose to serve the only true God. He instructed them on how they were to be a light to the world; how when they followed Him with all their hearts they would be blessed above all nations. He did miracles to prove His power and love for them so that the nations of the world would know there is a God who is in control of all creation. They did not have to depend on their own strength for deliverance, for with His hand He drove out the nations and planted the fathers of Israel. We can learn a lot from these passages. We do not have to be fearful, for our Lord fights our battles for us, and those are the battles that we never lose. Therefore, when we have trials, when we feel rejected, whatever it is that makes us feel defeated, we need only look to our Father and He gives us the victory.

Read Psalm 44:1-8
Psalm 121:1-2, Isaiah 26:4, Micah 7:15-20

Lord, deliver us from the evil one of this world. Give us strength to endure the darts of the enemy of our soul. You alone are holy and You alone have the ability to judge us. Show us mercy, for we are human and we easily fall. By faith, Your strength is sufficient for all our needs. Amen.

FEBRUARY 24
THROUGH THE DARKNESS

Psalm 44:22: Yet for Your sake we face death all day long; we are considered as sheep to be slaughtered.

In researching the time period when this psalm was written, although inconclusive some scholars discern it was during a time of great persecution of God's people. Although they did not turn away from Him then, they felt He was nowhere to be found, that He was asleep and possibly indifferent to the suffering that was taking place. The last verse of this psalm proclaims, "Rise up and help us; redeem us because of Your unfailing love." When we become followers of Christ, we might have a mistaken understanding that life will no longer be filled with heartache or trouble. Actually, the opposite is true. We are hard-pressed on every side but not crushed; perplexed but not in despair; persecuted but not abandoned; struck down but not destroyed. It is through our times of hardship that we learn to depend on the Lord. Through our darkest times, He keeps our lamp burning and He brings us through by His mighty, outstretched arm.

Read Psalm 44:9-26
2 Samuel 22:29, Psalm 18:28-29, 2 Corinthians 4:8-10

Father, You have said You will never leave nor forsake us. May we hold on to this truth, especially in our darkest moments through life. Draw us close to You and let us never lose hope in Your unfailing love. Amen.

FEBRUARY 25
FOREVER AND EVER

Psalm 45:6: Your throne, O God, will last forever and ever; a scepter of justice will be the scepter of Your kingdom.

As with many of the psalms, there are probably several ways in which this psalm can be interpreted. The one consistent theme is that of a wedding song where the Lord bestows upon the royal couple His righteousness. In turn, He requires that through the generations they remember where they, the royal couple, received their glory from. There are many responsibilities that come with being a follower of Jesus Christ, the foremost of which is to love the Lord our God with all our heart, soul and mind. When we do this, the love of God, through the power of His Spirit, leads us down paths of righteousness that we never thought possible. Our walk with the Lord boils down to trust. When we trust Him and believe Him, when we serve Him with our whole heart, as did the royal couple in this psalm, we will one day be blessed with a crown of glory because of our faith in Jesus Christ.

Read Psalm 45
2 Timothy 4:8, James 1:12, 1 Peter 5:4, Revelation 2:10, 3:11-12

Holy Lord, You alone are the Giver of life. We do not always understand Your ways but we can always trust that Your way is the way of truth and life and You will never do anything to harm us. Keep us on the narrow path of righteousness as we journey through life. When we wander, bring us back to You. Amen.

FEBRUARY 26
EVER-PRESENT HELP IN TROUBLE

Psalm 46:1: God is our refuge and strength, an ever-present help in trouble.

When everything is going well in our lives we sometimes become complacent and take things for granted. Then disaster in one form or another comes: our house burns down and we lose all of our earthly possessions. We experience an earthquake, tornado or hurricane. A loved one is suddenly snatched away from us by death. We are uncertain about how to try and fix these things, but we needn't fix anything at all. It is in these times that our Lord does His greatest work. He is a refuge for the oppressed and a stronghold in times of trouble. We must be on our knees in the good times and bad, seeking the face of Almighty God and praying for His help and direction. In our time of crisis, we realize how little control we have and it should draw us even closer to Him.

Read Psalm 46
2 Samuel 22:3 & 31, Psalm 9:9-10

Holy Lord, thank You that no matter our circumstances in life, You are always by our side. You wait for us to call upon Your mighty name. When we do, You lift us up into Your presence and give us Your perfect peace. We thank You and praise Your mighty name. Amen.

FEBRUARY 27
THE THRONE OF GOD

Psalm 47:7-8: For God is the King of all the earth; sing to Him a psalm of praise. God reigns over the nations; God is seated on His holy throne.

We have probably all seen the pomp and circumstance that surrounds the Queen of England during special times in the Royal Family such as royal weddings or coronations. When the queen sits on her throne, the aura about her is majestic and peoples come from all over the world to partake in these special times. There is another throne in Heaven which eye has not yet seen, and the Lord God Almighty sits upon it and sees all that the nations do. There is no place that we can hide from the Lord, for Heaven is His throne and the earth His footstool. Who among us can build a greater place for our Lord to dwell than His throne, or what other resting place could we provide for Him? There is no earthly throne like God's Heavenly Throne. The Prophet Ezekiel saw what looked like a throne of sapphire and the figure of a man who looked like glowing metal and a brilliant light surrounded him. Like the appearance of a rainbow in the clouds on a rainy day, so was the radiance around Him. It is so majestic, so powerful; there are no words to adequately describe it. In the end of time, there will be a river of the water of life, as clear as crystal, flowing from the throne of God and the Lamb down the middle of the great street of the city and on each side of the river will stand the tree of life, bearing 12 crops of fruit, and the leaves are for the healing of the nations. We know the end of the story, and eye has not seen nor ear heard what the Lord has prepared for those who love Him.

Read Psalm 47
Isaiah 66:1-2, Ezekiel 1:26-28, Acts 7:49-50, 1 Corinthians 2:9, Revelation 22:1-2

Holy Lord, who sits on Your throne in the heavens above, help us to keep our minds and hearts stayed upon You and never lose sight of Your truth that this world is not our permanent home but that You have prepared a place for us. When we are discouraged, bring this to our remembrance and let us never forget the hope that we have in You. Amen.

FEBRUARY 28
TO THE END

Psalm 48:14: For this God is our God forever and ever. He will be our guide even to the end.

A guide is someone who has knowledge of a particular subject in order to impart that knowledge to others. There are guides in museums to tell us about the artifacts and treasures that are inside. There are also tour guides to take us into unfamiliar territory. They help us expand our horizons by showing us landmarks and sharing historical facts about what we are seeing. We couldn't get through life without a guide of some kind. There are guides on psychology, parenting, music, archeology; the list is endless. There are also those who guide people by misleading them and leading them astray. In the days of the great Exodus from Egypt, the Lord went ahead of His children in a pillar of cloud to guide them on their way and by night in a pillar of fire to give them light, so they could travel by day and night. The Lord leads the blind by ways they have not known; along unfamiliar paths He guides them. He turns the darkness into light before them and makes the rough places smooth. He guides us with His counsel, and afterward He takes us into glory.

Read Psalm 48
Exodus 13:21, Psalm 73:24, Isaiah 9:16 & 42:16

Precious Jesus, thank You for guiding us through life. What love You have shown to us by fulfilling all of Your promises. Thank You for overcoming death, hell and the grave and giving us the hope of everlasting life. Thank You for being with us every step of the way on life's journey. Amen.

MARCH 1
FALSE HOPE IN RICHES

Psalm 49:10: For all can see that wise men die; the foolish and the senseless alike perish and leave their wealth to others.

Money makes the world go round. It's what makes us get up in the morning to go to work. It's what we use to provide for our families and the luxuries in life. No matter how much we have, though, it's never enough. Rich, poor, foolish, wise, we all work for or find ways to make money, and then we die and leave it to others. We can use money for everything except to buy an eternity with God. The psalmist says those who trust in their wealth and boast of their great riches cannot redeem themselves or the life of another or give to God a ransom so that he should live on forever and not see decay, for no payment is ever enough. In death, it is only God who can redeem our lives from the grave and take us to Himself.

Read Psalm 49:1-15
Ecclesiastes 5:15-16, Acts 8:20, Philippians 3:14, 1 Timothy 6:7

Heavenly Father, help us to keep our eyes on the prize of eternal life, the crown of glory in eternity, and not be caught up in the things which can be attained in this world, all of which pass away. Amen.

MARCH 2
RICHES WITHOUT UNDERSTANDING

Psalm 49:20: A man who has riches without understanding is like the beasts that perish.

The definition of understanding is the power to distinguish truth from falsehood, and truth is the real state of things; fact; reality; actual being or nature. Jesus Christ is the way, the truth and the life. No one comes to the Father except through Him. He is the basis of all truth, a firm foundation on which to stand. At the time of judgment, He will judge the great and small before the great white throne based on the truth. The one who has gained great riches on this earth without the truth is like a beast. The beasts of the earth cannot reason like human beings. They exist by sheer instinct or with the help of others, and then they perish. Jesus said to a rich man who inquired as to how to inherit eternal life that he must sell everything he had, give it to the poor and he would have treasures in Heaven. The rich man was saddened by this response and walked away. Jesus then turned to His disciples and said that it is easier for a camel to go through the eye of a needle than for a rich man to enter the kingdom of God. The disciples were amazed by this answer and inquired as to who then could be saved. Jesus said to them that with man this is impossible but not with God; all things are possible with God. The truth is that the rich man had to have a willing heart and not put his possessions before a relationship with God. He could only do this with God's help because, as Jesus explained, what is impossible for men is possible with God, meaning that rich people can find salvation through Christ and enter the gates of Heaven just like anyone else. Those who use riches for their own desires are without understanding as to why they have been entrusted with great wealth.

Read Psalm 49:16-20
Mark 10:17-27, John 14:6, Revelation 20:11

Lord, open our eyes to see what we put first in our lives. Direct our thoughts, for as a man thinks so is he. Help us to put You uppermost in our lives. Guide us in our finances. Help us to get out of debt so that we can help not only ourselves but others in need. We ask for wisdom and understanding so that all we do glorifies You. Amen.

MARCH 3
RULER OF ALL

Psalm 50:12: If I were hungry I would not tell you, for the world is mine and all that is in it.

The Lord speaks and summons the heavens and the earth. He knows every bird in the mountains. The cattle on a thousand hills are His. When we call upon Him in the day of trouble, He delivers us. The Lord has so many attributes it would take a lifetime to know them all. Everything we see, everything we have, every breath we take, it all belongs to Him. When we realize the vastness of our God, He is limitless in His power. The amazing thing is, He loves us so much and He is constantly calling us to a closer walk with Him so that every moment of our lives we can rest in the knowledge that no matter what we face each day, He is with us. He does not willingly bring affliction or grief to the children of men. He brings us through the trials. He only asks that we trust Him to do so.

Read Psalm 50:1-15
Psalm 62:7-8, Isaiah 40:28, Lamentations 3:31-33

Mighty Creator of all things, seen and unseen, thank You for revealing Yourself to us. When we consider the work of Your hands, it is awesome indeed and we know that You and You alone are worthy of our praises. Praise the Lord, the Almighty God! Amen.

MARCH 4
NO HIDING PLACE

Psalm 50:21: These things You have done and I kept silent. You thought I was altogether like you. But I will rebuke you and accuse you to your face.

In today's verses, the Lord turns His attention to the manifestly wicked among His people. These were like the ones that Jesus spoke about in the New Testament. He told the crowd and His disciples that everything the Pharisees do is done for men to see; that on the outside they appear to people as righteous but on the inside they are full of hypocrisy and wickedness. They tie up heavy loads and put them on men's shoulders but they themselves are not willing to lift a finger to move them. They deceived themselves into thinking that God was altogether like them, but in the end He will rebuke them and accuse them to their face. He is righteous and holy and not like those who are one way on the outside and another on the inside. When the Lord comes, He will bring to light what is hidden in darkness and expose the motives of men's hearts.

Read Psalm 50:16-23
1 Samuel 16:7, Matthew 23:2-7, 27-28, 1 Corinthians 4:5

Father in Heaven, reveal any hidden sins and secrets that we harbor in our hearts. Help us to live righteous lives so that what everyone sees on the outside is who we are on the inside. We pray for the light of Jesus Christ to shine through us. Help us to be witnesses of Your love and mercy. Amen.

MARCH 5
A BROKEN AND CONTRITE HEART

Psalm 51:17: The sacrifices of God are a broken spirit; a broken and contrite heart, O God, You will not despise.

David had many wives, which was not uncommon in that day, yet he desired another man's wife. He not only committed adultery but murder. When he was confronted with his sin, He cried out for God's mercy saying, "Hide Your face from my sins and blot out my iniquity. Create in me a pure heart and renew a steadfast spirit within me. Do not cast me from Your presence or take Your Holy Spirit from me. Restore to me the joy of Your salvation and grant me a willing spirit, to sustain me." He knew that God would hear and answer him. When we desire more than we already have, when we don't take time to pray and stay in constant communion with the Lord, we become blinded and yield to our own lusts and temptations. We allow the enemy of our souls to creep in and take us away from the things of God. There is hope in our failings, though, for we have a high priest who is able to sympathize with our weaknesses, One who was tempted in every way just as we are, yet He was without sin. When we acknowledge our sin and come humbly and honestly before the Lord, He is faithful and just to forgive us our sins and bring us back into His glorious presence.

Read Psalm 51
Hebrews 4:15-16, James 1:13-15, 1 John 1:9-10

Lord, in the beginning, when You created man, he decided to go his own way, separate from You. It has continued this way through the generations. Forgive us when we wander away and sin against You. Hear our humble cry and have mercy on us. Amen.

MARCH 6
GOD'S RIGHTEOUSNESS

Psalm 52:6-7: The righteous will see and fear; they will laugh at him, saying Here now is the man who did not make God his stronghold but trusted in his great wealth and grew strong by destroying others.

Many of the psalms speak of the boastings of man in his own strength but that in the end it all comes to nothing. We have a choice to make while on this earth, to either serve the Living God or not. If we choose to go our own way, we will trust in something or someone else. When we come to the end of life, we die without Him. We cannot save ourselves from the sins we committed throughout our lifetime or the judgment that awaits us. Some say it is possible by living a "good life." But what is good and who makes that determination? The answer to that question lies in God's Word. Jesus tells us that no one is good, except God alone. The psalms give us unique insight into the righteousness of God and what those who believe in Him can expect, as well as those who do not. It is a fearful thing to fall into the hands of the Living God, for He is the discerner of our every thought and action.

Read Psalm 52
Psalm 14:1, Isaiah 2:22, Mark 10:18, Romans 1:16-17, 1 Thessalonians 2:4

Gracious Father, You love Your creation so much that You made a way for us to reconcile with You through Jesus Christ, Your Son, who gave His life for us. Let us never lose sight of that precious gift that You have given. Amen.

MARCH 7
THE FOOL

Psalm 53:1: The fool says in his heart there is no God.

There was a rich man who had such abundance that he decided to build storehouses so he could live carefree. But God called him a fool, for he had stored up riches for his earthly life but made no provision for his spiritual life. All his earthly possessions were left to others. A fool is a person deficient in judgment, one who acts absurdly or stupidly; a simpleton; a dolt. Without God in our lives, this is what we are. We make our own judgments, our own gods and we decide what is right and wrong. There is no rock, no foundation for this, so when the next guy comes along, he or she makes their own judgments, has their own gods and ideas. And if the other guy doesn't agree, well, then look out; there could be trouble. Our God is the solid rock of righteousness. He spoke the world into existence and breathed life into mankind. He is the One who gave the law to Moses, and He alone is good. When we trust in ourselves, we are subject to the whims of the world and to death, not only in this life but in the life to come. When we trust in Jesus, His provision is enough and He gives us true life in Him, both now and throughout eternity.

Read Psalm 53
Psalm 74:18, Luke 12:15-21, Luke 18:18-19

Heavenly Father, who was, who is, who is to come, have mercy on us. Forgive us when we turn from You and go our own way. Draw us back to You so that we will have a firm foundation on which to stand. You alone are good. Help us to emulate Your goodness. Amen.

MARCH 8
DELIVERANCE FROM ALL TROUBLES

Psalm 54:7: For He has delivered me from all my troubles, and my eyes have looked in triumph on my foes.

As long as there is life on earth, there will be a battle between good and evil. God is good. Satan is evil. The battle that we don't see with our eyes is spiritual and it is the battle that determines our eternal destiny. As Americans, we are blessed in many ways that other parts of the world are not. In our beginnings, the foundation of our country was built on freedom, freedom to worship and serve the Holy God of Abraham, Isaac and Jacob; the Holy Father who gave us Jesus Christ as our Savior, who forgives our sins and delivers us from death and hell. In today's age, many no longer acknowledge this. Self-righteousness and pride abound. It is each man for himself. God's way is to love our neighbor as we love ourselves. Jesus said, "Do not let your hearts be troubled. Trust in God, trust also in me."

Read Psalm 54
John 14:1, Galatians 1:4-5, Ephesians 4:22-24

Lord, who alone is good, there are many things in life we do not fully understand. Open our eyes to the spiritual battle that is taking place so that we might see why it is so necessary to stay close to You and to continually pray for ourselves and others. Amen.

MARCH 9
FLEEING FROM ADVERSITY

Psalm 55:6: I said, "Oh, that I had the wings of a dove! I would fly way and be at rest."

King David had been exiled from Jerusalem. There were plots and conspiracies against him. His own son was gathering the people so that he could be king. Ungodliness prevailed in the city and David fled for his life because of his enemies. He was so distraught, even unto death, and wanted to fly away as a dove and find a place of rest. There have been or will be times in our lives when adversity overtakes us to the point of wanting to escape it all. That is the easy way out. We rarely want to confront adversity in our lives so we remove ourselves from it and pretend all is well. But it is through our greatest times of heartache and despair, when we cry out to our God, that we draw near to Him because we realize He is the only source of strength we have. He helps us and upholds us with His righteous right hand. To escape from our problems does not make them disappear. To endure them and allow our Lord to bring us through them makes us stronger.

Read Psalm 55:1-11
Isaiah 41:10, 2 Corinthians 13:4

Lord, may we not yield to our natural tendencies to flee adversity. Help us to come boldly to Your throne of grace and trust that You will bring us through and make us stronger and wiser in the process. Amen.

MARCH 10
GOD NEVER FAILS

Psalm 55:22: Cast your cares on the Lord and He will sustain you. He will never let the righteous fall.

There are times when we think we know someone else so well, that they are so much like us we are like one and then, boom, something happens that makes our world fall apart and we realize that wasn't the case at all. We have been betrayed, perhaps by an unfaithful spouse, a dishonest business partner, a trusted friend. Jesus Christ is the only person that we can truly know, that we can have an intimate relationship with and trust with everything pertaining to our lives. We can have such a relationship because He is who He says He is. He did what He said He would do. He has never lied and He never will. In our good times we should love and praise Him, and in our bad times we will trust Him to bring us through the trials that try to destroy us. King David's most trusted friend betrayed him by leaving the king and going to the son who was trying to overthrow him. The king said if it had been anyone else, he could have dealt with it but not his most trusted confidant. Then David turned to his Lord because He knew that justice would prevail in the end.

Read Psalm 55:12-23
Psalm 34:18, Jeremiah 9:4 & 11:20

Thank You, Father, for revealing Yourself to those who cry out to You for justice and mercy. May we always know that no matter the circumstances of life, You always do what is right and just. Amen.

MARCH 11
TRUST IN HIM

Psalm 56:3-4: When I am afraid, I will trust in You. In God whose word I praise, in God I trust, I will not be afraid. What can mortal man do to me?

When all we do, say and think is grounded in our faith in Jesus, we have no reason to fear. Our goal as Christians is eternity. On this earth, mankind craves for eternal peace and happiness. This is sometimes referred to as Nirvana, but that is not the peace and happiness that our Lord offers. Our souls are eternal and whether we acknowledge it or not, we will live forever. Once we are born upon this earth, there will never be a time when we do not exist. It is appointed to men once to die but after this is the judgment. There is a battle unseen to the human eyes for the soul of every man, woman and child. Jesus said to not be afraid of those who kill the body but cannot kill the soul. Rather, be afraid of the One who can destroy both soul and body in hell. We can trust that the Lord guides us through our trials, for we will have them, and when our lives are over our reward is everlasting life with Jesus, our Savior.

Read Psalm 56
1 Chronicles 5:20, Isaiah 12:2, Matthew 10:28, Hebrews 9:27

Our hope is in You, Lord. You have called us by name and we have answered. Walk with us every second of every day so that we will never lose sight of You, the One who keeps us secure in all circumstances of life. Amen.

MARCH 12
STRENGTH IN GOD

Psalm 57:2: I cry out to God Most High, to God, who fulfills His purpose for me.

Lifting weights is one way to tone our bodies and get in shape. The more consistent we are, the stronger we become. Each day, we build endurance and can accomplish more until we reach our goal and maintain it. This is a physical strength that comes with commitment and discipline, but it doesn't give us the strength we need to deal with the challenges of life. Asking the Lord to use His strength is the best way to meet any challenge we face. At the time David wrote this psalm, He was a cave dweller. God had anointed him king instead of Saul but he was in hiding. At one point in time, David was in a position to kill Saul. Saul had gone into a cave to relieve himself, not knowing that David and his men were far back in the cave. David crept up to Saul unnoticed and cut off a corner of Saul's robe, but he did not lift his hand against Saul because he was the Lord's anointed. He knew that the Lord would avenge the wrongs that had been done against him. When the Lord delivered David out of King Saul's hand, he shouted with praise and thanksgiving. We must draw our strength from the Lord and not from any physical strength that we might have. In doing so, we can face anything with a freedom that only He can give.

Read Psalm 57
1 Samuel 24:3-13, 2 Samuel 22:33, Nahum 1:7, 1 Timothy 4:8

Heavenly Father, Your strength is made perfect in weakness. Help us to rely only on Your strength and not our own. When we have been hurt, help us not to seek revenge but trust that You will be the judge and show mercy when mercy is due. Amen.

MARCH 13
A CRY FOR JUSTICE

Psalm 58:11: Then men will say, Surely the righteous still are rewarded; surely there is a God who judges the earth.

People go to trial with an adversary to seek justice. The judge hears both sides and renders a decision based on the entirety of the evidence before him or her. One side will be happy and the other won't, but hopefully justice will have been served by the judge who tried the matter. Courts were established to help individuals bring their cause before a disinterested but educated and knowledgeable judge who can render the appropriate justice. In today's psalm, David asks his accusers, of whom there were many, whether or not they were acting according to justice. Some held their tongues and by their silence gave consent to the injustices being perpetrated against David. But David knew that the Lord would vindicate him because He knew the hearts of those who set out to cause him harm. We may not have a cause worthy enough to go before an earthly judge, but we can be certain there is a God in heaven who will one day render justice to all who have ever lived.

Read Psalm 58
Deuteronomy 32:35, Amos 5:15, Romans 12:19, Colossians 3:25

Lord, in the midst of our struggles and also in our times of joy, hold us close to You that we never lose sight of Your presence in our lives. May we always be mindful that You are the judge of us all. Amen.

MARCH 14
SEE WHAT GOD WILL DO

Psalm 59:9: O my strength, I watch for You; You, O God, are my fortress, my loving God.

King David had many enemies, especially King Saul. David knew where his source of strength came from but he was still a man with all the emotions that a man has, and so he poured his heart out to the only One he knew could help him. We can learn so much from the psalms when we meditate upon them. They teach us that we need not pour our hearts out to others but to God alone because He is the One we can trust to do what is just. In the Old Testament, before Jesus came, there was no knowledge of salvation in Christ and so the cries of God's people were for revenge against their enemies now! There are times in our lives when we cry out to God for revenge now because of the injustices that we see.

We must remember that the Lord is not willing that any should perish but that all would come to everlasting life. Scripture tells us that there will be judgment, that no evil will go unpunished. We must endure to the end and pray for God's love and strength so that all who seek Him will call upon His name.

Read Psalm 59:1-9
Job 8:3-6, Matthew 24:13, 2 Timothy 2:12

Lord, may we look to You as our source of strength in time of trouble and distress so that in the midst of heartache we can hold our heads high and trust that through You everything is going to be all right. Amen.

MARCH 15
PRIDEFUL MAN

Psalm 59:12: For the sins of their mouths, for the words of their lips, let them be caught in their pride.

Pride goes before destruction, a haughty spirit before a fall. There is no better example of that than Nebuchadnezzar, king of Babylon. During his reign, he had a dream of what God was about to do to him. After Daniel interpreted the dream, he admonished the king to renounce his sins by doing what is right so it may be that his prosperity would continue. Twelve months later, the king was walking on the roof of the royal palace and said, "Is not this the great Babylon I have built as the royal residence, by my mighty power and for the glory of my majesty?" The words were still on his lips when a voice came from heaven and the dream which the king had came to pass. Because of his pride, he was driven away from people to live with the wild animals. He ate grass like cattle. His body was drenched with the dew of heaven until his hair grew like the feathers of an eagle and his nails like the claws of a bird. At the end of the Lord's appointed time, Nebuchadnezzar's sanity was restored and he praised the Most High and honored and glorified Him who lives forever and ever. Most likely we will not be changed into an animal because of our pride, but this story is an example of how the Most High is sovereign over the kingdoms of men and gives them to anyone He wishes. When we consider His greatness, it should make us so humble that pride has nowhere to take up residence in our lives.

Read Psalm 59:10-17
Proverbs 16:18, Daniel 4:28-37, James 4:10

Holy, Holy, Holy, Lord God Almighty, Creator, Redeemer, friend. Guide us by the light of Your presence. Engulf us by Your Spirit and help us to trust You no matter life's circumstances. We ask to be humble before You so that only You can lift us up. Amen.

MARCH 16
THE LORD'S BANNER

Psalm 60:4: But for those who fear You, You have raised a banner to be unfurled against the bow.

Banners are unfurled in order to draw attention to a particular cause or group of people. They are often embroidered with signs and symbols that have a particular meaning. In the Old Testament, each tribe of Israel had a distinguishing banner for their clan or family. Isaiah prophesied concerning the coming of the Messiah and said, "In that day, the Root of Jesse will stand as a banner for the peoples; the nations will rally to him and his place of rest will be glorious. . .He will raise a banner for the nations and gather the exiles of Israel; He will assemble the scattered people of Judah from the four corners of the earth." When the Lord raises a banner to be unfurled against the bow, this indicates His presence, His protection and aid to His people. Our banner is the Word of God which guides us into all truth. No prophecy of Scripture came about by the prophet's own interpretation. For prophecy never had its origin in the will of man but men spoke from God as they were carried along by the Holy Spirit. All Scripture is God-breathed and useful for teaching, rebuking, correcting, and training in the righteousness of God so that the man and woman of God may be thoroughly equipped for every good work.

Read Psalm 60
Isaiah 11:2 & 10, 2 Timothy 3:16, 2 Peter 1:20-21

Holy Lord, lift Your banner high above us so that we see Your glorious presence. When we look toward Heaven, open our eyes to see all that You have created and know that You are God. Help us to hide Your word in our hearts so that we do not sin against You. You are high and lifted up and we praise Your Holy Name. Amen.

MARCH 17
LIFE LIFTER

Psalm 61:2: From the ends of the earth, I call to You. I call as my heart grows faint; lead me to the rock that is higher than I.

No matter where we are or what we are doing, we can speak to the Lord. He hears us. He knows us by name and loves to hear our voices call out to Him in prayer and praise. He wants us to commune with Him and find peace in His presence no matter our circumstances. His love pours out from the heavens and He shields us with Himself. We cannot always comprehend what is going on in our lives but when we trust our Lord we can rest in the knowledge that all is well. When we grow faint and weary, He lifts us up, not necessarily physically but always spiritually. Our Lord is spirit and this is where eternal life flows from. This is the part of us that will live forever in eternity, our spirit. When that time comes, we will be rejoicing with our Savior. He is a continual light for all who call upon His name. We will be lifted high above the things that now bring us down and we will live in His presence forevermore.

Read Psalm 61
Mark 13:13, John 4:24

Lord, You raise us up when we are down. You shower us with Your love when we seek You with all our hearts. You are awesome. We love You and thank You for all You have done and are doing. Amen.

MARCH 18
OUR FORTRESS IN TIMES OF TROUBLE

Psalm 62:5-6: Find rest, O my soul, in God alone; my hope comes from Him. He alone is my rock and my salvation. He is my fortress. I will not be shaken.

A fortress is a wall of protection that surrounds a city and makes it difficult for the enemy to penetrate. As long as the fortress stands, the people inside are safe. At times, there are defects in the fortress walls which if not tended to and repaired can cause the whole wall to tumble. This is akin to life. We must nurture our relationship with the Lord or the wall of protection He offers comes tumbling down. When we give ourselves completely to maintaining the fortress, it never falls. Our Lord tells us that if we make Him our fortress we will never be shaken. When the enemy attacks, our Lord is in control. When we feel overwhelmed, we must look straight into the heavens and proclaim that the Lord God Almighty is our fortress and He never fails. He always brings us through the challenges we face.

Read Psalm 62
Psalm 18:2, 28:2 & 59:16, Jeremiah 16:19-21

Lord, there are times when we think we are strong enough to do everything on our own. Bring us back to You so we may never forget where our real strength comes from. You and You alone are the fortress that we need to protect us. Amen.

MARCH 19
THIRSTING OF OUR SOULS

Psalm 63:1: O God, You are my God. Earnestly I seek You; my soul thirsts for You; my body longs for You in a dry and weary land where there is no water.

Though the fig tree does not bud and there are no grapes on the vines; though the olive crop fails and the fields produce no food, though there are no sheep in the pen and no cattle in the stall, yet I will rejoice in the Lord. I will be joyful in God my Savior. There are times in our lives when we thirst because of the dry desert before us, and this is not only a physical thirst but a spiritual thirst of our souls. Our Lord lifts us above the deserts when we see no end to the dryness as we look out on its vast sands. He takes us to the oasis where our souls are renewed by His living and eternal water of life. He rejuvenates us and quenches our thirst when we trust in Him, for His miracle power transforms our lives.

Read Psalm 63
Isaiah 55:1, Habakkuk 3:17-18, John 7:37

Merciful and loving Father in Heaven, You look upon Your children and ask who will seek Me with all their heart and trust Me with every aspect of their lives? May we be the ones who answer when You call. Fill our souls and quench our thirst with the fullness of Your presence. Amen.

MARCH 20
HEARTFELT CRY

Psalm 64:10: Let the righteous rejoice in the Lord and take refuge in Him; let all the upright in heart praise Him.

There is One to whom we can go with our innermost thoughts, One we can cry out to who hears us and does not hold our words against us. He is our Lord, our Savior, our Comforter, our Deliverer. There are two forces at work in this world, and even though the world denies this it does not change the truth of it. We either believe in God or we don't. Even those who are seemingly good, if they have not chosen the ways of the Lord they have chosen their own way and made their own rules for life. There is a way that seems right to a man but in the end it leads to death. There is no hope because they have not trusted in Jesus for their eternal souls. Without a Savior, we cannot save ourselves from what awaits all of us in death. Those who are defiant and argue to their last breath that God does not exist will know the truth when they step into eternity. Those who call upon His name, who trust Him, have the hope that He guides them each day and that at the end of life He will be there to usher them into His presence and eternal kingdom.

Read Psalm 64
Proverbs 14:12, Matthew 19:25-26, Acts 16:30-31

Savior, who hears the cries of those who believe in Your Name, encircle us with Your heavenly angels and protect us from the temptations of this world. Amen.

MARCH 21
ABUNDANCE IN HIM

Psalm 65:9: You care for the land and water it; You enrich it abundantly. The streams of God are filled with water to provide the people with grain. For so You have ordained it.

Today's psalm begins with praise to the God in Zion, the One who hears prayer and forgives our transgressions The Lord answers with awesome deeds of righteousness He cared for the land and watered it He crowned the year with His bounty: the meadows covered with flocks and the valleys mantled with grain. Apparently it was a year of bountiful harvest and there was much to be thankful for. David knew what the Scriptures said and He saw the results of his prayers. He knew that His God was real and not some mere abstraction. He knew that He is the God that all men need because He is full of compassion and mercy. The Lord draws up the drops of water which distill as rain to the streams. He scatters His lightning about Him, bathing the depths of the sea. This is the way He governs the nations and provides food in abundance.

Read Psalm 65
Job 36:27-31, James 5:11

Almighty Lord, the world was formed when You spoke, and all that is in it. We praise You and thank You that You have called us to know You, Creator of all things both seen and unseen. We love You. There is no God like You. Amen.

MARCH 22
PRAISE HIM

Psalm 66:20: Praise be to God, who has not rejected my prayer or withheld His love from me.

The Bible was put together from over 15,000 manuscripts. The prophecies of the Old Testament that told about the birth of Jesus by a virgin came to pass, as well as many others that foretold His coming. When we read God's word with believing minds and a receiving heart, we learn about the goodness of our Lord and the consistent, unconditional love He has for His people. He calls us to come to Him, to know who He is. When our hearts are broken and we see no end to our hurt, He pours His love into our wounds to heal us. He waits patiently for our prayers. He rejoices when we call on Him and trust Him for the answers. When we wake in the morning, we should shout to Him with our praises, for another new dawn has come, another new day to walk with our King of kings and Lord of lords. Magnify and glorify His holy, wonderful name.

Read Psalm 66
Deuteronomy 26:18-19, 1 Chronicles 16:8-12, Isaiah 7:14, Jeremiah 31:3

We praise You, Lord, the Giver of life. You who sits upon the throne in glory are worthy of our praises. There is no God like our God! Help us proclaim Your love and mercy and pray for all the nations of the world so they will seek You. Amen.

MARCH 23
THE YIELD OF THE HARVEST

Psalm 67:5-6: May the peoples praise You, O God; may all the peoples praise You. Then the land will yield its harvest, and God, our God, will bless us.

When we are in our prime of life, we feel untouchable, strong, like the whole world is ours and nothing can stop us from attaining our goals. It takes but one misfortune to change the course of our lives and all we thought we could accomplish has slipped beyond our grasp. With the Lord by our side all is not lost. He can take a hardship and turn it into a blessing, not only for us but for others. There is a well-known artist in the Christian community who at a young age had a life-changing experience. She dove into a shallow lake and broke her neck, and her body was paralyzed from the neck down. She is a quadriplegic. If anyone had a reason to be angry, it was her. But she put her trust in God. He gave her the ability to draw by putting a pencil in her mouth. She also sings, has recorded several musical albums and is a staunch advocate for those with disabilities. Her unfortunate accident allowed her to do for others what she otherwise might never have done. When we depend on our Lord and don't look to our circumstances, others see that He has given the strength to endure, because everyone's life has purpose and meaning.

Read Psalm 67
Psalm 37:25, Philippians 4:12-13

Lord, You are the never-changing One who knows all things, from whom nothing is hidden. Receive our praises, Almighty Father, and yield the harvest in our lives that we need. Help us to live in Your strength and power until the end of our days. Amen.

MARCH 24
HAPPINESS AND JOY

Psalm 68:3: But may the righteous be glad and rejoice before God; may they be happy and joyful.

As followers of Christ, we have everything to be happy and joyful about. Through Him, we have the answers to life. There are times when we cry out for justice right now against the wrongs that are so prevalent in the world. Our Lord hears our prayers, but we must trust Him that He will be the One to mete out judgment. He wants us to know Him in such a way that we can share with Him our innermost desires. When we are honest, we have freedom; freedom from the temptations of this world; freedom from sin; freedom from sadness. Even when life brings us down, we can rejoice always in the knowledge that we have a God who loves us and wants us to be happy. We can have true joy and sing to the Lord, for He has done glorious things. When we are burdened with the affairs of life, it is difficult to proclaim God's goodness and mercy to others. If we are joyful and carefree, others will desire to find out why and perhaps be drawn to our Lord.

Read Psalm 68:1-18
Isaiah 12:5, Philemon 7, 2 John 3-4

Lord, thank You for the joy of life. You give us the freedom to choose in this life whether to be happy or sad, burdened or free. May we choose the joy that You have set before us so that we will be a light to others. Amen.

MARCH 25
BURDEN BEARER

Psalm 68:19: Praise be to the Lord, to God our Savior, who daily bears our burdens.

Jesus said, "Come to me all you who are weary and burdened, and I will give you rest. Take my yoke upon you and learn from me, for I am gentle and humble in heart, and you will find rest for your souls." He is our burden bearer. We will face heartache in this world but we don't have to be burdened with it. We can live without a care because our Lord tells us to come to Him with our burdens and He will give us rest. Before we call, He answers and while we are still speaking He hears. By asking, we receive. We also come into closer communion and relationship with Him when we let Him know what's on our mind. We do this by spending time alone with Him because it is impossible to become friends with someone we do not speak with. The Lord patiently waits for us to call out to Him and to love Him. What a friend we have in Him who bears our burdens daily.

Read Psalm 68:19-35
Isaiah 65:24, Matthew 11:28-29

Lord, we allow ourselves to be burdened down by the cares and worries of this world. Help us realize that all of this is unnecessary because You are our burden bearer. You tell us to cast all our cares upon You because You take care for us. May our yoke be easy and our burden light in You. Amen.

MARCH 26
DROWNING IN DESPAIR

Psalm 69:1-2: Save me, O God, for the waters have come up to my neck. I sink in the miry depths, where there is no foothold. I have come into the deep waters. The floods engulf me.

When we are in the midst of life's problems, sometimes it is like being in deep water with nothing to stand on or take hold of, and we panic. It's during this time of panic when we can drown. The Apostle Peter saw someone walking on the water. When he realized it was Jesus, he called out to Him because he too wanted to walk on the water. Jesus told him to, "come." Peter began to walk on water, but then he lost sight of the Lord and cried out, "Save me." As he was about to go down, Jesus took his hand, led him back to the boat, and said, "You of little faith. Why did you doubt?" The Lord tells us time and time again that when we trust Him, He takes us safely to shore. We are all sinners and we all fail. It is when we believe in Jesus Christ as the rock to hold onto that we never have to panic. The worst that can happen in this life is death. He is waiting for us on the other side to usher us into His kingdom. When we become overwhelmed and panicky, we should come to Him, talk with Him, pray to Him, and then listen. There is a calming peace that says all is well; thank you for trusting Me.

Read Psalm 69:1-18
Psalm 107:28-29, Matthew 14:26-31

Lord, when problems overtake us like a flood, take us by the hand and bring us out of the deep waters. Give us peace and remind us that You are by our side and You calm the storms of our life. Amen.

MARCH 27
HEAVEN AND EARTH WILL PRAISE HIM

Psalm 69:34: Let heaven and earth praise Him, the seas and all that move in them.

Jesus was entering Jerusalem. His followers were rejoicing because they thought He had come to set up His kingdom. People spread their cloaks on the road as He went along and the whole crowd of disciples began joyfully to praise God in loud voices saying, "Blessed is the King who comes in the name of the Lord." Upon hearing this, the Pharisees wanted Jesus to rebuke His disciples. Instead, He replied, "If they keep quiet, the stones will cry out!" As He approached Jerusalem He wept over it, and then He entered the temple area and began driving out those who were selling saying, "It is written that My house will be a house of prayer but you have made it a den of robbers." After this, the chief priests and leaders among the people were trying to kill Him but could not find a way to do it. We know that eventually He did die, but He did it of His own accord, for the Father gave Him authority to lay His life down and to take it up again. When He does return, His kingdom will be an eternal kingdom, and heaven and earth will praise Him.

Read Psalm 69:19-36
Daniel 4:2-3, Luke 19:35-47, John 10:18

Lord, we know when Jesus appears, the veil over our eyes will be lifted and the mysteries of God known. We know that He is coming as a thief in the night and will set up His kingdom. Help us to live as though He is coming today so that when He does appear in the clouds we will be ready to meet Him in all His glory. Amen.

MARCH 28
OUR HELP AND DELIVERER

Psalm 70:4: But may all who seek You rejoice and be glad in You; may those who love Your salvation always say, "Let God be exalted."

There was a wicked man named Nabal who was surly and mean in his dealings. After the sheep were shorn, David sent his men to Nabal saying that because they did not mistreat Nabal's men and nothing was missing from them that they be allowed to partake in whatever could be found for them. His response was, "Who is this David? Who is this son of Jesse? Why should I take my bread and water and the meat I have slaughtered for my shearers and give it to men coming from who knows where?" David was furious and set out to go to battle with Nabal until his wife, Abigail, intervened and asked David to reconsider. At her pleading, he did not go to battle. When Abigail told her husband about these things, his heart failed him and it became like a stone. Then about ten days later, the Lord struck him and he died. This is an extreme example of God's judgment, but the Lord knows the hearts of all of us and it is up to Him what should happen and when. He is the God who fed the prophet Elijah by using ravens that brought him bread and meat in the morning and evening at the beginning of a long drought. He caused the enemies of Israel to turn upon each other when He brought confusion into their midst. We serve a mighty God, and though He loves all His creation He answers those who call upon His name.

Read Psalm 70
1 Samuel 25:36-37, 1 Kings 17:1-6, 2 Chronicles 6:40-42, Romans 11:26

Lord, You are our help in times of trouble. With Your strong arm You deliver and protect us. We pray for all of Your creation, for to know You is to know the One who gave us life. Keep us safe this day and all the days of our lives. Amen.

MARCH 29
THE SOLID ROCK

Psalm 71:3: Be my rock of refuge, to which I can always go; give the command to save me, for You are my Rock and my Fortress.

Jesus told us to build our faith on the solid rock, not the sand that is taken away with the waves of the sea; for the rock stands forever. He is the Rock. If we read this psalm slowly and meditate upon it, we see that our God is faithful and trustworthy to those who know Him and call upon His name. If everyone believed this, they would want to serve the Lord, Creator of all things, the One who loves us with an everlasting love. God's most beautiful creation, Lucifer, decided He wanted to ascend above the Most High God and be worshiped but this was impossible because God cannot be surpassed. He was so persuasive many of the angels in Heaven went with him. These were angels who did not keep their positions of authority but abandoned their own home and are bound with everlasting chains for judgment on the great day. When Jesus came, he made it possible to reconcile to our Heavenly Father. These are things that have to be believed in faith. They are written about in God's Holy Word so we can have insight into what is going on in this life. When we take hold of the firm foundation of Jesus, we are anchored to Him and will not go off course.

Read Psalm 71
Isaiah 14:12-15, Matthew 7:24-27, Jude 6

Holy, holy, holy is the Lord God Almighty. You are the solid rock of our salvation, the One we can count on, who never fails. Help us to keep our eyes on You and never lose sight of Your firm foundation, Jesus Christ, our Lord. Amen.

MARCH 30
RIGHTEOUS RULERS

Psalm 72:1-2: Endow the king with Your justice, O God, the royal son with Your righteousness. He will judge Your people in righteousness, Your afflicted ones with justice.

King David cried out to God for his son Solomon, who would soon take his place as King of Israel. He asked that through Solomon, the people would be cared for and blessed. Solomon was the wisest man on earth. When the Lord said he could ask for anything, he asked for wisdom to rule his people and the Lord answered. He gave Solomon a discerning heart to govern his people and distinguish between right and wrong, and said there would never be anyone else like him, and there wasn't. During Solomon's reign, he loved many foreign women and turned his heart after other gods. When he died, his son Rehoboam took the kingdom and he did that which was evil in the sight of the Lord. Throughout Old Testament history, there were righteous kings and evil ones. When the righteous thrive, the people rejoice; when the wicked rule, the people groan. Righteousness exalts a nation.

Read Psalm 72
1 Kings 4:29-34 & 11:1-4, Proverbs 29:2, Zechariah 7:9-10

Lord, we pray for our leaders. We pray that their decisions are not made because of selfish desires but for the good all. Open their eyes to see that when they seek You with all their hearts righteousness prevails and our nation will be at rest. Amen.

MARCH 31
FINAL DESTINY

Psalm 73:16-17: When I tried to understand all this, it was oppressive to me, till I entered the sanctuary of God; then I understood their final destiny.

Our destiny is eternal life with Jesus. We know this because He said that He is going to prepare a place for us, that He is coming back to take us to be with Him so that we may also be where He is. We know our destiny because we have read the roadmap that leads us there, the Word of God. We would never plan a trip without knowing what our destination is going to be, but that is how a lot of us live. We go aimlessly through life with no guidance or direction. But when we get the map that tells us where we are going, worry disappears and we become confident that we know where we are headed. He told us, "You know the way to the place where

I am going." We may make a wrong turn once in a while and there will be detours along the way, but when we have the map as our guide we know we will arrive. And when we do, the glory of the Lord is there. He takes our hand and brings us to our final destination, eternal life.

Read Psalm 73:1-17
Ecclesiastes 3:11, John 14:3-4

Eternal Judge of all creation, thank You for sending Jesus so that we do not have to pay the eternal price of our sins. Help us to be Your people so that the light of Your glory may shine through us and those who do not yet know You will see You in us. Help us to live righteously as You have called us to do and not be one way publicly and another privately. Amen.

APRIL 1
HEAVEN

Psalm 73:25: Whom have I in heaven but You? And earth has nothing I desire besides You.

Although Heaven is mentioned hundreds of times throughout the Old and New Testaments, there is very little description of what it is like. Occasionally we get a glimpse of it through the eyes of others. We know that the Lord sits enthroned between the cherubim and that all the multitudes of Heaven stand on His right and His left. We also know it is God's dwelling place and the place we all want to go to when we die. We know that the earthly tent we live in will one day be destroyed but we have a building from God, an eternal house in heaven, not built by human hands. Jesus made it clear that there is only one way to get there, and that is by believing He is the only begotten Son of God. He made it possible for all who believe in Him to one day go to Heaven. The kingdom of God is like hidden treasure in a field. When someone finds it, they sell all they have to buy the field. It's also like a merchant looking for fine pearls. When he finds one of great value, he sells everything to buy it. Our citizenship is in Heaven, and we eagerly await a Savior from there, the Lord Jesus Christ, who will one day transform our lowly bodies so that they will be like His glorious body. When we ask Jesus to become our Savior, we have every reason to rejoice because our names are written in heaven.

Read Psalm 73:18-28
Deuteronomy 3:24, 1 Kings 8:30, 2 Kings 19:15, 2 Chronicles 18:18, Matthew 13:44-45, Luke 10:20, 2 Corinthians 5:1, Philippians 3:20-21, Hebrews 12:23

Heavenly Father, we pray for a life full of Your presence. We thank You for Jesus, who shed His holy blood on the cross at Calvary for our sins. Lift us above the fray of life and help us keep our thoughts on You who sits on Your throne in Heaven, knowing that one day we will be with You for all eternity. Amen.

APRIL 2
WHEN WE WANDER

Psalm 74:17: It was You who set all the boundaries of the earth; You have made both summer and winter.

God chose Abraham to be the father of a people whose number could not be counted, and through him all nations of the earth would be blessed. He singled His chosen out from all the nations of the world to be His inheritance. But the children of Israel continually wandered away from their Lord, from serving the Holy One. They worshiped and sacrificed to other gods and turned their back on the One who promised lifelong and eternal blessings if they would serve Him. Let's think about what we spend our time on each day. Our first priority should be to set aside time for Him in order to draw closer to Him. To please Him, we must seek Him and believe that He is. We must live within the boundaries He has set; not to be restricted but to remain safe and secure. Just like the children of Israel, there are times when we leave our first love. He allows us to wander wherever our own desires lead us but He continually calls us back to Him. He is faithful to respond to our cries for help when we realize we have drifted.

Read Psalm 74
Genesis 18:18 & 22:17-18, 1 Kings 8:38-39, 53 & 61

Lord, keep us from wandering away and desiring the things of this world. Renew our hearts. Search us. Fill us anew with Your Spirit and help us to make the desires of Your heart our desires. Amen.

APRIL 3
HE WHO HOLDS THE PILLARS FIRM

Psalm 75:3: When the earth and all its people quake, it is I who hold its pillars firm.

A thousand years are as a day to the Lord. He rejoices in creating every day. He laid the foundations of the earth. He knows the abode of light and where darkness resides, and takes them to their places. He knows the paths of their dwellings. He has seen the storehouses of the snow and hail which He reserves for times of trouble. He knows the way to the place where the lightning is dispersed and the place where the east winds are scattered over the earth. He has wisdom to count the clouds. He knows when the mountain goats give birth and watches when the doe bears her fawn. At His command, the eagle soars and builds its nest on high. There is no one who has a claim against the Lord that He must pay. Everything under heaven belongs to the Lord. We have no reason to fear when we realize that our God has done all of these things, and much more. Let's draw close to the One who holds the pillars firm, for we are safe in His loving arms.

Read Psalm 75
Job 38:19-24, 37, 39:1-2, 27, 41:11, 2 Peter 3:8

Lord, show us how to pray in power and authority by the One true God who can supply all of our needs, wipe away all of our tears and mend our broken hearts. We ask You to come into our lives in a mighty way with Your limitless supply of love and mercy. Amen.

APRIL 4
GOD'S PERFECT PLAN

Psalm 76:1: In Judah, God is known; His name is great in Israel.

There was a time when the whole world had one language and a common speech. The people were in the process of building a tower that reached to the heavens when the Lord looked down and said because there is only one language, there is nothing the people plan to do that will be impossible for them. So He confounded their language so they could not understand each other and scattered them over the face of the whole earth. He chose Abram (later known as Abraham) to leave his country and people and go to the land the Lord would show him and He would make him a great nation and bless him. Abram answered the call. He was faithful even to the point of willingly sacrificing his son to the Lord. Through the generations, a great nation was born known as Israel and they worshiped the God of Abraham, Isaac and Jacob. They were not always faithful to Him but they were chosen by Him. Through the lineage of Judah, the Messiah was born and He proclaimed the way to God. He taught us that God is our Father and He loves us so much that He sent His Son to die for our sins. When we take that leap of faith to trust Him, our lives are never the same.

Read Psalm 76

Genesis 11:1-9, Genesis 12:1-2, Deuteronomy 7:6, Matthew 1:17

Lord, thank You for Your plan from the very beginning. You give us freedom to choose our destiny. Open our hearts to receive Your promise of salvation. Keep us close by Your side. Hold our hand when necessary. Pick us up when we fall. Encourage us when we are sad and rejoice with us when we are happy. We want You to be not only our Lord but our friend. Amen.

APRIL 5
HOW GREAT IS OUR GOD

Psalm 77:13: Your ways, O God, are holy. What god is so great as our God?

There is no other god formed before the God of Heaven, nor will there ever be one after Him. There is no image to compare Him to. Men conjure up idols and make their own gods out of things that cannot see or hear. A craftsman casts it and a goldsmith overlays it with gold and fashions silver chains for it. A man too poor to present such an offering selects wood that will not rot. He looks for a skilled craftsman to set up an idol that will not topple. There is no breath to be found in idols fashioned by the hand of man. But do we not know, have we not heard, has it not been told from the beginning, have we not understood since the earth was founded, that the Lord sits enthroned above the circle of the earth? Today's Psalm cries out as though God has forsaken His people but then His glory shines forth and His acts of old are remembered. When we look to our circumstances, we may sometimes feel like the Lord is nowhere to be found, but He is there. There is no god as great as our God.

Read Psalm 77
Isaiah 40:25-26, 43:10 & 44:12-20, Jeremiah 10:3-5, Hebrews 1:10

Lord, we praise Your holy name. There is no idol made by human hands that speaks, hears and sees or that is holy, pure and worthy of praise. Nothing can compare to You. If we have any idols in our life, show us so that they are removed and nothing stands in the way of worshiping the great and mighty God that You are. Amen.

APRIL 6
TEACHING THE NEXT GENERATION

Psalm 78:5-6: He decreed statutes for Jacob and established the law in Israel, which He commanded our forefathers to teach their children so the next generation would know them, even the children yet to be born, and they in turn would tell their children.

The law of God began when Moses was called to Mount Sinai where he met the Lord. The Ten Commandments were a result of that encounter. The Lord wrote them by His own hand and Moses took them down the mountain to the people. If we were to live by these commandments alone, there would be harmony in the world. But there remains a veil under the old covenant, and it has not been removed because only in Jesus Christ is it taken away. His laws are now written on our hearts and it should be a natural thing to teach our children about the God whom we serve. Human nature being what it is, though, this does not always happen, and so our children go the way of the world if we do not teach them. Since the beginning of time, man's heart has rebelled against His Creator because he believes he knows how to live his own life without Him. If we were to seriously contemplate this, we would realize how short life is. Fame and fortune may come in one's lifetime but it is so fleeting. When the rich and famous succumb to old age, many become recluse. We hear stories of their sad lives, for nothing can satisfy the deep longing in our souls except a personal relationship with Jesus Christ. He fills that longing with His love when we give our lives to Him.

Read Psalm 78:1-39
Deuteronomy 4:9 and 30:9-10, 2 Corinthians 3:2-3 & 3:14, Hebrews 8:10

Lord, write Your law on the tablets of our hearts so that we will love and obey Your commands. Help us be the light of God to our children so they too will desire to follow You and Your precepts. Keep us on the narrow path that leads to the ways of righteousness for all generations. Amen.

APRIL 7
DO NOT TURN AWAY

Psalm 78:56: But they put God to the test and rebelled against the Most High. They did not keep His statutes.

God's chosen people had been slaves to Pharaoh, the King of Egypt, for many years. The Lord sent Moses to set His people free. He showed His mighty hand by sending many plagues upon the Egyptian people, even taking the firstborn of every household until Pharaoh finally let God's people go. As they traveled through the desert, they began to murmur against the Lord. They had no vision of what He planned for them. They could only see where they were at the moment, and to them it was not good. Though they witnessed many miracles, their hearts were hardened, and instead of entering the promised land, they wandered in the wilderness for 40 years until the generation that came out of Egypt was dead and the next generation came up to inherit the land flowing with milk and honey. It's awesome to know what the Lord will do to set His children free from slavery. He did it then for the children of Israel and He does it now for those who believe on His Son, Jesus Christ.

Read Psalm 78:40-72
Exodus 3:6, Amos 2:10, Acts 7:2-7

Lord of Mercies, thank You for setting us free from the slavery of sin. We ask that You continually search our hearts so that we do not turn from You back to our old ways. Help us to be truthful about our faults, confess our sins, ask forgiveness and walk in the Presence of Your Glory, through Christ our Lord. Amen.

APRIL 8
HELP US, O GOD

Psalm 79:9: Help us, O God Our Savior, for the glory of Your name, deliver us and forgive our sins, for Your name's sake.

God's chosen people were persecuted and killed by their enemies. The temple had been utterly destroyed and blood flowed like water in the land. There was no one to bury the dead. It was a time of despair and helplessness, so it seemed. The author of this psalm, who was the chief musician at the time of David, saw Jerusalem go to rubble under the reign of Solomon, King David's son, when he turned from the Living God to worship strange gods. In the midst of all the destruction that was taking place, Asaph, not only a musician but a priest from the tribe of Levi, cried out to Almighty God to show mercy on His people despite their rebellion against Him. It is no different for us today. We see things around us at times that might make us wonder where our righteous and loving God is, especially when cruelty and devastation exist. But we forget that there is a continual battle being fought for the souls of mankind, which is why Jesus came into the world as a light so that no one who believes in Him should stay in darkness. It is up to each of us to choose whom we will serve. When we choose our Lord, we need not fear what surrounds us because His promises are true. He is good and his love endures forever.

Read Psalm 79
2 Chronicles 5:12-14, Psalm 121:7-8, John 12:46

Lord, as we cry out to you for mercy, remember that we live in a fallen and sometimes cruel world and that it is only by Your mercy and grace that we are lifted up. Renew us by Your strength and keep us ever mindful of Your Presence. Amen.

APRIL 9
RESTORE US

Psalm 80:3: Restore us, O Lord God Almighty; make Your Face shine upon us, that we may be saved.

In verses 3, 17 and 19, there had been a falling away of God's people. They were pleasing themselves and worshiping other gods, to the point where the Lord gave them over to their own ways and it was quickly leading the children of Israel to destruction. Their only hope was to return to their God so He would save and restore them. There have been times in our lives when we have turned away from God and gone our own way. It may not even be intentional. We get busy with our work, our families, the computer and we don't take time to sit quietly before Him and seek what pleases Him instead of ourselves. The Lord has a way of getting our attention. He draws us back to Him so that our relationship will be restored and we can once again know the fullness of His unconditional love.

Read Psalm 80
Psalm 23:3, Joel 2:25 (KJV), Romans 1:28

Heavenly Father, You breathed into us the breath of life and we became a living soul. May we never forget that you are the Creator and we are the created. Thank You for Your mercy and for restoring us to You through Your Son. Amen.

APRIL 10
THE PROMISES OF GOD

Psalm 81:13-14: If My people would but listen to Me, if Israel would follow My ways, how quickly would I subdue their enemies and turn My hand against their foes.

Esther, who was a Jewess, was queen to King Xerxes, who ruled over 127 provinces stretching from India to Cush. The king gave Haman, the son of Hammedath, a seat of honor higher than that of all other nobles.

All the royal officials at the king's gate knelt down and paid homage to Haman, except for Mordecai, a Jew, who was the cousin of Queen Esther. This enraged Haman and he looked for a way to destroy not only Mordecai but all of the Jews throughout the whole kingdom of Xerxes. He talked the king into sending out a decree to destroy all the Jews on a certain date and time. When Mordecai learned of this, he tore his clothes, put on sackcloth and ashes and went out into the city, wailing loudly and bitterly. Upon hearing this, Esther sent clothes for him to put on but he would not accept them. She called for a three-day fast saying that when the fast was complete she would go to the king even though it was against the law. When she approached the inner court of the palace in front of the king's hall, the king was sitting on his royal throne. He held out to her the gold scepter, and so Esther approached the king with a request to meet him and Haman for a banquet that she had prepared. When they came to the banquet the second day, Esther revealed to the king all that Haman had planned concerning the destruction and slaughter of the Jews in the land. The king was furious and ordered that Haman be hanged on the gallows he had prepared for Mordecai. An edict was sent out by the king granting the Jews in every city the right to assemble and protect themselves. Their sorrow was turned into joy and their mourning into a day of celebration. Haman intended that the Jews be destroyed. Instead, his plan turned out to be his own destruction. God has called a people to be His own. There is an enemy, Satan, who wants to destroy God's people. In the end he will be thrown into the lake of burning sulfur and tormented day and night, but everyone who looks to the Son and believes in him shall have eternal life.

Read Psalm 81
Esther 1:1, 3:1-2, 3-6, 8-10, 4:1-2, 4, 15-16, 5:1-4, 7:1-6, 10, 8:11, 9:22, John 6:40

    You, O Lord, are worthy of all praise. Your promises are true and will come to pass. Thank You for Your holy word that reveals Your truths. Help us to be pure before You so that at Your coming we will be prepared for that glorious day when You return to rule and reign forever. Amen.

APRIL 11
CORRUPT JUDGES

Psalm 82:8: Rise up, O God, judge the earth, for all the nations are Your inheritance.

    There was a time in Israel when the Lord raised up judges to save His people who had been overtaken by raiders in the land. But they would not listen to the judges and they prostituted themselves to other gods and worshiped them. They turned away from the God of their fathers and disobeyed His commands. The judges were to look to God for guidance but they began administering their own form of justice, without regard to God's laws, and corruption soon prevailed. When we make our own judgments without God, we become arrogant and proud, but He constantly calls us back to Him. When we answer His call, confusion and self-absorption disappear and there is peace in our lives. We may not be called to judge a nation or people but we are called upon to make judgments and, with His guidance, we make the right ones. The time is coming when He will judge all the earth. May He find us faithful to Him when that day comes.

Read Psalm 82
Judges 2:16-19, Hosea 11:1-2, Acts 17:31

Judge of all the earth, we pray for wisdom and understanding so that as we are called upon to make decisions, we can have certainty that You are guiding us to make the choices in life that give glory and honor to You. Keep us ever mindful of Your ways so that we do not depart from them. Amen.

APRIL 12
ASAPH'S CRY

Psalm 83:18: Let them know that You, whose name is the Lord, that You alone are the Most High God over all the earth.

Asaph, the chief musician, cried out and asked God not to be silent, not to be quiet or still. See how the enemies are astir, how your foes rear their heads; with cunning they conspire against Your people; they plot against those You cherish. He ended by saying, "Let them know that You, whose name is the Lord, that you alone are the Most High over all the earth." No matter how desperate our situation, we must never lose sight of the One who can keep us from all harm, the One who loves us so much that when we cry out to Him He hears and answers us. He heard the cry of Asaph and He will surely hear us as well.

Read Psalm 83
Psalm 145:19, Lamentations 3:25-26

Heavenly Father, You are the judge of all the earth. You have said You are not willing that any should perish but that all would come to repentance. Hear our cry, as you heard the cry of the chief musician, and cover us with Your mighty hand of protection. Draw us close to You, we pray. Amen.

APRIL 13
NOTHING WITHHELD

Psalm 84:11: For the Lord God is a sun and shield; the Lord bestows favor and honor; no good thing does He withhold from those whose walk is blameless.

When we praise the Lord and lift Him up, our hearts are filled with His presence and our burdens lifted. It is when we cease to praise Him and do not look to Him for our source of strength that we become overwhelmed. As a child, we trusted our parents to provide for us; to be there when we cried, to feed us when we were hungry, to fulfill our needs. As we grow older and more independent, we forget all that our parents did for us. The Lord asks us to come to Him as children, to depend on Him for all our needs, wants and desires. He asks us to talk to Him as we would our best friend, to share our heart with Him and believe that He answers, and then to praise and thank Him for what He is doing and what He has done. Our Father in Heaven has endless treasures and He desires to give them to us when we serve Him with all our hearts.

Read Psalm 84
Psalm 7:17 & 138:4-5, Jeremiah 33:9, Matthew 18:3-5

We praise You, Heavenly Father, for You are worthy of all praise. You are righteous and holy. There is no other God like You. Let our praises fill Your throne room to overflowing and may our hearts be filled with Your presence and peace. Amen.

APRIL 14
FAITHFULNESS

Psalm 85:11: Faithfulness springs forth from the earth; and righteousness looks down from heaven.

All good and perfect things come from above, from our Lord on High. We are His greatest creation and He yearns for us to seek and love Him. From the time the Lord chose the children of Israel to be His inheritance, He gave them instruction on how to live their lives. If they followed the Lord and kept His commandments, they were blessed. If they went their own way, worshiped other gods and engaged in all sorts of immoral acts, they were cursed. No matter their status, He waited for His people to be faithful so that His righteousness would flow to them and bless them. It's the same today. When a person becomes a believer in Christ, all of His promises are theirs to claim. Jesus said that if we know Him, we know the

Father. The blessings that flow from our faithfulness to Him are limitless, both now and in eternity.

Read Psalm 85
Deuteronomy 11:26-28, Romans 12:2

Heavenly Father, may we be ever faithful to You and Your calling on our lives. Keep us on the straight and narrow so we never stray far from Your presence. Amen.

APRIL 15
CHOICES

Psalm 86:11: Teach me Your way, O Lord, and I will walk in Your truth; give me an undivided heart; I will glorify Your name forever.

We can choose to serve Almighty God, who sits on His throne and looks to and fro through all the earth seeking those who love Him, or we can choose the ways of the world that tell us we are in control of our own destiny and there is no God. For those who choose their own way, they serve the flesh and not the spirit. For those who believe in Christ, there is a peace that comes with trusting Him. We have a friend in Jesus who sticks closer than a brother. We have someone who loves us so much that He gave His life for all so that we do not have to suffer the consequences of sin, which is eternal darkness where there is weeping and gnashing of teeth. The New Testament proclaims there were over 500 witnesses to Jesus' resurrection. He told us He is the way, the truth and the life. Anyone who chooses to believe this not only knows Him but knows the Father who sent Him.

Read Psalm 86
Matthew 8:12, Luke 16:23-24, John 7:17-18, 1 Corinthians 15:6

Lord, guide us to make the right choices in life. Give us the ability to hear Your voice in the midst of all the other things that draw us in many different directions. May we never lose sight of You. Amen.

APRIL 16
GLORIOUS CITY OF GOD

Psalm 87:3: Glorious things are said of You, O city of God.

Zion originally referred to a mountain in Jerusalem and also to the land of Israel. It later became synonymous with the capital of Jerusalem. God's temple was built there as a place of worship for His people, and the Ark of the Covenant was placed there. It has been a city of peace and a city of desolation. Daniel cried out to the Lord for Jerusalem, "O Lord, listen! O Lord, forgive. . .Do not delay because Your city and Your people bear Your name." The Lord called His people to arise and shine for the light has come and the glory of the Lord rises upon Zion. Nations will come to your light and kings to the brightness of your dawn. The glory of Lebanon will come to you, the pine, the fir and the cypress together, to adorn the place of His sanctuary, and He will glorify the place of His feet. No longer will violence be heard in the land, nor ruin or destruction within its borders but the walls will be called Salvation and the gates Praise. The Lord will return to Zion and dwell in Jerusalem. It will be called the City of Truth and the mountain of the Lord Almighty will be called the Holy Mountain.

Read Psalm 87
Isaiah 60, Daniel 9:16-19, Zechariah 8:3

Father, may the spirit of Jerusalem be in our hearts. Help us remember that one day You will set up Your kingdom in the glorious city of God, and on that day there will be everlasting peace. Fill us with the brightness of Your dawn and cover us with Your truth. Amen.

APRIL 17
HEAR ME IN MY DISTRESS, O LORD

Psalm 88:3: For my soul is full of trouble and my life draws near the grave.

This is a sorrowful and heartfelt psalm. The psalmist is in great distress and cries out to His Lord. In the midst of his painful circumstances and seeming as though his prayers are going unanswered, he directs his petitions straight to God Almighty. He knows there is no god in heaven or on earth like his God, who keeps His covenant of love with his servants who continue wholeheartedly in His way. When we find ourselves in such dire need, we must get on our knees in prayer, knowing that He hears our every word. Unlike the psalmist who cried out to God that in death there is no hope, that there are no praises that rise up to Him, we have our hope in the death and resurrection of Jesus Christ, who came to preach good news to the poor, to proclaim freedom for the prisoners, recovery of sight for the blind and to set the captive free. His message is that of unconditional love and forgiveness. In our darkest hour, let's not lose hope. He is with us, and we can rest knowing that all is well in Him.

Read Psalm 88
Exodus 8:10, 2 Chronicles 6:14, Psalm 13:5, Luke 4:18-19

Lord, we cry out to You in our darkest hour and ask that You pour forth Your light, lift our burdens and give us Your everlasting peace that, yes, all is well with our soul. Amen.

APRIL 18
GOD'S FAITHFULNESS

Psalm 89:8: O Lord God Almighty, who is like you? You are mighty, O Lord, and Your faithfulness surrounds You.

The first 18 verses of this psalm give a description of Almighty God. He is more awesome than all who surround Him. The Lord is a compassionate and gracious God. He is slow to anger, abounding in love and faithfulness. He tells us we cannot even look upon Him because He is so holy and that if we were to see Him we would die. Yet, before sin entered the world, Adam and Eve walked and talked with Him in the cool of the day. We can talk with Him today. We may not physically see Him because God is spirit, but we can personally know Him. Jesus said if you believe I am who I say I am, when you see me you see the Father. The Trinity is a mystery to us right now but it is the way God designed it. It is by faith we believe this truth. To think that today we can talk with our God because of what Jesus did, we are a blessed generation.

Read Psalm 89:1-18
Exodus 34:6, 1 John 5:7 (KJV), Revelation 1:8

Awesome Lord, You have given us life at this time in history for Your plan and purposes. Help us always to look to You and realize our time is short on this earth and we should proclaim You always, not necessarily in words but in the way we live our lives for You. Amen.

APRIL 19
ESTABLISHING THE THRONE

Psalm 89:29: I will establish his line forever, his throne as long as the heavens endure.

The Book of Matthew begins with the genealogy of Jesus, who is called the Son of David, who is called the son of Abraham. Jesus is referred to as the Son of David 14 times in the New Testament, which is another title for Messiah, the promise to come. The Almighty chose David to be king over His people and declared that He would build a house for him. He told David He would raise up his offspring to succeed him and that his throne would be established forever. The Lord declared through the prophet Jeremiah that the days are coming when He will raise up to David a Righteous Branch, a King who will reign wisely and do what is right and just. Jesus is the One and His name will be called the Lord Our Righteous. Mary, the mother of the Lord, was told the Son she was bringing into the world would be great and would be called the Son of the Most High; He would sit on the throne of his father David and reign over the house of Jacob forever, and His kingdom will never end. Jesus Himself spoke to John and said, "I am the Root and the Offspring of David and the bright Morning Star." He is coming soon to rule as the King of kings and His throne will be established forever.

Read Psalm 89:19-37
1 Chronicles 17:10-14, Jeremiah 23:5-6, Matthew 1:1, Luke 1:31-33, Acts 13:23, Revelation 22:16

Father, Help us to keep our eyes fixed on Jesus Christ, Your Son, knowing that He will one day return to set up His kingdom. We pray for endurance, strength and wisdom to remain faithful to You until that day comes. Amen.

APRIL 20
FULLY TRUSTING THE LORD

Psalm 89:47: Remember how fleeting is my life. For what futility You have created all men!

The psalmist is once again in great distress. Jerusalem has been ravaged and plundered, its walls broken through; no one is ruling from the throne of David. God's people are in turmoil and their enemies seemingly have the upper hand. So the cry is: Where are You, God? Have you forgotten Your promises to Your people? Why have You utterly deserted us? We sometimes look at life in a similar manner. When all is crumbling around us – we've lost loved ones, been told we have an incurable disease, finances have dried up and the bills keep coming in – we ask: Where are You, God? Why are all these things happening to me? We are not seeing the whole picture when we focus on our particular situation at any moment in time. We judge our circumstances with partial knowledge, not seeing things as He does. This is dangerous because these are the times we panic and make rash decisions. We must wait to hear from our Lord because He is in the midst of our battles. It is when we wait on Him and trust Him that He does His magnificent work.

Read Psalm 89: 38-52
Numbers 11:23, Psalm 31:23-24

Lord, forgive us for the times we have not trusted You. When our situations seem hopeless, help us to draw close to You. As You stretch forth Your hand to guide us, may we never let go, knowing that You are always faithful. Amen.

APRIL 21
LIFE QUICKLY PASSES

Psalm 90:10: The length of our days is seventy years – or eighty, if we have the strength; yet their span is but trouble and sorrow for they quickly pass, and we fly away.

Before God chose Moses to bring His people out of slavery, his life was full of grandeur living in Pharaoh's palace. He left it all to lead a life of complete faith and trust in God Almighty. He was a very humble man, more humble than any man on the face of the earth. We are also chosen of God. Our time on this earth is no mistake. He knew exactly what He was doing from the moment we were formed in our mother's womb. Like Queen Esther, who knows but that she came to her royal position for such a time as she did. She is one example of many who God used. Because of her obedience to Him, God's people were saved from annihilation. We can choose to believe Him, serve Him, seek Him, so that our journey to the end may be rewarded with eternal life, or we can choose to live for ourselves and deny His existence and sovereignty and at the end of the journey be in eternal darkness where He can never be found. In our youth, it seems the whole world is attainable; yet when the years pass we realize that we are only here for a short while and when we die all that we lived for, thought about and worked for no longer exists. Our time is over. Those who come after then live their lives and make their choices.

Read Psalm 90
Numbers 12:3, Esther 4:14, Isaiah 44:24

All-knowing and merciful Father, we sometimes forget how short our lives are. Lead us on Your chosen path for us so that we live to serve You and others all the days of our lives. Amen.

APRIL 22
THE GOD WHO RESCUES

Psalm 91:9-10: If you make the Most High your dwelling, even the Lord, who is my refuge, then no harm will befall you; no disaster will come near your tent.

The Lord is the God who rescues. He rescued His children from the hand of the Egyptians and Pharaoh. He told Moses when His people went to battle in their own land they would be remembered and rescued from their enemies. During the war between the house of Saul and the house of David, the Lord promised David He would rescue His people from the hand of the Philistines. Isaiah prophesied that the Lord Almighty would shield Jerusalem like birds hovering overhead; He would pass over it and rescue it. When the Apostle Peter was in prison and the Lord sent his angel to set him free, he declared, "The Lord has rescued me from Herod's clutches." The Lord rescued Timothy from all kinds of things that happened when he preached in Antioch, Iconium and Lystra. The Lord has done all of these things and much more. He knows how to rescue godly people from trials and to hold the unrighteous for the day of judgment.

Read Psalm 91
Exodus 18:9-10, Numbers 10:9, 2 Samuel 3:18, Isaiah 31:5, Acts 12:11, 2 Timothy 3:11, 2 Peter 2:9

Lord, thank You for rescuing us from our sins and the judgment that awaits us. You alone are worthy and because of Your love for us You have made it possible to be righteous in Your sight. Thank You for sending Jesus to set us free. Amen.

APRIL 23
GOD'S GREAT WORKS

Psalm 92:5: How great are Your works, O Lord, how profound Your thoughts.

The heavens declare the glory of our Lord. The sun, the stars, the moon, without them there could be no life on earth. Every detail is thought out with precision. The atmosphere, gravity, atoms, neutrons, and things we do not even know exist, they hold the world together and provide our needs. Human nature causes us to think the world exists for our pleasure, but we cannot control one thing that makes life happen. In acknowledging Him, seeking His face, and praying, He reveals His plan for our lives moment by moment until old age, when we can look back and say: Wow, what a marvelous thing You have done, O Lord. Amid my trials and mistakes, You brought me through. When things went well, You were there. Now it is time to go home and leave the world to the next generation. May His glory continue to shine and may those He draws to Him answer the call, until that promised day when the Savior, Jesus Christ, appears.

Read Psalm 92
1 Samuel 2:2, Psalm 19:1

Thank You, Lord, for Your great works, for speaking the world into existence and for the gift of life and the hope of eternity with You. Glorify Yourself in us that we might show others Your love and mercy and they too will seek the Lord, Creator of all things. Amen.

APRIL 24
ETERNITY AWAITS US

Psalm 93:2: Your throne was established long ago; You are from all eternity.

What awaits us in eternity is incomprehensible. There is no sin in eternity, and the Lord Himself will be our light. His majesty is revealed and the darkness that is in this world will be gone from His glorious kingdom. The psalms were written over a span of many, many years. The Savior had not yet come. Still, for those who believed in the Almighty God, there was hope that no matter their circumstances, He would provide in their lifetime and the lifetime to come. The Lord spoke to His people through the prophets and they proclaimed His sovereignty and love. They had visions of His glory on the throne. The awesome thing is that today we can have an even more intimate relationship with our Heavenly Father than the prophets and people of old could ever have imagined. We are blessed to have His word, the teachings of Jesus, and the Holy Spirit. It is all available to us, and the rewards for following Him are eternal.

Read Psalm 93
Isaiah 6:1, John 14:16-17, Revelation 22:5

Heavenly Father, who sits on His throne and knows all things, give us a vision of Your eternal glory that we will stay focused on You, be filled with Your Spirit and proclaim Your Word to all who want hear. Amen.

APRIL 25
ALL KNOWING

Psalm 94:9: Does he who planted the ear not hear? Does he who formed the eye not see?

There is a saying that we cannot judge a book by its cover. The title only tells a part of the story. It isn't until we read the pages that we discover what is really going on. We can then make an informed decision about whether the title really reflects the story. We often live like the cover of a book. On the outside we smile, say we are happy and everything is just fine, thank you very much. The truth is we have inner turmoil and don't want anybody to know. These are the things we cannot conceal from God, who searches our hearts. The Pharisees, who loved money, sneered at Jesus, but He said to them, "You are the ones who justify yourselves in the eyes of man but what is highly valued among men is detestable in God's sight." He also said that they were concerned about a cup or dish being clean on the outside but that inside they were full of greed and wickedness. We serve an all-knowing God and nothing can be hidden from Him.

Read Psalm 94
Luke 11:39 & 16:15, Acts 15:8, Romans 8:27

With Your right hand of righteousness, Lord, hold us up. You created us in Your image and You love us so much. We ask that You continually search our hearts and reveal any sin against You. Help us to confess our sin so that You, who are faithful and just, will forgive us. Amen.

APRIL 26
THE WORK OF HIS HANDS

Psalm 95:4: In His hand are the depths of the earth, and the mountain peaks belong to Him.

The Lord has arranged every part of the body just as He wanted them to be. There are many parts but only one body. The eye cannot say to the hand, "I don't need you," and the head cannot say to the feet, "I don't need you." There should be no division in the body and its parts should have equal concern for each other. Though we need every part of our body, the hands serve many purposes. Without them, the daily tasks we take for granted would be difficult, if not impossible, to accomplish. We are like clay in the Master Potter's hands. He takes a clump and molds it the way He sees fit, some for special purposes and some for common purposes, but we are all precious in His sight. His hands also bring comfort and lift us up when we are down. As Jesus was hanging on the cross, He called out with a loud voice, "Father, into your hands I commit my spirit." We can only imagine the Father's reaction as He heard those words. He must have reached down from Heaven to the bruised and bloody body of His Son, wrapped His arms and hands around Him, pulled Him to His chest and said, "Well done, my Son. Now take Your place at the right hand of my throne."

Read Psalm 95
Psalm 111:7, Isaiah 64:8, Luke 23:46, Romans 9:21, 1 Corinthians 12:18-21, 25

What an awesome God You are, O Lord. We lift our hands to praise You, to worship You, to give ourselves fully to You. Teach us moment by moment the joy of serving You fully! May this day, and all days, be filled with Your Presence and as Your light shines through us, may others be drawn to You. Amen.

APRIL 27
GREAT IS THE LORD

Psalm 96:4-5: For great is the Lord and most worthy of praise; He is to be feared above all gods. For all the gods of the nations are idols, but the Lord made the heavens.

We set up idols in our hearts when we don't turn to God for help. We may not even realize that's what we are doing, but when we depend on something beyond ourselves it is a form of worship. But the Lord will not yield his glory to another or His praise to idols. They are a detestable thing in the eyes of the Lord. Most of them are inanimate objects that have no life in them. The Lord tells us not to turn to idols for they can do us no good. They can't rescue us because they are useless. Some people turn to spiritual readers or mediums thinking they can look into the future, but this too is something the Lord says to stay away from. Only He knows what the future holds. When times are good, we are to be happy. But when times are bad, consider this: God has made the one as well as the other and no one can discover anything about their future. We should live in the moment with Him instead of hurting from the past, worrying about the future or being so consumed with busyness that we don't even take time to slow down. There is no room for fear of the unknown because He is the master of the unknown. Let's rejoice in our Savior, in our Father, in the Spirit, for they are worthy of our praise.

Read Psalm 96
Leviticus 19:4 & 31, 1 Samuel 12:21, Isaiah 42:8 & 45:11, Ecclesiastes 7:14

Lord, You alone are God. Your Name is majestic and holy. You sit upon Your throne and listen to the prayers of Your children. Help us to live in the present where You are and not long to know the future. Take away any idols, known or unknown, that we have allowed to be in our lives. You are our future and You are worthy of our praise. Amen.

APRIL 28
HE IS THE LIGHT

Psalm 97:11: Light is shed upon the righteous and joy on the upright in heart.

In the beginning, the earth was formless and empty and darkness was over the surface of the deep and God said, "Let there be light," and He separated the light from darkness. Light dispels darkness and what we could not see is now in plain view. Christians have the light of Jesus Christ that allows them to view the spiritual part of life that once was unknown. Darkness and despair should never be our companions, for the light of our Lord shines upon those who call on His name. Let's ask Him to search our hearts and reveal any darkness we are carrying, any unforgiveness we have against anyone, any pride, or if we are seeking revenge because of a perceived or real wrong. The Almighty God of the universe loves His children. He wants every part of our being to be yielded to Him so He can use us for His kingdom. In times of weariness, may we never forget that the light of His presence guides us through our times of darkness.

Read Psalm 97
Genesis 1:1-4, John 8:12 & 11:10, Ephesians 5:13, 1 John 1:7

Precious Lord of Light, thank You that we need not fear the darkness for You are our light and will always be with us to guide us through. For You are the Most High over all the earth, You are exalted far above all gods. We love You and praise Your Holy Name. Amen.

A Daily Devotional of God's Unending Love

APRIL 29
SING TO THE LORD

Psalm 98:9: Let them sing before the Lord, for He comes to judge the earth. He will judge the world in righteousness and the peoples with equity.

Singing praises to the Lord makes us focus on Him and His glory. It takes our eyes off of ourselves. Thousands of songs have been written in worship to the Lord. Many tell a story of His faithfulness. King David was always singing praises to the Lord. He was so excited as the ark of the Lord was entering the city that he danced before the Lord. He sang a song of praise after he was delivered from the hands of his enemies and from the hand of Saul, ending with the words, "Therefore, I will praise You, Lord, among the nations. I will sing praises to Your name." Singing is a form of worship that allows us to come into His presence with total abandon. Lifting our hands while singing fills our souls and we surrender our burdens to Him. In our time of prayer, we should incorporate singing. He doesn't care if we sing off key, for He looks at our hearts. Sing for joy, O heavens, shout aloud, O earth beneath, burst into song, you mountains, you forests and trees. The Lord has redeemed Jacob and displayed His glory in Israel.

Read Psalm 98
2 Samuel 6:14 & 22:50, Isaiah 44:23

Lord, we lift our voices in song to praise You. We thank You that You lift our burdens and bring us into the glory of Your presence. Help us to take time each day to pray, to read Your Word, to bare our hearts and souls to you. Help us to always remember that You are the judge of all the earth. We praise You, Almighty God. Amen.

APRIL 30
KNOWING HIM

Psalm 99:5: Exalt the Lord our God and worship at His footstool. He is holy.

Abraham, Moses, Samuel, Isaiah, and many more, have one thing in common. They knew and loved the Lord with all their hearts. Abraham was the father of God's chosen people. Moses led God's people out of bondage from Egypt. Samuel and Isaiah were prophets of old who spoke the word of the Lord to bring His children back to Him. We can also have that close relationship with our Heavenly Father. Right before Jesus was arrested, He looked toward Heaven and prayed for His disciples. His prayer was not for them alone but for those who, through their message, also believe in Him. He prayed that all of them may be one as He and the Father are one. To be one with another person is to know them intimately, and that is what Jesus Christ wants for us. He continued His prayer, "May they also be in us so that the world may believe that you have sent me. I have given them the glory that You gave me, that they may be one as we are one: I in them and You in me." There is one God and one mediator between God and men, the Lord Jesus Christ. He came to make the Father known to us in order that the love He had for Jesus would be in us and Jesus Himself would be in us.

Read Psalm 99
John 17:20-26, 1 Timothy 2:5

Lord, we ask that Jesus' prayer continue to be heard and that we truly become one with You. Draw us into Your presence and speak to our hearts and minds so that we will come to know You intimately. Amen.

MAY 1
THE GOOD SHEPHERD

Psalm 100:3: Know that the Lord is God. It is He who made us, and we are His. We are His people, the sheep of His pasture.

We are sheep and our shepherd is God Almighty. He keeps us in line when we stray. He knows our every need and makes provision for it. He shears us so that the old is taken away to make way for the new. If even one of us goes astray, He leaves the 99 and goes after the lost sheep until He finds it. He calls His friends and neighbors and says, "Rejoice with me. I have found my lost sheep." He searches our hearts continually so that we don't allow the things of this world and our sinful nature to take up residence. The pride of life and the things we seemingly accomplish on our own must not become uppermost because it is then that we go our own way and forget our loving shepherd. He is the faithful God, keeping His covenant of love to a thousand generations of those who love Him and keep His commands, and we should never wander away.

Read Psalm 100
Deuteronomy 7:9, Psalm 119:10, Isaiah 40:11, John 10:11

O Lord, we like sheep have gone astray. Thank You for being our Shepherd who searches for us until You find us and bring us back into Your fold. You are so faithful. As You lead us, help us not to wander away but to keep our eyes focused solely on You. We praise Your Holy Name. Amen.

MAY 2
A BLAMELESS LIFE

Psalm 101:2: I will be careful to lead a blameless life – when will You come to me? I will walk in my house with a blameless heart.

David had just become King of Israel. He was blameless before God and kept himself from sin. It was a great responsibility to rule over a kingdom and he knew it was an impossible task without the help of the Lord. He sang this psalm to his God, setting forth his intentions on how to rule the people. Though he later failed, in the beginning he set the standard for himself first and then for those whom he would surround himself. Noah was blameless among the people of his time and he walked faithfully with God. Job was blameless and a man who feared God. These are all people of the Old Testament who set an example for others. Today God keeps us strong to the end so that we will be blameless before Him on the day of our Lord Jesus Christ.

Read Psalm 101
Genesis 6:9, 2 Samuel 22:24-26, Job 1:8, 1 Corinthians 1:8

Lord, cover us each day with Your armor so that we might withstand all the fiery darts of the enemy of our souls and live blamelessly before You. We ask for discernment and wisdom in accordance with Your Holy Word so that we may glorify You in all we do. Amen.

MAY 3
HOPE IN DESPERATION

Psalm 102:17: He will respond to the prayer of the destitute; He will not despise their plea.

There was a wedding feast in Cana. Jesus, His mother and His disciples had been invited. It was the third day of the celebration and there was no wine. In those days, to run out of wine was a great embarrassment. It meant there had not been enough preparation for the festivities and the hosts would be distraught about the situation in which they found themselves. This may be how we feel at times. We are at the height of life, having a good time and celebrating. Then we reach the bottom of the barrel and there is no more wine to take out. We feel hopeless, but then something miraculous happens. Jesus' mother informed Him of the situation. At first He seemed reluctant to do anything about it but then he instructed the servants to fill all the barrels with water. The master of the banquet tasted the water that had now been turned into wine. He called the bridegroom aside and said, "Everyone brings out the choice wine first and then cheaper wine after the guests have had too much to drink, but you have saved the best until now." That is what Jesus does for us; He gives us hope in our desperation and we can expect His very best.

Read Psalm 102:1-17
Job 36:15, Psalm 142:5-6, John 2:1-10, 1 Timothy 4:10

Almighty and Merciful Father, thank You that we have hope in You. You know us and You are faithful to meet our needs. We ask for patience when our prayers are not always answered the way we want them answered. We know that all things work together for good for those who love the Lord. Increase our faith so we always trust You. Amen.

MAY 4
THE BEGINNING

Psalm 102:25 & 27: In the beginning You laid the foundations of the earth, and the heavens are the work of Your hands. . .But You remain the same, and Your years will never end.

God has always existed. He makes known the end from the beginning, the ancient times and what is still to come. There is no other god on earth who makes claim to the authority of God Almighty, and there will be none after Him. What He has ordained will come to pass. Jesus was chosen in the beginning, before the world was created, to redeem mankind from their sin. He came to earth and taught us how to live for Him. He revealed the end of time to John, who wrote the Book of Revelation. The seven seals of the last days will be required to be open before the end comes to pass. A mighty angel from Heaven proclaimed in a loud voice, "Who is worthy to break the seals and open the scrolls?" John wept because no one was found to be worthy, but one of the elders said, "Do not weep for the Root of David has triumphed and He is able to open the scroll and its seven seals. He is the one who was slain and with His blood He purchased man for God. He made them to be a kingdom and priests to serve our God and reign on earth." Jesus will reign on David's throne and over His kingdom, establishing and upholding it with justice and righteousness forever.

Read Psalm 102:18-28
Deuteronomy 4:35, 1 Kings 8:60, Proverbs 8:22-23, Isaiah 9:7, 43:11 & 46:10,
Revelation 5:2-3, 5 & 9

Almighty Father, who was and is and is to come, we have come from those who were before and others will come after us. Help us to realize that we are here for a short time and our purpose is to serve You, the all-knowing, all-loving God. Thank You for the words written in Your Book so that we can live in accordance with Your plan. Prepare us for the time when Jesus returns to reign upon the earth. Amen.

MAY 5
OUR DAYS ARE LIKE GRASS

Psalm 103:14-16: For He knows how we are formed. He remembers that we are dust. As for man, his days are like grass. He flourishes like a flower of the field; the wind blows over it and it is gone, and its place remembers it no more.

Our accomplishments are but a fleeting moment in life. Without God, we are never satisfied, even when we are the very best. He has given us an inborn desire to have a relationship with Him. Turning our lives over to Him is what satisfies the longing of our soul and it doesn't matter the great and wonderful things we accomplish if we keep focused on Him. We are body, soul and spirit and that which we nurture grows. Like grapes on a vine, if they are cared for properly, they flourish and become the finest of wines, but if they are not harvested at their peak they shrivel into raisins. They may still have value but their full potential is never reached. This applies to the way we live our lives The things we give the most attention to produce the best results. Our desire should be to do things that store up riches for eternity, for where our treasure is there will our heart be also.

Read Psalm 103
Psalm 39:4, Matthew 6:21, John 6:63, Romans 9:20, Hebrews 8:11

Lord, when we lift ourselves up, bring us down. We pray that pride and arrogance not overtake us. You give gifts to all of Your creation. It is up to us what we do with them. Will we use it for Your glory or our own? We pray for wisdom to know the difference and humility to accept the answer. Amen.

MAY 6
A FIRM FOUNDATION

Psalm 104:5: He set the earth on its foundations; it can never be moved.

It is the Lord God who created the heavens, the earth, the seas and all that is in them, and the world could not exist without Him. As we read and meditate on Psalm 104, we should be in awe at the wonder of our Mighty God. He is clothed in splendor and majesty and wraps Himself in light as a garment. At His rebuke, the waters fled and flowed down the mountains to their assigned places and He set boundaries that they could not cross. Every place He created has a purpose and fills a need. Even the crags of the hills where we might think no life exists, He has made it a place for the coneys. He provides trees for the birds to rest in, grass for the cattle to eat and plants for man to cultivate and provide food. There is not enough paper to write on to describe the awesome wonder of the God whom we serve. He is our Provider, our Comforter, and the solid foundation on which we must build our lives.

Read Psalm 104:1-18
Isaiah 42:5, Colossians 1:16, Hebrews 11:10, Revelation 10:6

You, O Lord, have eyes that see all mankind. You know our every thought. We cannot hide from You. Open our eyes to the wonder of Your creation that we might see all that You do and never lose hope knowing that You formed the earth and its foundations can never be moved. Amen.

MAY 7
THE WISDOM OF HIS WORKS

Psalm 104:24: How many are Your works, O Lord! In wisdom You made them all; the earth is full of Your creatures.

And God said, "Let the water teem with living creatures and let the birds fly above the earth across the vault of the sky." So God created the great creatures of the sea and every living and moving thing with which the water teems. And God said, "Let the land produce living creatures according to their kinds: livestock, creatures that move along the ground, and wild animals." There is no other god who spoke and things were created; some things so small a microscope is necessary to see them. Other creatures, like ants, are of little strength, yet they store up their food in the summer. Locusts have no king, yet they advance together in ranks. There are creatures that come out at night such as owls, crickets, bats and frogs. He has given us eyes to see His many wonders; ears to hear so that we may understand; a mouth and nose in order to breathe the breath of life; feet to carry us many places; and hands with which to create. From the time God created man on the earth, from one end of the heavens to the other has anything so great as this ever happened, or has anything like it ever been heard of? When we open our hearts and minds to the Lord, we can have a limitless life.

Read Psalm 104:19-35
Genesis 1:20-21, 1:24-25, Deuteronomy 4:32, Proverbs 30:25-28

Lord, we praise You who knows all things. Help us to realize how much we need You. We live in a lost world that did not even recognize the Savior whom You sent to set men free and bring them back into communion with You. Open our eyes to see and ears to hear all that You have for us, so that we can be the light of Christ in this dark world. Amen.

MAY 8
OUR PROVIDER

Psalm 105:17-19: And he sent a man before them, Joseph, sold as a slave. They bruised his feet with shackles. His neck was put in irons, till what he foretold came to pass, till the word of the Lord proved him true.

Joseph was the most beloved son of Jacob. His 11 brothers were jealous of him. When he told them of a dream he had, they laughed and said, "Do you intend to reign over us? Will you actually rule us?" They sold him into slavery, telling their father that he had been killed by a wild animal. In process of time, Joseph became head of Potiphar's household until his wife falsely accused him of raping her. He was then imprisoned and put in charge of all the prisoners by the warden. The baker and cupbearer of Pharaoh were imprisoned and both had dreams. Joseph interpreted the dreams and they came to pass. Joseph asked the cupbearer when he was restored to his position to remember him because he had done nothing to deserve being put in a dungeon. It wasn't until two years later that Pharaoh had a dream that no one could interpret and his cupbearer remembered Joseph and told Pharaoh about him. He was immediately summoned. When Pharaoh told Joseph the dream he interpreted it and Pharaoh made him second in command only to himself. Joseph was falsely accused and imprisoned, yet there is never a word of pity recorded or cursing toward God from him. It took many years before he was put in such a powerful position. Because of his obedience, the entire house of Jacob was rescued from famine. We don't always understand why hardships happen in our lives, but there is a reason for everything. Our God provides all of our needs and uses everything that happens to us for His purposes and glory when we depend on Him.

Read Psalm 105:1-22
Genesis 37:3-8 & 31-33, 39:1 & 11-22, 40:8-15, 41:1-16, & 41:39-43

You are our provider, Lord. Thank You so much for all You do; for the blessings that we do not even recognize or acknowledge. You are mighty indeed. Even before we ask, You know our requests. Thank You for Your provision and for Your unending love. Amen.

MAY 9
HE IS LIMITLESS

Psalm 105:42-43: For He remembered His holy promise given to His servant Abraham. He brought out His people with rejoicing, His chosen ones with shouts of joy.

All through the ages, and to this very day, our Heavenly Father has kept His promise to His chosen people, the descendants of Abraham. He called them out of Egypt after 400 years of bondage. At first, Pharaoh would not let them go. He knew if he did he would lose the slaves that labored for him night and day. The Lord began a mighty work in the land of Egypt, using Moses as His instrument. He turned the waters of Egypt into blood, killing all the fish. He sent teems of frogs, swarms of flies, turned rain into hail, struck down their vine and fig trees, sent locusts and grasshoppers to eat every green thing in the land. Each time Pharaoh's heart would be hardened until lastly, during the Passover, the firstborn of every Egyptian was struck dead and Pharaoh finally relented and let God's people go to the land that others had toiled for but that He had chosen for them. When we put our confidence and trust in the mighty God who did all of these things, He fights our battles for us. There is no limit to what He can do when we trust in Him.

Read Psalm 105:23-45
Genesis 7:17-18, Hebrews 3:2-6, 11:8-10, 11:24-28

You, O Lord, are worthy of all praise. You fight our battles for us, even those we do not know exist. Thank You for Your love and protection. Continually guide us by the power of Your Holy Spirit and help us yield to You. Amen.

MAY 10
HE NEVER FAILS

Psalm 106:2: Who can proclaim the mighty acts of the Lord or fully declare His praise?

There are not a lot of people who have personally witnessed the mighty acts of God but David was one who did, even before he assumed the throne as king of Israel. Not much is written about him as a young man but one account gives testimony to the mighty acts of God in his life. He was the youngest of eight boys. One day his father instructed him to take grain and bread to his brothers who had followed King Saul, who was at war with the Philistines. He reached their camp as the army was going out to its battle positions. There was a champion of the Philistines named Goliath. He was over nine feet tall, had a bronze helmet on his head, wore a coat of armor, and had a bronze javelin slung on his back. He shouted his usual defiance at the troops of Israel and they all ran from him in fear. Upon seeing this, David asked, "Who is this uncircumcised Philistine that he should defy the armies of the Living God?" So David was chosen to go up against Goliath. Now, David was only a boy, ruddy and handsome, and when Goliath saw him, he said, "Am I a dog that you come at me with sticks?" David responded, "You come against me with sword and spear but I come against you in the name of the Lord God Almighty." Reaching into his bag he took out a stone and slung it. He struck Goliath on the forehead. The stone sank into his forehead and he fell face down on the ground. When we put our trust in God, he slays all the giants in our lives, and we never cease to praise Him for His mighty acts.

Read Psalm 106:1-5
1 Samuel 17

Heavenly Father, we pray that You would fight all of our battles and overcome the giants we face in our lives. Help us to remember that You are our shelter in times of trouble and that our armor is prayer. You are worthy of all praises for You are mighty, faithful, merciful and loving. We praise Your holy name. Amen.

MAY 11
DO NOT FORGET

Psalm 106:9: He rebuked the Red Sea and it dried up; He led them through the depths as through a desert.

Moses led the Israelites out of Egypt in order to serve the Living God. As they journeyed towards the Promised Land, they came to the vast Red Sea and panicked as they looked behind them and saw Pharaoh and his army in pursuit. By the blast of the Lord's nostrils the waters piled up and stood firm as a wall and the people walked on dry land to the other side, but Pharaoh and his army were drowned as the walls of water came together. Despite this mighty work of God, the people soon forgot and rebelled against their Maker. Our walk with the Lord can be similar to this. In our times of trials, we call out to Him. He hears and answers. Then it is not long before we forget what He has done and we continue going our own way. In His mercy, He is ever faithful when we call on Him.

May we learn from our hardships and never forget where our deliverance comes from.

Read Psalm 106:6-15
Exodus 15:8-12, Joshua 2:10, Isaiah 51:10, Hebrews 11:29

Lord God of Mercy, as You look upon us, Your children, remember that we are human and easily fail. Help us to never forget where our strength comes from. When our pride lifts us up, help us remember that without You we are nothing. Amen.

MAY 12
GOD OF MERCY

Psalm 106:23: So he said he would destroy them had not Moses, His chosen one, stood in the breach before Him to keep His wrath from destroying them.

God created mankind to be in perfect communion with Him. He gave us the ability to think and reason, to make our own choices. He does not choose for us, for He desires a people who freely give themselves to Him with total abandon. Moses gave himself completely to God, who spoke to him and guided him to bring out His people from Egypt. Despite their eagerness to be set free from slavery they constantly rebelled against Moses and, thus, the Lord. They were envious and backbiters, to the point that while Moses was on Mt. Sinai receiving the Ten Commandments they made a golden calf to worship as their god. They were so rebellious that the Lord, in His anger, was ready to annihilate them. Moses intervened on their behalf and the Lord repented and did not destroy them. But there were consequences, and those who began the rebellion were destroyed. Moses was a type of Christ. Though not perfect, he was a deliverer of God's people. Christ is the mediator of a new covenant, that those who are called may receive the promised eternal inheritance. God has called us to a life of righteousness. May we keep our eyes firmly fixed on Him so we do not go back to the ways of the world.

Psalm 106:16-33
Exodus 32:7-14, Hebrews 9:11-15

Merciful Lord, we are so prone to our sinful nature that draws us away from You. Fill us continually with Your Holy Spirit so that we are always aware of Your Presence within us that gives us the strength to choose the way of righteousness. When we fail, give us the ability to realize what we have done that we might humble ourselves before You and ask forgiveness. Thank You for sending Jesus to set us free from sin. Amen.

MAY 13
A WHOLE HEART

Psalm 106:44: But He took note of their distress when He heard their cry.

The children of Israel had witnessed many miracles by God. Eventually they entered into the land which the Lord had promised them. He commanded them to destroy the heathen because they did not serve Him. Instead they took on their customs and idol worship to the point that they even sacrificed the blood of their innocent children to a god that they knew not. They became so blinded that they believed in a god who would require such a horrid act. They had gone the way of the world and forsook the God of their fathers. The Lord calls us out of the world; He doesn't want us to dabble in it because it is easy to fall back into our old ways of sinfulness if we do not wholeheartedly serve Him. We do not literally sacrifice our children to other gods on an altar, but if we are not serving Him we are serving something or someone else. We are visual beings and what we see with our eyes is very tempting. The world offers riches and fame, things which draw us away from Him. The Lord God Almighty expects His children to give their lives to Him. When we do, we gain our lives and the desires of this world no longer have a hold on us. We begin to see that life is so temporary but that He is the everlasting, eternal God. When we are tempted to turn from Him, may it bring great distress to our souls so that we cry out for Him to deliver us.

Read Psalm 106:34-48
2 Chronicles 6:24-27, Matthew 6:24 & 10:39

We lift our eyes up to You, Lord, who sits upon Your heavenly throne, the One who knows all things. Search our hearts, our minds, our souls, and reveal anything that displeases You so we can confess it and serve You with a whole heart. There is so much we don't comprehend about You. Help us to completely trust You even when we don't understand. Amen.

MAY 14
HE DELIVERS US FROM DISTRESS

Psalm 107:6: Then they cried out to the Lord in their trouble, and He delivered them from their distress.

Jesus appeared in the temple court and sat down to teach the people gathered around Him. The teachers of the law and the Pharisees brought in a woman caught in adultery. Scripture doesn't say anything about the man who was with her. They brought her before Jesus and said that the law of Moses commanded them to stone her. But Jesus bent down and started to write on the ground with His finger. He looked up and said, "If any one of you is without sin, let him be the first to throw a stone at her." One at a time, they all left until Jesus and the woman were there alone. Jesus looked at her and said, "Woman, your accusers are gone and no one has condemned you. Neither do I condemn you. Go now and leave your life of sin." Some surmise that this was Mary Magdalene, who followed Jesus closely from that time on. She was definitely a woman in distress, was almost to the point of being stoned to death, but Jesus rescued her and set her free. He does the same thing today. We are sometimes on the brink of disaster but Jesus intervenes when we cry out to Him in our trouble and delivers us from all of our distresses.

Read Psalm 107:1-22
Genesis 35:3, 2 Samuel 22:7, John 8:1-11

Heavenly Father, many times we fail You and we do not fulfill the plans You have for us, but You are ever faithful to pick us up and put us back on our feet. Help us to realize that if we are faithful to You, You have promised us an eternity with You where we will no longer endure the hardships of this earthly life. Praise Your Name! Amen.

MAY 15
HE WALKS WITH US

Psalm 107:43: Whoever is wise let him heed these things and consider the great love of the Lord.

Everyone is called to know and serve the Lord but not everyone answers that call. For those who do, all things are possible to those who believe. In the storms of life, as in the storms of the sea, it is not by pure coincidence or luck that we survive them. It is by divine providence. When the storms come raging, when all seems lost and we can find no means of escape, may we cry out to our God, "peace be still," and may the calmness of our Lord's mercies flow over us and soothe our souls, for it is only in and through Him that we find true peace in this life. When we walk in the dark where there is no light, we must trust in the name of the Lord. In the ways of the world this sounds like foolishness but to those who believe in the Lord, it is the truth of God. We should have no fear in giving Him all glory and honor so that those who hear and receive will know the wonder and faithfulness of the most Holy God whom we serve. By knowing Him, we are blessed in this life and in the life to come.

Read Psalm 107:23-43
Isaiah 50:10, Jonah 2:2, 1 Corinthians 1:18

Lord, thank You that You know our needs before we even ask. It is us who need to pray so that when we see Your answers it builds our faith and gives us boldness to share Your faithfulness and love with others. May we acknowledge You in all things and realize that there is a purpose and a plan and that nothing happens by chance. We pray for wisdom and ask that our lives be a reflection of Your love. Amen.

MAY 16
HE IS FAITHFUL

Psalm 108:4: For great is Your love, higher than the heavens; Your faithfulness reaches to the skies.

God is true to His promises and His word. He is consistently loyal and trustworthy. He is always faithful. We serve a God who stretches out the heavens like a canopy and spreads them out like a tent. He made the earth and created mankind upon it. His own hands stretched out the heavens and marshaled their starry hosts. He created the heavens above to rain down righteousness. The earth opens wide to let salvation spring up and let righteousness grow with it. The love He has for us is higher than the heavens. That is a lot of love, and it is ours for the taking.

Read Psalm 108
Isaiah 40:22, 45:8 & 45:12

Almighty God, thank you for Your faithfulness. There is nothing we can hide from You who has created all things. Bring us into Your presence and draw us to You so we will keep our eyes on eternity, where You have prepared a place for us. We praise Your Holy Name and give You thanks. Amen.

MAY 17
GOD'S SILENCE

Psalm 109:1: O God, whom I praise, do not remain silent.

Silence is not a welcome response when we want answers. In today's psalm, David was once again in the midst of enemy territory surrounded by what he called wicked and deceitful men who had opened their mouths against him with lying tongues. He was a man of prayer and asked the Lord that the days of his enemies be few; that their children be fatherless; that creditors seize all they have and strangers plunder the fruits of their labor. These are drastic requests to a God whom we know as merciful and loving. We are not told the outcome of this prayer, but even as David praised his Lord all he "heard" was silence. Times have changed since Jesus came to set men free, for we all have access to the throne of God because of Him. He does not answer prayers of revenge and hatred against another. The time for judgment is coming soon enough. He does hear everyone's prayers, though, and His perceived silence at times does not indicate His inability to answer. Patience is a virtue and the time is coming when He will be silent no longer.

Read Psalm 109:1-20
Isaiah 65:6, Habakkuk 1:13, Galatians 6:7

Almighty God, we pray for patience when we perceive You are silent, for You hear the prayers of Your children. Help us to prayer in accordance with Your will, knowing that You are the judge of everyone. What we see on the outside is not always what is happening on the inside, but You know. Help us to trust You and serve You with all of our hearts. Amen.

MAY 18
UNLIMITED SUPPLY

Psalm 109:30: With my mouth I will greatly extol the Lord; in the great throng I will praise Him.

There were times in King David's life that he was so weary and distraught, even unto death. He felt as if he could not go on one more day. He fasted and prayed and there seemed to be no answer. In his weakness, he cried out to the Lord, who saw his need and heard that cry, and suddenly David's countenance changed. He knew that though he was weak, the everlasting God Almighty was strong. He knew that the Lord saves in accordance with His unending love. We have such hope in this life as well, when we turn all of our dreams, our desires, our distresses, our happy and contented times, over to our Lord. He answers with His unlimited supply. The best times of answered prayer are when we wait on Him. Those are the times when we can look in wonder and awe at what He has done. He loves to bless His children and walk hand in hand with them through life's journey. When this happens, the glory of His presence fills us to overflowing.

Read Psalm 109:21-31
Psalm 147:5, John 3:34, 2 Corinthians 1:3-5, Philippians 4:19

O Lord, help us to be fully committed to serving You in every aspect of our lives. It is You who chose us to be here at this particular time. Help us to realize that life is not all about us, for we are here for only a short time and then eternity awaits us. May all we think, say, and do be according to Your will. Amen.

MAY 19
A HIGH PRIEST

Psalm 110:4: The Lord has sworn and will not change His mind. "You are a priest forever after the order of Melchizedek."

Melchizedek was a high priest in the Old Testament. It is said that he had no mother or father, no beginning or end. We know very little about him but Scripture tells us that Jesus is a high priest after the order of Melchizedek. Today's psalm reveals Jesus. After His death and resurrection, He ascended into Heaven and is now seated at the right hand of our Father where He intervenes continually for those who serve Him. We are His emissaries until the day He returns. When He returns, it will not be as at the first when He was born as a baby, grew into a man and eventually died for our sins on the cross at Calvary. No! When He returns the second time, every eye will see Him, every knee will bow and every tongue will confess that He is indeed the Lord of all creation. He will come to bring judgment upon the earth and rule the nations with a rod of iron. The prophecy of this psalm will one day come to pass, of this we can be certain, because the Lord has sworn it and He will not change His mind. For this reason, we have confidence in our faith in Jesus Christ. He is full of majesty and has promised those who believe in Him that they will reign with Him forever in His kingdom.

Read Psalm 110
Hebrews 5:5-10, 1 Corinthians 15:24-28, Philippians 2:10-11

Almighty God, Eternal Lord, Savior, King of kings and Lord of lords, we thank You that from the very beginning You had a plan of salvation and redemption for Your creation. Jesus, You are our High Priest, who sits at the right hand of our Father in Heaven. You have sent Your Holy Spirit to guide us in the ways of truth and righteousness. Lead us continually by Your presence and help us to be yielded to You until that day when we see You face to face. Amen.

MAY 20
THE VASTNESS OF OUR GOD

Psalm 111:10: The fear of the Lord is the beginning of wisdom; all who follow His precepts have good understanding. To Him belongs eternal praise.

Let's ponder the great works of our Lord as we delight in His presence today. His deeds are glorious and majestic. His righteousness endures forever. He is gracious and compassionate. He shows the power of His works, and the works of His hands are faithful and just. His precepts are trustworthy and steadfast forever and ever. He provides redemption for His people. His name is holy and awesome. To Him and Him alone belongs eternal praise. There is no one else to whom such attributes belong. When we read this psalm, our hearts should be rejoicing because of the great and wonderful God whom we serve. He made it possible to know Him intimately by sending Jesus Christ to die for us so that we are reconciled to Him. By the Holy Spirit, He dwells in us when we invite Him into our lives and hearts. By faith we believe it and receive it. Praise His Holy Name!

Read Psalm 111
1 Samuel 12:24, 1 Chronicles 16:29-31, Job 28:28, Isaiah 33:6

Majestic and Glorious Heavenly Father, You are wonderful indeed. Your ordinances are sure and altogether righteous. Give us a desire to seek You as we would seek a great treasure, for You are more precious than the finest gold and sweeter than any honey from the comb. Guide us by Your loving and faithful hand. Amen.

MAY 21
FAITH IN THE MIDST OF TURMOIL

Psalm 112:7: He will have no fear of bad news; his heart is steadfast, trusting in the Lord.

There are parallels in Psalm 111 and Psalm 112. God's righteousness is proclaimed in the former and the righteousness of man in the latter. It is only through Him that we have righteousness, for there is none righteous of himself. The life of King Hezekiah is an example of God's perfect righteousness. Hezekiah trusted in the Lord. There was no one like him among all the kings of Judah, either before him or after him. He held fast to the Lord and did not cease to follow Him. The Lord was with Him and he was successful in whatever he undertook. The king of Assyria threated him. He sent his commander and said to those in Jerusalem, "Do not let Hezekiah deceive you. He cannot deliver you from my hand. Do not let Hezekiah persuade you to trust in the Lord when he said, 'The Lord will surely delivery us.'" Hezekiah sought the Lord through the prophets. The Lord said to him, "I have heard your prayer concerning the king of Assyria. He has insulted and blasphemed the Holy One of Israel." And that night the angel of the Lord went out and put to death 185,000 men in the Assyrian camp. Hezekiah never lost faith that his God was in control and all would be well. We can also endure hardships and remain faithful, and we can rest in the knowledge that He will bring us through. All things are possible to those who believe and trust in Him. The righteousness of His saints will endure because it springs forth from God's righteousness.

Read Psalm 112
2 Kings 18:5-7, 18:28-30, 19:20-22 & 19:35, Mark 9:23, 1 John 1:8

Lord, thank You for being steadfast. There is certainty in serving You. We ask for Your strength to come through the battles of life in victory. May we never lose sight of the glory that comes from You and You alone, Most Holy, Heavenly Father. Thank You for loving us. Amen.

MAY 22
WHO IS LIKE THE LORD?

Psalm 113:5: Who is like the Lord our God, the One who sits enthroned on high.

There are many gods and prophets that represent different religions but most, if not all, of them are dead. Their teachings are kept alive by those who follow them, but none of them are the Living God of Abraham, Isaac and Jacob. He is a jealous God who commands us not to worship any other god. In the song of Moses, he recited these words in the hearing of the whole assembly of Israel, saying, "They make Him jealous with their foreign gods and anger Him with their detestable idols." Amaziah was a king of Judah who brought back the gods of the Edomites after a battle. He set them up, bowed down, and burned sacrifices to them. The Lord sent a prophet to him saying, "Why do you consult this people's god which could not save their own people from your hand?" The Lord's jealousy is righteous. He is a consuming fire, and because He is giving us a kingdom that cannot be shaken, we should worship Him with reverence and awe, withholding nothing of ourselves.

Read Psalm 113
Exodus 34:14, Deuteronomy 4:24, 31:30 & 32:16, 2 Chronicles 25:14-15, 27-28, Psalm 40:4, Hebrews 12:28-29

We thank You, Heavenly Father, for this beautiful day. We pray for the ability to live in the present moment with You by our side. May we put the past behind us and learn from our mistakes, and may we not worry what the future holds. Help us to be content in our circumstances, knowing that You are with us, that You know all of our needs and that You meet them according to Your riches in glory. Amen.

MAY 23
TREMBLE AT HIS PRESENCE

Psalm 114:7: Tremble, O earth, at the presence of the Lord, at the presence of the God of Jacob.

Should we not fear the Lord and tremble in His presence? He made the sand as a boundary for the sea, an everlasting barrier it cannot cross. The waves may roar but they cannot cross it. There will come a time when the fish of the sea, the birds of the air, the beasts of the field, every creature that moves along the ground and all the people on the face of the earth will tremble at His presence. He is the God who shakes the earth from its place and makes the pillars tremble. He performs wonders that cannot be fathomed and miracles that cannot be counted. In the last days, the earth will reel like a drunkard and sway like a hut in the wind. The sun will be darkened and the moon will not give its light. The stars will fall from the sky and the heavenly bodies will be shaken. Then the Son of Man will come on the clouds of the sky with power and great glory. The Lord will roar from Zion and thunder from Jerusalem. The earth and the heavens will tremble but the Lord will be a refuge for His people.

Read Psalm 114
Job 5:9, 9:6 & 10, Isaiah 24:20-23 & 44:6-8, Ezekiel 38:20, Joel 3:16, Matthew 24:29-30

All powerful and Mighty Father, You who can remove the mountains at Your command, remove the doubt from our minds and help us to surrender totally to Your will. May we never lose sight of the truth that with You nothing is impossible and You delight in the prayers, petitions and praises of Your people. Amen.

MAY 24
THE HIGHEST HEAVENS

Psalm 115:3: Our God is in heaven; He does whatever He pleases.

The Lord God is the great I AM. He made the heavens, even the highest heavens, and all their starry host. He gave life to everything and the multitude of heaven worships Him. With His great power, He made the earth and its people and the animals that are on it and He gives it to anyone He pleases. There is no other god who loves His children so much that He sent His Son to earth as a man to have Him become a sacrifice for ALL mankind. We do not have to do anything to receive this gift. It is freely given to us if we only believe. He cares deeply and profoundly for our lives and our souls. He provides not only our physical needs but our spiritual ones as well. He said to seek first His kingdom and His righteousness and all these things will be given to you. He rides across the highest heavens, the ancient heavens, and thunders with a mighty voice. The heavens, even the highest heavens, the earth and everything in it belong to Him.

Read Psalm 115
Deuteronomy 10:14, Nehemiah 9:6, Psalm 68:33, Jeremiah 27:5, Matthew 6:33

All-knowing, all-seeing, all-hearing, al- merciful Father in Heaven, we rejoice that You have called us by name, that You have put Your seal on our foreheads and that we have every reason to believe and understand that our lives are secure and safe in Your loving hands. As we read the precious Word of God every day, fill our hearts and minds anew with the knowledge of who You are, the great I Am who lives and reigns forever and ever. Amen.

MAY 25
HE HEARD MY CRY

Psalm 116:1: I love the Lord, for He heard my voice; He heard my cry for mercy.

Hannah was one of two wives of Elkanah. Year after year he went to worship and sacrifice to the Lord Almighty. Whenever the day came to sacrifice, he gave Hannah a double portion because he loved her. But the Lord had closed her womb, and because of this her rival, who had sons and daughters, provoked her until she wept and would not eat. In bitterness of soul, she wept much and prayed to the Lord. She made a vow, saying, "Almighty God, if you will only look upon your servant's misery and not forget your servant but give me a son, I will give him to You all the days of his life." Eli, the priest, saw her and thought she was drunk because her lips were moving but he did not hear her voice. Hannah replied, "Not so. I am deeply troubled and was pouring out my soul to the Lord." Eli told her to go in peace and prayed that the God of Israel would grant her what she asked Him. In the course of time, Hannah conceived and gave birth to a son, whom she named Samuel. She brought him to Eli, the priest, to serve in the temple all the days of his life. Hannah kept her vow to God because of His mercy upon Her, and He blessed her with six additional children. This example of God's mercy gives us hope that He hears the prayers of His children. If we believe, we will receive whatever we ask him prayer.

Read Psalm 116
1 Samuel 1:1-28 & 2:5, Matthew 21:22

Lord, sometimes it is difficult to express our prayers in words. Thank You for knowing our every need even before we ask. Reveal any unbelief we harbor in our hearts, for Jesus said if we have the faith of a mustard seed we can move mountains. Help our unbelief and increase our faith in You. Amen.

MAY 26
EXTOL HIM

Psalm 117:1: Praise the Lord, all you nations; exalt Him, all You peoples.

This is the shortest Psalm, yet it says a lot. If all the nations of the world praised and extolled the one true God, we would have heaven on earth. Righteousness exalts a nation but sin is a disgrace to any people. Sin separates us from God and takes our thoughts away from Him. Paul wrote to the Romans to accept one another just as Christ accepted them, in order to bring praise to God. If we took into account the needs of others before ourselves, there would be no lying, stealing or harm to another. If all nations praised God and looked to Him for answers, there would be no wars. This would be a foretaste of the eternal glory that awaits us in Heaven. We can have this peace within ourselves when we put our trust in Him.

Read Psalm 117
Proverbs 14:34, Luke 2:14, Romans 15:7, Philippians 2:4

Lord God Almighty, the One who breathed life into Your creation, help us to keep our focus on You always. We pray for the nations of the world that they may come to serve You and experience the peace that there is in knowing and trusting the eternal God of all creation. Amen.

MAY 27
OUR MIGHTY GOD

Psalm 118:16: The Lord's right hand is lifted high; the Lord's right hand has done mighty things.

Our lives sometimes go down paths we have no control over. Our first inclination may be to blame God for anything we think is a burden. He does not promise that our lives will be trouble free, but He does promise to always be with us and bring us through. It's when we don't trust Him that our lives become miserable because we try to solve things on our own, or we harbor hate or anger or lust in our hearts. He is a God of unlimited resources, a God of freedom and truth. He is so mighty and powerful that at the blast of breath from His nostrils the foundations of the earth lay bare. The only thing we can do by the breath of our nostrils is blow our nose! When Elijah called on his God, the fire of the Lord fell and burned the sacrifice that he offered; He licked up the water in the trench while the worshipers of Baal called on their god who did nothing. The voice of the Lord is like the roar of rushing waters. He is so mighty, so awesome, so trustworthy, never changing and when we call on Him, He never, ever fails us.

Read Psalm 118:1-18
2 Samuel 22:14-16, 1 Kings 18:38-39, Ezekiel 43:2

All Powerful, All-Mighty King, Savior, Father, God Almighty, Your name is worthy of all praise. You alone are the One who never fails for You have all the resources necessary at your disposal to provide for Your children. When we call upon You, You answer. If the answer does not seem forthcoming, You are still answering. Give us a measure of faith to believe the path You lay before us is the one we should unquestionably take. Bless Your Holy Name. Amen.

MAY 28
JESUS, THE CORNERSTONE

Psalm 118:22-23: The stone the builders rejected has become the capstone; the Lord has done this, and it is marvelous in our eyes.

Jesus came to save the lost sheep of the house of Israel. He sent His disciples out, not to the Gentiles but to the house of Israel, to preach the message that the kingdom of heaven was near. One day Jesus was teaching the people in the temple courts and preaching the gospel to the chief priests and teachers of the law. He told them a parable about a man (God) who planted a vineyard. He rented the vineyard to some farmers (house of Israel) and went away for a long time. At harvest time, he sent servants (prophets) to the farmers, who beat the servants, treated them shamefully and sent them away empty-handed. The owner of the vineyard then sent his son (Jesus) saying perhaps the farmers would respect him. But when they saw him, they killed him, saying, "The inheritance will be ours." The owner of the vineyard killed those he had rented the vineyard to and gave it to others (Gentiles). The stone (Jesus) that the builders (house of Israel) rejected has become the capstone. The kingdom of God has been taken away from them and given to a people who will produce its fruit. Now everyone who calls on the name of the Lord will be saved.

Read Psalm 118:19-29
Matthew 10:5-6, 15:24 & 21:43, Luke 20:1-17, John 12:40, Acts 2:21

Jesus, thank You for coming to set men free from sin. You are our cornerstone, the Rock upon which we can build our lives. Teach us to pray. Reveal the true nature of God so that our faith increases. Gently guide us into the ways of righteousness. Fill us anew with Your Holy presence so we may live to the fullness of all our Father has planned for us. Amen.

MAY 29
HIS COMMANDMENTS

Psalm 119:2: Blessed are they who keep His statutes and seek Him with all their heart.

Before Jesus came, there was the Law of Moses to guide His people. The first commandment, Thou shalt have no other gods before me, tells us that if we love the Lord our God with all our hearts, minds and souls He will truly be our God. His ways are not burdensome. If we follow Him with all of our hearts, our lives will be full of His presence; we will have joy and peace beyond the understanding of the world. He has given us the commandments for our own protection. Thou shalt not commit adultery, there should be no burden in obeying this command. We take vows in marriage that are meant to last a lifetime. When they are broken by infidelity or abuse, it results in heartache and turmoil to not only the person who engages in such conduct, but the spouse, the children, the grandparents, and friends. Jesus said He came to fulfill the law, not to destroy it. He also says we are His friends if we do as He commands. This life is not a joyride to do as we please, though this is what the world teaches. Our God is a holy, merciful and just God. He has made a way to follow His commands, which leads to eternal life.

Read Psalm 119:1-8
Deuteronomy 11:13-15, Matthew 11:30, John 15:14

Lord, You are the Giver of Life. The world has no desire to serve You, but the whole purpose of life is missed when we do not seek You. Help us to not be influenced by the things that soon pass away. Help us store up treasures in Heaven where moth and dust do not destroy. Thank You for the gift of life. May we use this gift in a way that glorifies You. Amen.

MAY 30
LIVING ACCORDING TO GOD'S WORD

Psalm 119:9: How can a young man keep his way pure? By living according to Your Word.

Life is full of temptations. They come to us as pleasure and power. When we give into these temptations, we are never satisfied. Our human nature always wants more so we fill our lives with many things trying to satisfy the inner longings and desires we have. We go from one thing to another until we come to the end of life. But it doesn't have to be this way. The Lord has given us instructions so we can overcome the temptations that barrage us every day. When we live according to His Word, we are not deceived by the serpent's tricks like Eve was, and our hearts are not lead astray from sincere and pure devotion to Christ. He waits for us to call upon Him to lead us each day. When we wake up and go our own way without spending time with Him, our souls are empty. Seeking and following Him keeps our lives pure while on this earth, and forevermore.

Read Psalm 119:9-16
2 Samuel 22:22, Romans 13:14, 2 Corinthians 11:3

Lord, we are so blessed to have Your Word as a guiding light. In days of old, this was impossible. There was no ability to produce multiple copies of the Bible, and even if they were available most could not read. Help us to apply Your Word to our lives so when temptation comes knocking at our door, we can resist it because of Your Holy Word. Amen.

MAY 31
OPEN EYES

Psalm 119:18: Open my eyes that I may see wonderful things in Your law.

The god of this age has blinded the eyes of unbelievers so they cannot see the light of the gospel of the glory of Christ, who is the image of God. Believers in Christ renounce secret and shameful ways. They should not use deception nor distort the word of God. Paul was blinded on the road to Damascus. After three days, Ananias went to the house where he was staying and laid hands on Paul. Immediately something like scales fell from his eyes and he could see again. It was a transformation that we can all experience. From that day forward, Paul preached the gospel of Christ. His spiritual eyes were open to the kingdom of God and Christ crucified. When we seek the things of God with all of our hearts, He opens our eyes in a way that we desire to seek His righteousness and holiness. We delight in His Word and keep His commands because we know this pleases Him.

Read Psalm 119:17-24
Acts 9:18, 2 Corinthians 4:2-4 & 4:18

Lord, may we see what surrounds us, for Your beauty is everywhere. You create new every day. We are such a minute part of Your creation, yet You call us to serve You, and You love us unconditionally. Open the eyes of our hearts. We want to see You. May we never be blind to what is plainly before us when we live by the power of Your Spirit. Amen.

JUNE 1
UNDERSTANDING HIS PRECEPTS

Psalm 119:27: Let me understand the teaching of Your precepts, then I will meditate on Your wonders.

We are flesh. God is Spirit. We are finite. He is infinite. We live by time. He is timeless. Our resources are limited. His are limitless. A time is coming and has now come when worshipers will worship the Father in spirit and truth for they are the kind of worshipers the Father seeks. The precepts of the Lord are right, giving joy to the heart. His commands are radiant, giving light to the eyes. Praying and waiting quietly on the Spirit of

God, we gain understanding of His precepts and it draws us closer to the One who loves us with the richness of His righteousness.

Read Psalm 119:25-32
Proverbs 19:8, John 4:23

Lord, forgive us for not seeing as You see and thinking as You think. We limit You when we try doing things on our own. Help us trust You, to have faith in Your ability to meet all of our needs. In our times of distress, send Your peace so that we do not try and fix whatever we perceive needs fixing. There is nothing You can't provide if we allow You to do it. Amen.

JUNE 2
OBEYING GOD'S LAW

Psalm 119:34: Give me understanding and I will keep Your law and obey it with all my heart.

Moses went up to God and He called out to him from the mountain. The Lord said to tell the house of Jacob and the people of Israel, "Now if you obey me fully and keep my covenant, then out of all the nations you will be my treasured possession." The Lord also told them to follow His decrees and be careful to obey His laws and they would live safely in the land. These were His promises to His people, and even though they turned from Him He said, "When you are in distress and all these things have happened to you, then in the later days you will return to the Lord your God and obey Him, for the Lord is a merciful God and He will not abandon or destroy you or forget the covenant with your forefathers." He knows we stray from His ways, but He brings us back into communion with Him when we call upon Him.

Read Psalm 119:33-40
Exodus 19:3-6, Leviticus 25:18, Deuteronomy 4:30-31

Lord, take our hearts and our minds and transform them so that our desire is to seek Your ways and not our own. It is a constant struggle, for the things of this world are tempting and give promises of fame and fortune. You, though, are the solid rock into which we need to anchor. Search our ways and show us where we are lacking that we might confess our sin before You and draw closer to You as we pray, read and meditate upon Your Holy Word. Amen.

JUNE 3
FREEDOM

Psalm 119:45: I will walk about in freedom for I have sought out Your precepts.

Freedom always comes with a price. Our military serves selflessly, even to the point of death, to keep us free. To be free is to have liberty; to not be in bondage; exempt or liberated from slavery, imprisonment or restraint from the power or control of another. God's precepts free us from sin and death, and that freedom also came with a price, which is the blood of Jesus Christ. We are free from the burden of sin and should live as free people. Jesus said that if we hold to His teachings, we are his disciples and we will know the truth and the truth will set us free. This freedom is not to be used as a cover-up for evil but to now live as God's slaves. Letting go of the things that bind us—like anger, hatred, unforgiveness, self-centeredness—sets us free to live the way our Heavenly Father intends. We become slaves to righteousness, which leads us into a personal relationship with our Heavenly Father, whom we will one day be with forever.

Read Psalm 119:41-48
Isaiah 61:1, John 8:32 and 36, Galatians 5:1, 1 Peter 2:16

Heavenly Father, Your Word tells us that whom the Son sets free is free indeed. We are free from our sin and the sin of the world. We are free to serve You with all of our hearts, souls and beings. Draw us closer to You so that we may continue to enjoy this freedom which You have so generously bestowed upon us. Amen.

JUNE 4
HIS PROMISE

Psalm 119:50: My comfort in my suffering is this: Your promise preserves my life.

Ever since man's fall into sin, God has made a promise of salvation and redemption. He proclaimed that even though His creation had given into their own desires and chosen their own way, there would be a Redeemer to save men's souls. All through God's Word, there is the story of good and evil, a continual battle for the souls of each and every human being who has been born on this earth. Those in the Old Testament knew there would be a Savior and even to this day there are those who believe the Messiah will one day come. The good news is that He has come. When Jesus spoke His final words on the cross, "It is finished," the veil in the temple was ripped in two and a new dawn had broken. Christ had accomplished His mission. His message is that of reconciliation, love, mercy, and grace. Our Father in Heaven is so awesome and He waits patiently for His children to receive His promise. It is real and it is everlasting.

Read Psalm 119:49-56
1 Kings 8:56-58, Galatians 3:22

Father, thank You for Your promise of salvation and redemption. Without the perfect sacrifice of Jesus Christ, we would be lost forever with no hope. Thank You for shining His light in the world and in our lives. Help us in our weaknesses and forgive us when we fail You. We praise and bless Your holy, wonderful name. Amen.

JUNE 5
OUR GRACIOUS GOD

Psalm 119:58: I have sought Your face with all my heart; be gracious to me according to Your promise.

When we meet someone we would like to know better, we make time to be with them. By talking and sharing things about each other, the bond between us grows stronger and we become friends. It is no different when we want a relationship with Jesus. If we want to know Him, we need to spend time with Him. He is spirit and we do not see Him physically, but when we talk with Him and spend time reading the Bible, He responds to us and we begin to know Him in a way that transcends any friendship on this earth. He is the One who calls us by name and who loves us with a love we can never experience from another human being. The love of God is pure and holy. When we experience that love, we want more. By pursuing the Father, the Son, and the Holy Spirit as we would pursue something so precious we would never want to lose it, they reveal themselves to us. Once we experience the true love and presence of God in our lives, we can never be the same. He molds our lives into His image so that we reflect His love and mercy to others, and He gives us a vision of the eternal life that awaits us in Heaven.

Read Psalm 119:57-64
Matthew 7:7-8, Romans 5:5, 2 Corinthians 3:18

Gracious Father, thank You for Your Word that gives us the instruction we need in life and that also reveals who You are. As we read Your word, may it penetrate deep into our hearts, minds and souls so that in every situation that comes our way we will know how to pray not only for ourselves but for all with whom we come in contact. Praise Your holy name. Amen.

JUNE 6
IN TIMES OF AFFLICTION

Psalm 119:67: Before I was afflicted I went astray, but now I obey Your Word.

Naaman was commander of the army of the king of Aram. He was a valiant soldier and highly regarded, but he was afflicted with leprosy. There was a young girl from Israel who served Naaman's wife and she told her about Elisha, the prophet, who could cure him. Naaman went to Elisha, who sent him a messenger saying, "Go wash yourself seven times in the Jordan and your flesh will be restored." Naaman was outraged for he thought Elisha would come himself, call on the name of the Lord and cure his leprosy. His servants prevailed upon him to go to the Jordan, and he did. He dipped seven times and his flesh was restored and became clean like that of a young boy. In his affliction, Naaman took action and his need was met. He proclaimed that there was no God in all the world except in Israel. Then there were the Egyptians who mistreated God's children who cried out to Him. He brought them out of their affliction with a mighty hand and outstretched arm to a land flowing with milk and honey. The Spirit of God often speaks to us in a way that directs us what to do. By taking action, it results in answer to our prayers. We are to be joyful in hope, patient in affliction and faithful in prayer.

Read Psalm 119:65-72
Deuteronomy 26:7-9, 2 Kings 5:1-3 &10-15, Romans 12:11-12

Heavenly and Gracious Father, remember that we are human and many times our thoughts and actions are counter to what You desire for us. In our times of darkness, in our deepest needs, send forth Your loving hand to take our hand and walk with us. Help us remember that You will never leave nor forsake us, that You hear our prayers and You answer. Hold us close to Your side so we remember to put our trust in You. Amen.

JUNE 7
HE FORMED US

Psalm 119:73: Your hands made me and formed me; give me understanding to learn Your commands.

The Lord fashioned and made the earth. He did not create it to be empty but formed it to be inhabited. He planted a garden on the east, in Eden, and the man He formed He put there. He said it was not good for man to be alone so He made a helper suitable for him and called her Eve. They sinned against the One who gave them life and were sent out of the garden. Since that time, people have been looking for a way to once again commune with their Creator. He chose a people to serve Him but they acted corruptly toward Him and became a warped and crooked generation. Moses asked them, "Is this the way you repay the Lord? Is He not your Father, your Creator, who made you?" We are not our own for we were bought at a price with the precious blood of Jesus Christ. The One who formed us wants us to know Him and love Him.

Read Psalm 119:73-80
Genesis 2:8 &18, 3:23, Deuteronomy 32:5-6, Isaiah 45:18,
1 Corinthians 6:20

Lord, life is a precious gift. May we always remember that You are the Giver of life. We had no say in being born and we have no say when we will die. We pray for insight into Your ways so we might have a greater understanding of who You are. Amen.

JUNE 8
ALWAYS FAITHFUL

Psalm 119:86: All Your commands are trustworthy; help me for men persecute me without cause.

It's not for certain at what stage of life King David was when he wrote this psalm. It's clear he is in great distress, but he looked to the Lord for his source of strength and renewal of life. In our good times, we don't always remember our Lord or even consider that each day's blessings come from Him, but in our time of need we realize we are incapable of finding answers and we call out to God. Believers in Christ know He hears their cries. It is essential to know the promises in God's word and hide them in our hearts because it is during those times of despair and stress that we need to lean on what we know our God has said. He is not slack in His promises. He is not a man that He should lie and He is ever faithful to deliver us. Even when we suffer to the point of death, we have hope of an eternal glory with Him. Sometimes it is difficult to look past our present circumstances which seem as though they will never end, but when our hope is in Him we have no need to fear for though our soul faints with longings, our hope is in His Word which never fails.

Read Psalm 119:81-88
Numbers 23:19, Psalm 119:11, Proverbs 2:1-5

Heavenly Father, we praise You in the good times and in the bad. When we are down, lift us up into the stillness of Your presence that we might rest in the comfort that only You can give. In our weakness, You are strong and when we wait upon you, those are the times we see the mighty works of Your hand. Increase our faith that we might live life to its fullest in You. Amen.

JUNE 9
ETERNAL WORD OF GOD

Psalm 119:89: Your word, O Lord, is eternal; it stands firm in the heavens.

The consistent theme of Psalm 119 is that man is weak but God is strong and that reading His Word gives knowledge that the Lord is our source of strength and salvation. We are assured that He is always with us; He upholds us with his right hand of righteousness and He loves us with an everlasting love that nurtures us while on this earth and in the eternal life to come. His word is immovable, for it is truth, and the truth always stands while a lie crumbles to the ground when it is discovered. God has no ulterior motive to His love for us. He is like parents who want the best for their children. He may know their needs before they even ask, but they need space to grow and not be smothered. We are God's children and He wants to bless us, but He never forces His will or ways on us. He waits for us to ask. Standing firm in the Word and staying close by His side keeps us from falling back into the ways of this world. There are many temptations to draw us away from Him. Heaven and earth will one day pass away but God's Word will stand forever.

Psalm 119:89-96
Psalm 48:10, Isaiah 41:10, Mark 13:31

Eternal Father, who was and is and is to come, this is a concept that is difficult to grasp at times but we know it is the truth. Give us a strong desire to be in Your Word and learn of You. You Word breathes life into our souls and gives us the faith we need to endure to the end. We long to know You in the fullness of Your everlasting love, for it is our source of strength. Amen.

JUNE 10
HIS WORDS ARE SWEETER THAN HONEY

Psalm 119:103: How sweet are Your words to my taste, sweeter than honey to my mouth.

More knowledge about a myriad of subjects exists today than we could possibly learn in a lifetime. If we stop to consider this, we realize how finite we are and how infinite our God is. In His Son Jesus Christ are hidden all the treasures of wisdom and knowledge. If this is the truth, we should desire to search the Word of God so that we can discover these sweet, hidden treasures. All the knowledge in the world will not give us eternal life, but the knowledge of the tender, merciful words of Christ will. Even though King David lived centuries before Christ, in his heart he knew Him. He knew that His God whom he served had a plan to save mankind from their sins. He searched the Scriptures. He meditated all the day long on their precepts. We can have this communion with our Lord when we seek Him with our whole heart, when we meditate upon and read His word and pray for understanding and wisdom so that we can apply it to our lives. When we live like this, others see the manifestations of the sweet aroma of Christ in us and hopefully desire it for themselves unto everlasting life!

Read Psalm 119:97-104
Proverbs 16:23-24 & 24:14, 2 Corinthians 2:14-15

Heavenly Father, thank You for Your Word. Open our hearts to receive all You have for us so that we might be filled with understanding of Your ways, for Your ways lead us in paths of righteousness for Your Name's sake. Amen.

JUNE 11
HIS PATH LIGHTS THE WAY

Psalm 119:105: Your Word is a lamp to my feet and a light for my path.

The Word of God is like a lamp. If it just sits on the table and is never turned on, it has no purpose except perhaps as a piece of furniture. It's only when the switch is turned on that it serves its true purpose. Many people have a Bible in their homes but they never open it and read the words written on the pages that are full of instruction for life. But when we have the Word of God in our hearts, especially from the time we are very little, it lights the path that leads to eternal life. The light that shines forth from knowing God's Word is like the first gleam of dawn, shining ever brighter until the full light of day. We are not some cosmic accident that came about by a random act of nature. We did not come from tissue in our mother's womb. We were formed in the womb specifically and purposefully, for our God does nothing by mistake. His glory covers the heavens, His praise fills the earth, and His splendor is like the sunrise. He lines the path before us with His forgiveness, His tender mercies, and His love. His Word is truth and the truth of God sets us free from the grasp of sin so that we can walk the path which leads to eternal life.

Read Psalm 119:105-112
Proverbs 4:18, Jeremiah 1:5, Habakkuk 3:3-4, Romans 6:22

Lord, at times we find it difficult to choose the way You have laid before us. We are filled with doubts, worry and unbelief. During these times, envelope us with Your loving presence and bring to our minds Your words of comfort and truth. Your path leads to righteousness and we need not fear when we choose it because You are always guiding us by Your merciful and outstretched hand. Praise Your holy, wonderful Name. Amen.

JUNE 12
HOPE IN HIS WORD

Psalm 119:114: You are my refuge and my shield. I have my hope in Your Word.

As long as there is breath, there is life. As long as there is life, there is hope. There was a man who had two sons. He divided his property among them. The youngest one got together all that he had and set off for a distant country. There, he squandered all that he had on wild living. There was a severe famine in that whole country and he began to be in need. He hired himself out to a citizen of that country who sent him to the fields to feed his pigs. He was so hungry that he filled his stomach with the pods that the pigs were eating because no one gave him anything to eat. When he came to himself, he remembered his father and said, "How many of my father's hired men have food to spare and I am starving to death!" He headed back to his father's house in humility to ask forgiveness, not seeking to be restored as the man's son but as one of his hired men. While he was still a long way off, his father saw him and was filled with compassion for him. He ran to his son, threw his arms around him and kissed him. He called out to his servants to bring the best robe and put it on him; put a ring on his finger and sandals on his feet. He declared a feast and celebration, for his son who was dead was alive; he who was lost had been found. We are all sinners saved by grace. We live in a fallen world and are surrounded every day by temptations, and there are times when we yield to those temptations. But our Lord is never angry with us. He loves us with an unconditional love. He watches and waits for us to return to Him. When we do, there is rejoicing in the presence of the angels of God.

Read Psalm 119:113-120
Micah 6:8, Luke 15:10-24

Father, we come humbly to You today and ask that You search our hearts and minds. If there is anything that hinders our walk with You, reveal it by Your Holy Spirit. We thank You for the blood of Jesus that washes away all of our sins and gives us a pure heart. May our desires be Your desires and may Your plan for us be fulfilled according to Your most precious Word. Amen.

JUNE 13
I AM YOUR SERVANT

Psalm 119:125: I am Your servant; give me discernment that I may understand Your statutes.

King David's relationship with God was so unique. All around him were naysayers against the word of God. They were continually devising ways to deceive and trick the king and to take away his authority but this never deterred him from serving the Lord. It made him even more determined to read the Scriptures so he could learn and understand the ways of the God whom he served. He never wavered in his faith, and he knew that when his oppressors came, the one source of strength that would sustain him was his love for the Word of God which told him that the Lord would uphold him with His righteous right hand. This is the example we should strive for, to have complete trust and faith in the ability of our God to keep us safe. David considered himself a servant even though he was a king; as well did Jesus, who left His home in glory to take on the nature of a man. He too proclaimed His servanthood, yet He is Lord of all. Our Father in Heaven is not a taskmaster who takes out a whip and beats his servants into submission but a master who gives instructions with love and mercy and allows His servants full latitude to follow their master and know His ways. They are the ways of eternal life and freedom from sin.

Psalm 119:121-128
1 Chronicles 17:18, Mark 9:35, Philippians 2:5-8

Heavenly Father, Your word tells us we cannot serve two masters, meaning the world and You. We must choose whom we will serve. As for me and my house, we will serve the Lord. The things and desires of this world pass away but Your Word endures forever. Renew our hearts each day and fill our minds with understanding that we may serve You always and forevermore. Amen.

JUNE 14
UNFOLDING OF YOUR WORD

Psalm 119:130: The unfolding of Your words gives light; it gives understanding to the simple.

God's Word is like a folded piece of paper. We can look at it and ponder it but not until we unfold it do we discover what is inside. The words written on the paper are what reveal the story. When we open the Word of God, it is our instruction book for life. The cover has only a title but the chapters and verses are the substance that guides our footsteps so that sin does not rule over us. The pages are full of historical facts and genealogies; stories of different people that tell about God's grace and mercy; the faults and failures of God's people and how each time they cried out to Him He answered. It's a story about the fall of mankind and redemption; a story of hope and a future with the Creator of the world. We are unable to redeem ourselves from sin, which is why Jesus came. He is our help in time of trouble, our deliverer, our strength. It is by the power of His blood we have forgiveness of all of our sins. We are tried and tempted many times. When we hide the Word of God in our hearts, we know what He expects of us and we will not want to sin against Him.

Read Psalm 119:129-136
Psalm 49:7 & 119:37, 1 Corinthians 1:26-31, Galatians 3:13-14

O Lord, may Your words penetrate our hearts like beams of sunlight and dispel the darkness of our minds. Give us understanding so that our desire might be to please You and not sin against You. Help us live for You and not be distracted or swayed by those who would lead us away from You. Keep us safe from harm and lead us by Your Holy Spirit. Amen.

JUNE 15
HIS STATUTES ARE TRUSTWORTHY

Psalm 119:138: The statutes You have laid down are righteous; they are fully trustworthy.

The Lord has established statutes by which His people must live. He does this for their own protection, for He Himself needs no laws. The law of the Lord is perfect, refreshing the soul. The statutes of the Lord are trustworthy, making wise the simple. We are the ones who make laws complicated, especially civil laws. According to one politician, the Internal Revenue Code and regulations add up to more than a million words and is nearly seven times the length of the Bible. It is impossible for the average taxpayer to understand and accurately apply its provisions. This is done purposely by lawyers and politicians, mainly for their own benefit. As God's people did in the Old Testament, they rejected His decrees and the covenant He made with their ancestors and the statutes He had warned them to keep. They followed worthless idols and themselves became worthless. We must give to Caesar what is Caesar's, but we must also give to God what is God's. His statutes are our heritage forever and they are the joy of our heart.

Read Psalm 119:137-144
2 Kings 17:15, Psalm 19:7 & 119:111, Matthew 22:21

Heavenly Father, life gets complicated with so many rules and regulations by those in authority. We pray for wisdom to know what is Yours and what is Caesar's, for Your statutes are the ones we must follow. Guide us by the power of Your Holy Spirit and keep us from wandering from the truth of Your Word and the statutes that You have established. We put our trust in You and thank You for all things. Amen.

JUNE 16
HIS STATUTES LAST FOREVER

Psalm 119:152: Long ago I learned from Your statutes that You established them to last forever.

God's boundaries do not confine us to some sort of cage where we have no freedom. They actually have the opposite effect. They give us guidance on how to keep ourselves from a lot of heartache and trouble. If we all lived by the Ten Commandments, we could have full and joyful lives. By having no other gods before us, we worship the One True Living, all-knowing, all-merciful, all-powerful, all-loving God. By resting on the

Sabbath, we bring rest to our minds and bodies. By honoring our parents, we learn how to honor others and ourselves. By not taking God's name in vain, we give Him reverence and believe He is holy. By not murdering, committing adultery, stealing, lying or coveting what others have, we protect ourselves from consequences of such conduct, as well as those who may also be affected by our actions. This was the law given to man by God, yet it is impossible to keep these commands by our own strength. True freedom comes by believing in the One who came to set the captive free. He is the One who gives us the ability to live by God's statutes that have been established to last forever.

Read Psalm 119:145-152
Joshua 24:14-15, Isaiah 30:21, Galatians 5:16-26

Heavenly Father, we pray for the desire to follow Your precepts. As we read the Bible, open our minds to understand Your ways so that we will walk in them. Your ways bring joy and fullness to life. When we stray, quickly bring to our minds Your statutes which are everlasting and true. Forgive us our sins and bring us back to You. Amen.

JUNE 17
HIS WORDS ARE TRUE

Psalm 119:160: All Your words are true; all Your righteous laws are eternal.

After His resurrection and appearance to His disciples, Jesus was taken up before their very eyes and a cloud hid Him from their sight. Suddenly two men dressed in white stood beside them saying, "Men of Galilee, why do you stand here looking into the sky? This same Jesus will come back in the same way you have seen Him go to Heaven." These are encouraging words to believers in Christ because we know He is coming back. As lightning that comes from the east is visible even in the west, so will be the coming of the Son of Man. He will come on the clouds of the sky, with power and great glory. No one knows that day or hour, not even the angels in Heaven, nor the Son, but only the Father. Therefore, we are to keep watch because we do not know on what day the Lord will come. It will be a time of great rejoicing. Those who are invited to the wedding supper of the Lamb will be blessed for these are the true words of God.

Read Psalm 119:153-160
Matthew 24:27, 30, 36 & 42, Acts 1:10-11, Revelation 19:9

Heavenly and Merciful Father, as we read Your Word each day, draw us closer to You so that we may look to those things which are eternal. At times we are consumed with our present circumstances and forget that all of this is temporary and will one day pass away. But You are faithful, always by our side; You are forever and Your Word is truth. Amen.

JUNE 18
PEACE IN TURMOIL

Psalm 119:165: Great peace have they who love Your law, and nothing can make them stumble.

In the midst of turmoil we can have peace. When we stumble and fall, we can have peace. When all is well with our souls, we can have peace. The peace of God transcends all understanding and that is why Christians have faith in God. It is not necessary to understand all His ways, but we trust that all of His ways are righteous. There are times, like Daniel, when we are in a den of hungry lions and we feel like we are going to be eaten alive. But then the Spirit of God intervenes and shuts the mouths of the lions so they cannot harm us. Our minds might not be able to grasp all we are reading in the Bible, especially in the Old Testament when God becomes angry with His chosen people to the point that He destroys or scatters them, but He is always merciful. When His people turned back to Him with a repentant heart, He forgave and blessed them. At times, we may question what life is all about and why there is suffering and heartache. One day, the answers to these questions will be known. In the meanwhile, the peace of God, which transcends all understanding, will guard our hearts and minds in Christ Jesus.

Read Psalm 119:161-168
2 Chronicles 33:12-13, Isaiah 26:3, Daniel 6:21-22, Philippians 4:7

Peace, peace, wonderful peace that flows down from the Father above. We thank You that we do not have to worry when we trust in You, for Your peace is with us. Help us to never doubt this promise that You have given us. When we are peaceful in the midst of turmoil, Your light shines through for others to see. And when they see our peace, our prayer is that they will desire You in their lives and also experience Your peace. Amen.

JUNE 19
STRAYING LIKE LOST SHEEP

Psalm 119:176: I have strayed like a lost sheep. Seek Your servant, for I have not forgotten Your commands.

Sheep are docile animals. Without a shepherd, they are vulnerable to attack by predators, unable to defend themselves. They have a tendency to wander away from the flock when they graze. In the New Testament, sheep are referred to almost 50 times. Jesus called Himself the Good Shepherd. He said, "I know my sheep and my sheep know me," and "I lay down my life for the sheep." A shepherd tends diligently to his flock. He watches over and protects them. Without a shepherd, we are all like sheep that have gone astray and we have each turned to our own way. For believers in Christ, we are the sheep who have now returned to the Shepherd and Overseer of our souls. We know we need someone to watch over and protect us. Unlike sheep, we have the ability to think and reason, to make choices. The world is full of things that lead us away from God, but when we have His statutes hidden in our hearts, we recognize the voice of our Shepherd when He calls us back to Him. He pardons our sins and forgives our transgressions. He treads our sins underfoot and hurls our iniquities into the depths of the sea.

Read Psalm 119:169-176
Isaiah 53:5-6, John 10:14-15, 1 Peter 2:25

Lord, we are Your sheep; You are our shepherd. As a shepherd watches over His flock, we pray that You would watch over us. You have drawn us to You and called us by name. Help us not to wander from the path of righteousness, which leads us in Your ways. Thank you for the light of Your presence that shines when we walk hand in hand with You. Amen.

JUNE 20
HE HEARS AND ANSWERS

Psalm 120:1: I call on the Lord in my distress and He answers me.

Cain and Abel were brothers. When the harvest was ready, it came time to sacrifice to the Lord. Abel's sacrifice was acceptable to God but Cain's was not. Cain became angry and killed Abel and then lied to the Lord about doing it. This is the first recorded murder. The evil in man's heart became so bad, it grieved the Lord that He had made man and His heart was filled with pain. Each man was a god unto himself. They were spiritually dead and did whatever they wanted to fulfill their lustful desires. When God looked down and saw this, He flooded the entire earth and only Noah and his family were saved in an ark which God directed him to build. After the waters receded, the Lord established His covenant with Noah and said, "Never again will all life be cut off by the waters of a flood; never again will there be a flood to destroy the earth." It is not our Father's desire to destroy man, for He created us in His image. There have been those who have chosen to follow Him with all their hearts: Joseph, Abraham, Isaac, Jacob, Moses, Samuel, David, Esther, the prophets; and those in the New Testament, Matthew, John, Mary, James, Paul, to name a few. Life was not easy for them and they suffered much because of their beliefs. He gave His servants the fortitude to withstand their hardships because they had faith in the Lord God Almighty. As we go through life, may we be continually mindful that when we call upon the Lord in our distress, He answers.

Read Psalm 120
Genesis 4:4-5, 4:8, 6:6, 9:11, Psalm 34:7, Acts 14:22

Almighty Father, when all is going well we tend to take for granted that You are with us, but we don't always pursue You during these times the way we do during our distresses. Help us to remember that You want to be a part of all we do. Take us into Your loving presence and guide us that we might walk in the way that pleases You. Amen.

JUNE 21
HE NEVER SLUMBERS NOR SLEEPS

Psalm 121:3-4: He will not let your foot slip. He who watches over You will not slumber. Indeed, He who watches over Israel will neither slumber nor sleep.

God gives us the shade of His right hand so that the sun will not harm us by day nor the moon by night. He watches over our coming and going, both now and forever. He never slumbers, nor sleeps. He is available no matter the time of day. We don't need a cell phone to call Him or worry that He won't answer. He views the ends of the earth and sees everything under the heavens. But woe to those who go to great depths to hide their plans from the Lord, who do their work in darkness and think He does not see or know what they do. Nothing is hidden from His sight. He sees the big picture and knows the minutest details of our lives, even the number of hairs on our head. In the words of a favorite hymn: His eye is on the sparrow and I know He watches me.

Read Psalm 121
Job 28:24, Psalm 121:5, Isaiah 29:15, Matthew 10:30

Our Father, who never slumbers nor sleeps, look with delight upon us, Your children. Bring us into Your presence and give us a greater understanding of Your precepts. It is upon these precepts that our faith increases. Each day presents its challenges, but You are with us in them all. Help us to trust in Your ability to bring us through. Amen.

JUNE 22
JERUSALEM

Psalm 122:6: Pray for the peace of Jerusalem. May those who love You be secure.

Jerusalem, the Holy City of God, the place where He dwells, it is the high and holy place where His people come to worship. In our present day, Jerusalem is the center of much media attention. There is a battle as to whose capital it should be between the Jews and Muslims. There are questions as to whether It should be a divided city or one city. There is much controversy in that part of the world; yet the Bible is clear on how significant this city is to the Lord. It is the city that He chose for His people. When Jesus returns, He will stand on the Mount of Olives and split it in two from east to west, and He will rule and reign from His throne in Jerusalem for a thousand years. The nations of the earth will come to Jerusalem to worship Him. After the thousand years, Satan will once again be loosed into the world for a short time. There will be another falling away, but then the end will come and God's judgment will be declared. There will be a new city of Jerusalem coming down from Heaven prepared as a bride beautifully dressed for her husband. It is a place where God dwells with man in perfect peace. There will be no more death, no more crying, no more pain. He will make everything new. This is our eternal hope in Him.

Read Psalm 122
2 Chronicles 6:3-6, Ezra 1:3, Jeremiah 3:17, Zechariah 14:4 & 8-9, Revelation 20:7-8 & 21:2-4

Lord, God Almighty, there is much controversy in this world about the significance of Jerusalem and who it belongs to. We need not concern ourselves with the affairs of what man thinks. We know that the city is Yours and one day You will reign from Your throne in Jerusalem. Even if we have never been there, we know from Your Word the importance of this place to You throughout the ages. We know Your Word is true and will come to pass. Until that day, our prayer is for the peace of Jerusalem. Amen.

JUNE 23
GOD'S HEAVENLY THRONE

Psalm 123:1: I lift up my eyes to You, to You whose throne is in Heaven.

The throne room at Neuschwanstein Castle, Bavaria, Germany, is breathtaking. The porticos and artistry that surround where the throne was to be placed brings a foretaste of Heaven to one's mind. King Ludwig, who had the castle built, had visions of grandeur where he would rule his kingdom from his throne. Because of his untimely death, his dream went unfulfilled. There is a heavenly throne room that far surpasses anything that man can create. The One who sits on the throne has the appearance of jasper and carnelian. A rainbow encircles the throne and it is surrounded by 24 other thrones that seat the 24 elders. From the throne comes flashes of lightning and peals of thunder. Before the throne there is what looks like a sea of glass, clear as crystal. There is nothing on earth comparable to the throne of God. The robes of those who come out of the great tribulation are washed in the blood of the Lamb and they are before the throne of God serving Him day and night. The Lamb is at the center of the throne and leads them to springs of living water where He wipes away every tear from their eyes.

Read Psalm 123
1 Kings 22:19, Revelation 4:2-6, & 7:17

Heavenly Father, whose dwelling is in Heaven, we pray for revelation of Your truths. Many times we are so bogged down with the things of life that we can't ever imagine that there is a God in Heaven who sits upon His throne. Increase our faith in You. If we have now only a small measure, please give us more. By Your Spirit, teach us how to pray more effectively, with certainty and trust that You hear and answer. We love You and thank You for Your love for us. Amen.

JUNE 24
THE NAME

Psalm 124:8: Our help is in the name of the Lord, the Maker of Heaven and earth.

Each one of us has a name. Our name identifies who we are as an individual. Someone can call our name and we answer. There are billions of people in the world and together we are a mass of humanity, but when our name is used we are set apart and called out from the crowd. In the time of the Great Exodus from Egypt, Moses was called by name to bring forth the children of Israel out of slavery so that they would once again be free to worship their God. After God gave him instructions on how to accomplish this great task, Moses asked the Lord what he should tell them when they inquired about who sent him and what is His name, to which God responded, "I am who I am. . .I am has sent me to you." When God gave Moses the Ten Commandments, He said, "You shall not misuse the name of the Lord Your God." His name, above all names, is holy. His name, above all names, is worthy of honor and praise. When Mary and Joseph were engaged to be married, the Lord appeared to Joseph and instructed him to name the child Jesus because He will save His people from their sins. When the final judgment comes and the books are opened before the Lord, we will want our name to be found written in the Book of Life.

Read Psalm 124
Exodus 3:13-14 & 20:7, Isaiah 57:15, Ezekiel 36:22-23, Matthew 1:21, Acts 4:12

The power of Your Name, O Holy and Righteous Lord, when we stop to think on this, it is fantastic. When we call on Your Name, You hear and answer. When we lift up Your Name, we come into Your presence to worship. We thank You that You have called each of us by name and that You knew us even before we were born. Teach us Your ways and draw us closer to You. Give us wisdom and understanding, for Your Holy Name's sake, that You might be glorified. Amen.

JUNE 25
UNSHAKEABLE TRUST

Psalm 125:1: Those who trust in the Lord are like Mount Zion, which cannot be shaken but endures forever.

According to Hebrew tradition Mount Zion "sits to eternity" neither bowing down nor moving to and fro. It cannot be removed. Our trust in the Lord God Almighty should be like Mount Zion, immovable, but our human tendencies trust in those with whom we surround ourselves and the things we possess. In Job's distress he said, "If I have put my trust in gold or said to pure gold that you are my security or if I have rejoiced over my great wealth, the fortune my hands have gained, then let briers come up instead of wheat and weeds instead of barley." He knew that trust in God was real security and not that which is fleeting. No matter our circumstances, we are more than conquerors through Him who loved us. We can be utterly forsaken and everything precious to us taken away, but neither death nor life, neither angels nor demons, nor anything else in all creation can separate us from the love of God that is in Christ Jesus our Lord. There are so many reasons to have faith and trust in God. He is eternal. He knows what went before and He knows what lies ahead. He makes our feet like the feet of a deer and enables us to go to the heights. By the power of the Holy Spirit, we can trust that what He says is the truth. The more we seek Him, the more time we spend with Him in prayer, the more we realize this unshakeable truth.

Read Psalm 125

Job 31:24 & 28, Habakkuk 3:19, Romans 8:38-39

Your Word, Lord, is truth. When You say You will do something, we can have full assurance and trust that You will. Draw us into Your Holy Presence. Increase our faith so we may never doubt nor wander away from You. Help us not to be swayed by what we see or by our circumstances; help us to be on our knees before You, seeking Your Presence in our lives so that all You have planned for us will be fulfilled. Amen.

JUNE 26
JOY

Psalm 126:3: The Lord has done great things for us and we are filled with joy.

A righteous man may have many troubles, but the Lord delivers him from them all. There may be times when we lose all hope, become discouraged and think we will never be able to get out of our present distresses. Then we fall to our knees and cry out to our God for help, for guidance, for deliverance and He hears our plea. By no act of our own, He lifts our burdens and sets us free. This happens by trusting Him to work things out. By praying and waiting upon Him, things begin to happen. When He speaks, we must take action. This should bring unspeakable joy from within our very souls. The One who sets us free from the bonds of sin and gives us a new hope of eternal glory is the same One who looks down from the throne, sees our circumstances, and hears our prayers. The joy that comes from trusting Him renews us. The joy of the Lord is our strength. He is with us. He is mighty to save. He takes great delight in us. He quiets us with His love and rejoices over us with singing.

Read Psalm 126
Nehemiah 8:10, Psalm 34:19, Isaiah 12:3, Zephaniah 3:17,
1 Thessalonians 5:16

Your joy, Lord, is unspeakable and full of glory. Forgive us when we do not trust You completely and think we can fix things on our own. There is a saying: The definition of insanity is doing the same thing over and over again and expecting a different result. Help us not to be stubborn, obstinate and insistent that we can do things our way. Reach down from Heaven, change our thinking, open our eyes to see and ears to hear You in all aspects of our lives; that we might have the peace that passes all understanding as we wait patiently upon You to hear and answer. Amen.

JUNE 27
UNLESS THE LORD BUILDS THE HOUSE

Psalm 127:1: Unless the Lord builds the house its builders labor in vain. Unless the Lord watches over the city, the watchmen stand guard in vain.

When the Lord builds our house—in other words, our life—we have a firm foundation on which to stand. His ways are sure and certain. They do not change with the wind. We can depend on Him. When we do anything without Him, it may stand for a time, but only for a time because everything in this life one day perishes. The only thing remaining is that which has been built on His Word. Heaven and earth shall pass away but His Word will never pass away. If we stop to contemplate our lives, we realize how little control we actually have. We have no choice where we are born or who we are born to. We begin to grow from infancy into childhood, then adolescence, then adulthood. There is not one thing we can do about it. It's God's plan and it happens to all of us. We grow to an old age and then we die. We cannot choose not to grow old and we cannot choose not to die. We are born into a sinful world because of the disobedience of one man. God no longer walks in the Garden of Eden with His creation but they now have to seek Him in order to have a relationship with Him. When we seek Him, we find Him. When we make Him our foundation and build our lives upon His ways, He has promised eternal life where we will dwell with Him forever.

Read Psalm 127
1 Samuel 2:8, Isaiah 28:16, Matthew 7:26-27

How firm the foundation when we trust in You, Lord. We can build our lives upon You because You are trustworthy. You say it and it comes to pass. You have proclaimed it and it is. Thank You for Your plan of salvation and for sending Jesus to die for our sins. Thank You that we can count on what He taught us while He walked on this earth. We pray that You would guide us continually into Your Presence so we might do Your will and glorify You with our lives. Amen.

JUNE 28
BLESSINGS

Psalm 128:1-2: Blessed are all who fear the Lord, who walk in His ways. You will eat the fruit of your labor; blessings and prosperity will be yours.

The Lord commanded the children of Israel to obey His decrees and to fear the Lord their God so they would always prosper and be kept alive. It was a fear that kept them from going astray because they knew the consequences when they wandered away. He required this because of His holiness. There are many blessings that come from following His commands. Blessed are the poor in spirit and those who are persecuted because of righteousness for theirs is the kingdom of Heaven. Blessed are those who mourn for they will be comforted. Blessed are the meek for they will inherit the earth. Blessed are those who hunger and thirst for righteousness for they will be filled. Blessed are the merciful for they will be shown mercy. Blessed are the pure in heart for they will see God. These are blessings not only for the children of Israel. Scripture foresaw that God would justify the Gentiles by faith and announced the gospel in advance to Abraham so those who have faith are blessed along with Abraham, the man of faith.

Read Psalm 128
Deuteronomy 6:24, Matthew 5:3-10, Galatians 3:6-9

Lord, at times we go our own way not even realizing that we have forgotten You. Bring us back to Your outstretched arms that wait to embrace us. Teach us how to live in the present moment and not to worry about what the future holds. Teach us to trust all of Your ways so that our lives will be blessed and firmly established upon You. Then we can show others why Your way is the way of life. We love You and we praise You. Amen.

JUNE 29
THE LORD IS RIGHTEOUS

Psalm 129:4: But the Lord is righteous. He has cut me free from the cords of the wicked.

This Psalm is a lament of the hardships that Israel has endured. The Lord called them to be a great nation, to proclaim Him as their Lord and King. When they did this, they were lifted up and blessed. When they went astray, they were left to their own devices. They would cry out to their God and He would answer and deliver them. This is the history of the tribes of Israel. Compare this to the life of a Christian, a true follower and believer in the Lord Jesus Christ. When we answer His call on our life, there is a drastic change in us. We realize that life is not a mere chance or that perhaps in another life we will come back rich and famous. As we begin to search God's Word and pray, we come to the knowledge that He has a divine purpose for each person who is born, if only they will seek Him to know what that purpose and plan is. It is not easy to live this way in a world which constantly tries to disprove His existence. This battle will continue until Jesus Christ returns to reign from His throne in Jerusalem. Early Christians were tortured, fed to the lions and set on fire. They were drifters in the desert. The Apostle Paul was imprisoned, beaten and beheaded for his faith. All of the apostles, except for John, died at the hands of others because of their unwavering hope and faith in their Savior, Jesus Christ. He is a very real God who cares about everything in our lives. He is the lifter of our head and one day we are going to be with Him in glory.

Read Psalm 129
Psalm 3:3, Titus 1:2, 1 John 4:16-17

Lord, we pray for insight into Your everlasting ways that we might keep our eyes fixed on You. Our hope is in You. You have promised to never leave nor forsake us. Help us grow in our faith so we will never forget Your promises but continually proclaim them. Thank You for loving us and being a loving Father who has a plan for our lives. Amen.

JUNE 30
FORGIVENESS THROUGH THE BLOOD

Psalm 130:3-4: If You, O Lord, kept a record of our sins, O Lord, who could stand? But with You there is forgiveness; therefore You are feared.

The Holy God of Heaven cannot look upon sin. When sin entered the world, the first animals to be slain were in the Garden of Eden when God made garments of skin to cover man's nakedness. Through Abraham, God made a covenant that all nations would be blessed through him. Through Moses, He revealed the law and gave instruction on how to sacrifice animals for the remission of sins. But the Lord was not pleased with burnt offerings and sin offerings, for it became just a ritual. The animal sacrifices were an annual reminder of the sins of the people but it was impossible for the blood of bulls and goats to take away sins. In the New Testament, there was a child born of a virgin, who was sent by God and became the only perfect man to ever live. He was conceived in the womb without sin. He willingly laid down His life on a cross and shed His blood. We have been made holy through the sacrifice of the body of Jesus Christ once and for all. We have to do nothing, except come in faith believing this is true, and our sins are forgiven, thrown into the sea of forgetfulness to be remembered no more. This is how much our Father in Heaven loves us. He is not willing that any should perish but that all should come to Him.

Read Psalm 130
Genesis 3:21, Exodus 24:8, Leviticus 17:11, Romans 3:25,
Hebrews 10:1-10

How marvelous is Your Name, Holy Father, Giver of life, Forgiver of sins. Humble us in Your presence so we might experience the fullness of who You are. When we consider Your ways, they are the way of life. Help us to walk in them and never wander away. Thank You for sending Jesus. Thank You for Your plan of salvation so we can come into Your holy presence and worship You, our Lord, our King, our Mighty God, who loves us now and through all eternity. Amen.

JULY 1
YIELDING TO GOD

Psalm 131:1: My heart is not proud, O Lord; my eyes are not haughty. I do not concern myself with great matters or things too wonderful for me.

This is one of the shorter Psalms, yet one of the most difficult to interpret. It's like a culmination of who King David is and why the Lord considered him a man after His own heart. He was a mighty warrior and the King of Israel, yet he took no credit for himself. He knew he was anointed and any glory was given to God. He did not allow his accomplishments to make him proud. He concerned himself only with those things that pleased God. He was quick to admit his failures and ask forgiveness. These are qualities that we should long for. When we are yielded to Him, He pours out His Holy Spirit upon us; He renews us with His strength and He guides us down paths of righteousness for His Name's sake. The things of this world no longer have a hold on us and we look up to the heavens and declare the Lord is our strength, in Him alone will we trust. Our God cares deeply for us and He loves when we come into His presence and commune with Him, when we pour out all that is in our hearts and hide nothing from Him. He is a mighty Savior who can do anything and will do anything for those who call upon His name.

Read Psalm 131
2 Samuel 22:51, Psalm 23:3, Isaiah 40:31

Lord, Your ways lead us into righteousness. We pray for Your strength and wisdom so that our lives give glory and honor to You and You alone. When we fail, bring it to our minds quickly that we might ask forgiveness and be reconciled to You. Our lives are nothing without You. You are the Giver of life and hope of eternity. Amen.

JULY 2
THE TEMPLE

Psalm 132:4-5: I will allow no sleep to my eyes, no slumber to my eyelids til I find a place for the Lord, a dwelling for the Mighty One of Jacob.

King David had built himself a magnificent palace in which to dwell but he could not be satisfied with this until the Ark of the Covenant was found and restored to its proper place, the Temple of the Most High God. David found the Ark and there was great rejoicing among the people when it was brought back to Jerusalem. He gathered all the necessary supplies to build the Temple but the Lord forbad him from building it and the task fell to his son Solomon when he became King of Israel. Even though there is no building large enough for the Lord to physically dwell in, the symbolism of a temple brought the people together to worship the Lord and praise His Mighty Name. He chose Zion, Jerusalem, as the City of God, which it is to this day. How does this relate to us in this day and age? Scripture tells us that our bodies are the temple of the Holy Spirit. Therefore, in view of God's mercy, we should offer our bodies as a living sacrifice, holy and pleasing to God. When we are filled with the Holy Spirit, the promised Comforter of God, He comes into our lives and changes us from desiring the things of this world to desiring the things of God. By the power of the Holy Spirit, Jesus was raised from the dead. This is the same Spirit that dwells within us when we accept Jesus Christ as our Lord and Savior. He guides us by His love, reveals the secrets of the kingdom of God to us and helps us to pray when we don't know how or what to pray for.

Read Psalm 132
2 Samuel 6:13-15, John 14:26, Acts 17:24, Romans 12:1, 1 Corinthians 6:19

Heavenly Father, reveal Yourself to us by the power of Your Spirit. As we rise in the morning and seek You, fill us anew and guide us where You want us to go. Keep our eyes steadfast on You and Your Word that we may never forget that our bodies are the temple of the Holy Spirit and that You have called us to live righteously before You. Help us, for we are weak but in You we find the strength to live our lives for You. Amen.

JULY 3
THE LOVE OF GOD BRINGS UNITY

Psalm 133:1: How good and pleasant it is when brothers live together in unity.

There is power in unity. Jesus said where two or three are gathered in my name, there I am in the midst of them. Scripture tells us though one may be overpowered, two can defend themselves; a cord of three strands is not quickly broken. When we gather together in prayer, He fills us with His Spirit and suddenly we realize that being in unity with Him allows us to be in unity with every situation in our lives. Unity with our brothers and sisters in Christ brings great joy to our Lord. It is like the priest with anointing oil. He begins at the head and lets the oil flow down to the very hem of the garment, filling us with God's love so that we can selflessly love others. Unity is likened unto the dew of Mount Hermon that flows into Mount Zion and waters the hills with its moisture. It brings forth fruit and the people are filled with its goodness. In the Body of Christ, unity should be a goal that is uppermost. When we are unified, we are strong and able to withstand the trials and temptations that come our way. It is when we are divided that we fall. No matter our place in life, our religion, our nationality, our language, if we believe in Jesus Christ as our Lord and Savior we are unified here on earth and forevermore.

Read Psalm 133
Ecclesiastes 4:12, Luke 11:17, Romans 13:9-10, Ephesians 4:3

Heavenly Father, You are the great unifier. You are love, and where love exists there is peace and harmony for we put the needs of others above ourselves. We pray that the light of Your love would shine in our lives so we might live in unity with You until that glorious day when Jesus comes to rule and reign. It is then that true unity will exist and we will be with You forevermore. Amen.

JULY 4
LIFT YOUR HANDS

Psalm 134:2: Lift up your hands in the sanctuary and praise the Lord.

The church is our sanctuary, a place to be in God's presence and worship Him. In our church, the guitarists come out, the drums begin to sound and the singers lift their voices in praise to Almighty God. The congregation stands and everyone joins in the singing. Timothy tells us to lift up holy hands in prayer, without anger or disputing. We may be hesitant at first, especially if we are new believers in Christ. It's an unfamiliar gesture and might make us feel self-conscious. But once those hands begin to rise, it brings a freedom that makes us want to shout to the Lord in praise and thanksgiving. It is an act of total surrender, and we are letting go. It brings cleansing to the soul and takes the burdens from our hearts. When we stand praying, if we hold anything against anyone, it is a time to forgive so that our Father in Heaven may forgive us, and we should never look back. As long as we live, we will lift up our hands and praise Him, for He alone is worthy.

Read Psalm 134
Psalm 28:2 & 63:4, Mark 11:25, 1 Timothy 2:8

    Lord, we lift our hands high in worship and praise of You. There is no God like You. We thank You for Your presence in our lives. We thank You continually for Your love and blessings. Reach down and touch us in a way that transforms us into Your likeness and image so we might be the body of Christ until the time He returns in all His glory. Amen.

JULY 5
THE LIVING GOD

Psalm 135:13: Your Name, O Lord, endures forever, Your renown, O Lord, through all generations.

    Nebuchadnezzar, the king of Babylon, had made an image of gold. As soon as the sound of the horn was heard, the people were commanded to fall down and worship the image. Whoever did not fall down to worship it was immediately thrown into a blazing furnace. There were three Jews who had been set over the affairs of the province of Babylon who paid no attention to this edict and they did not worship the image of gold. This infuriated the king and the men were brought before him. He ordered that the furnace be heated seven times hotter than usual and commanded some of the strongest soldiers in his army to tie the men up. The furnace was so hot that the flames of the fire killed the soldiers when they threw the three men into the blaze. In amazement, the king leaped to his feet and said, "I see four men walking around in the fire, unbound and unharmed, and the fourth looks like a son of the gods." The king called the names of the three out of the furnace. When they came out, not a hair on their heads was singed, their robes were not scorched, and there was no smell of fire on them. He is the God of Abraham, Isaac and Jacob. He is not the God of the dead but of the living and He brings us through the fiery flames that at times try to burn us.

Read Psalm 135
Jeremiah 10:10, Daniel 3:1, 4-6, 13 & 24-27, Matthew 22:32

    Everlasting and Omnipotent Father, You are so vast that at times it seems impossible to find You! But Your Word is true. It says that when we seek You with all of our heart we find You. Thank You for this promise. Thank You for sending Your Holy Spirit who reveals Your truths to us. Cleanse us from all sin by the blood of the Lamb, Jesus Christ, and help us to always be in perfect communion with You. Keep us from all harm and cover us with Your veil of protection. Amen.

JULY 6
HIS LOVE ENDURES FOREVER

Psalm 136:26: Give thanks to the God of Heaven. His love endures forever.

There is only one God who divided the Jordan to the right and to the left when the prophet Elijah took his cloak, rolled it up and struck the water with it; who sent a chariot and horses of fire to take that same prophet up to Heaven in a whirlwind. Only one God performs such mighty miracles. He sent his prophet Elisha to the men of a city whose water was bad and the land unproductive. The Lord instructed him to throw salt into the water saying it would never again cause death or make the land unproductive. During a time when the king of Judah set out to help the king of Israel fight against Moab, the army had no more water for themselves or for their animals. The Lord came upon Elisha and said, "Make this valley full of ditches. You will see neither wind nor rain, yet this valley will be filled with water and your cattle and other animals will drink. This is an easy thing in the eyes of the Lord." When we fill our lives with His love and our goal is to give of ourselves to others, as Jesus gave Himself for all, we build up treasures in Heaven where moth and rust do not destroy and thieves do not break in and steal. A love that withstands time and space does endure forever and this is the love which God pours out on us. It fills our hearts with joy and gives us a vision of the glories that lie ahead. He is real. He rules and reigns from on high, and one day we will be with Him in His glorious kingdom where His love endures forever.

Read Psalm 136
2 Kings 2:8, 11 & 19-21, 3:6-9 & 16-18, 1 Chronicles 16:34, Ecclesiastes 3:14, Jeremiah 33:11, Matthew 6:20

Father, as You pour out Your love upon us, give us the capacity to receive it and believe it. There is no other God in Heaven or on earth like You. We can never hide anywhere where You cannot find us. Open our minds to receive this wonderful truth that Your love endures forever. It is not conditional upon anything that we do for You. It is just there for the taking. Wrap us in Your loving arms. Hold us close to Your bosom. The love that You so freely pour out on us, help us to pour out on others. Amen.

JULY 7
A TIME TO SING

Psalm 137:4: How can we sing the songs of the Lord while in a foreign land?

    Jerusalem, the Holy City, had been ravaged and destroyed to its very foundation. The remnant were exiled to Babylon where they were mocked and ridiculed. "Sing to us one of the songs of Zion," their captors shouted. Though disheartened, they would not profane their God in such a way as to sing and then be derided by the enemy. They would rather their right hand forget its skill and their tongue cling to the roof of their mouth so they could not speak. Their city had been destroyed by the enemies of God and they cried out for retribution, for justice, for the same treatment that they were given to be given back to their captors. In a way, this is a picture of the church of Jesus Christ. True believers in the Son of God are a thorn in the side of a sinful world. They read His Holy Word and follow His ways and do not give into the lusts and desires of this world. The church and its people are mocked for their belief in the God, and their lips are silent because of the unbelief. It is a spiritual battle that will continue until Jesus Christ returns to earth. We need not concern ourselves with whether evil will be judged, for the Lord God Himself will mete out justice. Our purpose is to glorify Him, stay true to His Word and as much as possible share the good news of hope, salvation, love and eternal life with all who will receive it.

Read Psalm 137
Job 4:16-17, Ecclesiastes 3:7, Matthew 7:6, Mark 8:36

    Heavenly Father, when we see and/or receive injustice, our first inclination is for vengeance. But Your Word teaches us that "vengeance is mine," says the Lord. No matter our situation, help us always, always to turn to You, for You alone are our help. You alone give us strength to endure our trials. You alone are merciful and mighty and able to sustain us. The rewards for faithfulness to You are eternal. Help us to remember that eye has not seen, nor ear heard the things that the Lord has prepared for those who love Him, who are called according to His purpose. Amen.

JULY 8
HE IS WORTHY OF PRAISE

Psalm 138:6: Though the Lord is on high, He looks upon the lowly, but the proud He knows from afar.

When we find the Lord, it is like finding a treasure that brings great wealth. Joy bubbles up within us and we shout praises. He is the richest treasure we could find. He saves us and makes us His own. When we come into communion with our Father, He is like a jealous parent who watches over His children, who protects them, who loves them; but those who reject Him He knows from afar. When we realize what He has done, how much He loves us, the plans He has for us, it should be an easy thing to praise and glorify his Holy Name. The more we do this, the more we want to know Him. There is no other god like our God. There will come a day that all, including the kings of this earth, will praise and glorify Him. We should seek Him while He can be found for in Him are hidden all the treasures of wisdom and knowledge. Praise His glorious Name!

Read Psalm 138
2 Samuel 22:4, Isaiah 45:3, Colossians 2:2-3, Hebrews 4:13

Lord, You are our Father. What a joyful thing to know the Creator of all things as our Father. Although You are high above the earth, You love us and consider us Your own. Thank You for Your Holy Word which reveals to us who You are. Thank You for sending Your Son Jesus Christ to die for our sins so that we might be reconciled to You and have boldness to pray to Your very throne. Thank You for Your precious Holy Spirit who reveals You to us, who assures us that there is no god like our God, who alone is worthy of our praises. Amen.

JULY 9
WE CANNOT HIDE FROM GOD

Psalm 139:7: Where can I go from Your Spirit? Where can I flee from Your presence?

Then the man and his wife heard the sound of the Lord God as He was walking in the garden and they hid from Him among the trees. But the Lord called out, "Where are you?" They thought they could hide from the Lord but they could go nowhere that He could not find them. There is not a thought we have or an act we commit that the Lord does not know about. Just like the House of Israel could not hide their sin from the Lord, neither can we. Though we dig down to the depths of the grave, from there His hand will take us. Though we climb to the heavens, from there He will bring us down. Though we hide from Him at the bottom of the sea, there He will command the serpent to bite us. In other words, He will find us no matter where we are. Instead of running from Him, we should run to Him, for we are all imperfect and we all fail. We might wonder why it is even necessary to pray if we can't hide anything from Him. It is because we do not know everything about Him and prayer brings us into communion with Him. Only by seeking Him with all of our hearts do we find Him. We have no friend, no deliverer, no Savior, no one else in the world who unconditionally loves us as does the Father, Son and Holy Spirit. They will never lead us astray.

Read Psalm 139:1-12
Genesis 3:9-10, Jeremiah 29:13, Amos 9:2-3

Holy, Holy, Holy are You, O God of mercy. We are in awe of who You are. Your ways lead to eternal life and we pray that You keep us close to You so that our eyes are fixed on what now is unseen but will one day be revealed. Search our hearts and search our ways. If there be anything hidden, bring it to the light so that we might confess our sins and be cleansed from all unrighteousness by the precious blood of Jesus, the Giver of life and Savior of our souls and the world. Amen.

JULY 10
FEARFULLY AND WONDERFULLY MADE

Psalm 139:13-14: You created my inmost being; You knit me together in my mother's womb. I praise You because I am fearfully and wonderfully made; Your works are wonderful. I know that full well.

We serve the God who knew us before we were ever born, while we were yet in our mother's womb. The human body is so intricate. There is the inside which we cannot see with our human eyes: the heart, the stomach, liver, gall bladder, appendix, the blood and water and oxygen that flows through our veins. This is what gives the body the ability to function. Every part of the body has a purpose. The skin covers all the inner parts. With our head, we can see, hear, smell, eat, talk and reason. Our hands make it possible to make and do things. Our legs and feet allow us to walk and go wherever we desire. Some people spend their lifetime learning about the body, how it functions, how to keep it healthy and youthful. We are not put on the earth to be selfish and fulfill our own desires but to live self-controlled, upright and godly lives. We are blessed abundantly when we freely give to others as He has given to us. We have not evolved over the centuries from apes. We were created by the Most High God for His pleasure, to commune with Him and serve Him. We are made in His image and we are fearfully and wonderfully made! Praise the Name of the Lord.

Read Psalm 139:13-24
Job 31:13-15, Psalm 22:10 & 51:6, Titus 2:11-14, 1 John 4:11

Thank You, Lord, that You knew us before we were even born, that You have a plan and a purpose for each of us, and that You love us and walk by our side every moment of every day. Help us to intentionally seek You each day so that our relationship with You grows stronger and our faith continually increases. Amen.

JULY 11
YOU ARE MY GOD

Psalm 140:6: O, Lord, I say to You, "You are my God." Hear, O Lord, my cry for mercy.

When the prophet Samuel came to anoint David king, his own father did not bring him in with his other brothers until Samuel asked him to do so. King Saul hated him and tried several times to kill him. His enemies continually looked for ways to destroy him. He gave into his lusts and committed adultery and murder. One of his own sons tried to kill him so he could become king. In every circumstance, through every hardship and trial, David called upon the name of his God. He delivered him from his enemies in battle and from the evil that surrounded him. He forgave his sin when he cried out for mercy. There is never a time when David lost faith in the abilities of his God. The answer may not have come right away but he remained faithful and always trusted God. He knew hardship and he knew his God could and would deliver him from it all. How do we react when controversy surrounds us and there is trouble on every side? We shouldn't panic and say, "How am I going to get out of this mess?" We should get on our knees before the God of the universe and believe that He delivers us. When we allow God to be in control of our lives, we become carefree in the sense of not having heavy burdens. He bears them all. We are tried and tested through life's journey, but when we turn those trials and tests over to Him our faith and trust grow stronger.

Read Psalm 140
1 Samuel 16:10-13 & 19:1-2, 2 Chronicles 20:15-17, Psalm 34:17, 1 Peter 5:7

Lord, no matter what good or bad happens in our lives, we ask for faith to believe that You deliver us from them all. In times of prosperity and in times of drought, we lift our voices in praise to You. Thank You for always being with us. We love You and praise Your holy name. Amen.

JULY 12
GUARD MY MOUTH

Psalm 141:3: Set a guard over my mouth, O Lord, keep watch over the door of my lips.

There is a saying, "Sticks and stones may break my bones but words will never hurt me." This is so far from reality, for the words that we speak and that are spoken to us determine the directions we take in life and the things we do.

St. Francis of Assisi said to always share the Gospel of Christ and use words when necessary. Our lives should so reflect the life of Jesus Christ and all that He taught us that just by the way we live others know there is something different. They should see peace and joy unspeakable that's full of glory so they will also desire the things of God. When we speak words of blessings to our children, their response is so different than if we are critical, cruel or controlling in what we say. When we encourage others to do their best and congratulate them on their accomplishments, it gives them the desire to continue on. When men speak lies, it affects not only themselves but those around them, and it creates terrible situations that at times are life altering. Our God spoke the world into existence. The Word became flesh and made His dwelling among us. He came from the Father, full of grace and truth. The Word of God is quick and powerful, and He knows the thoughts and intents of the heart. When we stand before the Lord at judgment, we will give account for every idle word that we have spoken. Words are powerful. Let's be quick to listen and slow to speak. May the words of our mouth glorify the One whom we serve.

Read Psalm 141
Proverbs 12:18-19 & 13:3, Matthew 12:36 (KJV) &15:10-11, John 1:14, James 1:26 & 3:8-10

Lord, You gave us two ears and one mouth. That is so we can listen twice as much as we talk! When we are confronted with situations where we want to lash out, help us to keep our mouths sealed unless and until You give us words to speak. When we are the recipient of someone's angry words, help us not to dole out the same thing in return. Give us a calmness and peace so that we might look at our situation the way You would and react in the way You would react. It is only then that there can be a resolution. We pray for wisdom. Amen.

JULY 13
OUR GOD OF MERCY

Psalm 142:1-2: I cry out to the Lord; I lift up my voice to the Lord for mercy. I pour out my complaint before Him. Before Him I tell my trouble.

Once we were not a people but now we are the people of God; once we had not received mercy, but now we have received mercy. He wraps the arms of His unconditional love around us when we lift up our voices to Him and tell Him our troubles. He extends His mercy to us and expects us to have mercy on others. There was a king who wanted to settle accounts with his servants. A man who owed him millions of dollars was brought to him but was unable to pay so the king ordered that he and his wife and children and all that he had be sold to repay the debt. The servant fell on his knees before the king begging, "Be patient with me and I will pay back everything." The king took pity on him, cancelled his debt and let him go. Sometime later that servant went out and found one of his fellow servants who owed him a few dollars. He grabbed him and began to choke him saying "Pay back what you owe me!" His fellow servant fell on his knees and begged him to be patient and he would pay him back. But he threw the man into prison until he could pay the debt. When the king heard of this he called the servant in and said, "You wicked servant. I cancelled all your debt. Shouldn't you have had mercy on your fellow servant just as I had on you?" So he turned him over to be tortured until he could pay back all he owed. We are to be merciful just as our Father in Heaven is merciful.

Read Psalm 142
Matthew 5:7 & 18:23-35, Luke 6:36 & 11:4, 1 Peter 2:10

Heavenly Father, thank You for Your mercy. We are all sinners who need a Savior. Sometimes we forget that it is by Your mercy we are saved. Take away the hardness of our hearts that would prevent us from being merciful to others and replace it with Your love. Amen.

JULY 14
TEACH US YOUR WILL

Psalm 143:10: Teach me to do Your will for You are my God; may Your good Spirit lead me on level ground.

Doing the will of God is acting without hesitation when He speaks. Noah did God's will when he built the ark. The Lord saw how great man's wickedness on the earth had become and that every inclination of the thoughts of his heart was only evil all the time; He proclaimed that He would wipe mankind from the face of the earth for He was grieved that he had made them. The Lord instructed him to bring two of all living creatures, male and female into the ark; and to take every kind of food that is to be eaten and to store it away as food for them and the animals. Noah did everything just as God commanded him. After the flood the Lord said He would never again curse the ground because of man; that as long as the earth endured, seedtime and harvest, cold and heat, summer and winter, day and night would never cease. Mary, the mother of Jesus, was greeted by the angel Gabriel telling her she had found favor with God and would conceive a child. She was perplexed by this salutation but when the angel explained how this would happen she said, "May it be to me as you have said." Noah saved mankind. Mary brought forth the Savior. There was a time when Joshua and Caleb were sent to spy out the land the Lord had promised to His children. When they returned, the people were afraid to go up against the inhabitants because they were told the people were stronger and taller than they were, with large cities and walls up to the sky. Joshua said not to be afraid but they would not listen. The Lord became angry with them when they would not go so they repented and said they would go but the Lord said, "Tell them not to go up and fight because I will not be with you. You will be defeated by your enemies." They went anyway and were defeated. His purposes are always accomplished when we follow His will and not our own, and it is pleasing in His sight.

Read Psalm 143
Genesis 6:5, 7 & 19-22, Genesis 8:21-22, Deuteronomy 1:28 & 41-42, Luke 1:26-30 & 34-38

Lord, help us to be obedient to Your will at all times. Help us not to question why You guide us in a way that we do not understand, because we know that You do not lead us astray. Draw us closer to You and help us focus on that which is eternal, believing that You bring us through all things until that day comes. Amen.

JULY 15
RESCUE US

Psalm 144:7: Reach down Your hand from on high; deliver me and rescue me from the mighty waters, from the hands of foreigners.

King David was a man of war. He was surrounded by enemies and foreigners. When he went to battle, he always called on the name of the Lord for strength, for wisdom, for help, and the Lord gave him the victory. At the end of his life he wanted to build a dwelling for the Most High God whom he served and trusted, who was there continually by his side, but the Lord spoke and said that he was not to build the temple because he had shed much blood and fought many wars. We can know our Heavenly Father as intimately as David did and even now more so because Jesus has come. We can receive His guidance every day of our lives when we listen for His voice. Our Father yearns for and desires a people who will love Him with all of their heart, even to the point of death, for in dying we are reconciled to Him forever. He is the only true God and He acts on behalf of those who wait upon Him, and we don't have to wait until we pass from this life to the next. As David taught us, He is our protector; He fights our battles when we trust Him. He strengthens us and gives us wisdom. He knew what He was doing when He created man and woman. It is not for us to question. He reaches His hand from on high and delivers and rescues us from the rough waters. When we follow Him with all of our hearts we are blessed because we are the people whose God is the Lord.

Read Psalm 144
Deuteronomy 4:36, 1 Chronicles 22:8, Isaiah 64:4, 1 Timothy 1:17

Father, thank You for Your promises. We are weak but You are strong. We thank You that when we call upon Your mighty name You are faithful to deliver us. Help us to realize it is not for us to understand all things but to trust and believe You. Keep us safe from the attacks of the enemy of our souls and protect us by Your strong right arm. Amen.

JULY 16
GLORIOUS SPLENDOR

Psalm 145:8-9: The Lord is gracious and compassionate, slow to anger and rich in love. The Lord is good to all; He has compassion on all He has made.

The psalmist cried out, "One generation will tell of your mighty acts. They will speak of the glorious splendor of Your majesty!" In the process of building the Lord's temple, David praised the Lord in the presence of the whole assembly saying, "Yours, O Lord, is the greatness and the power and the glory and the majesty and the splendor. For everything in heaven and earth is Yours." Job said that out of the north He comes in golden splendor; God comes in awesome majesty. The Almighty is beyond our reach and exalted in power. We should ascribe to the Lord the glory due His name and worship Him in the splendor of His holiness. Our minds cannot even grasp such splendor, such majesty, such holiness. There is nothing on this earth to compare to it. Yet, He has called us to serve Him, to love Him and to trust Him. He is all He proclaims to be. Not until He comes will we experience the light of His holy presence. After the end days, the lawless one will be revealed, whom the Lord Jesus will overthrow with the breath of his mouth and destroy by the splendor of His coming.

Read Psalm 145:1-12
1 Chronicles 29:11, Job 37:22-23, Psalm 29:2, Isaiah 63:1,
2 Thessalonians 2:8

You are so holy, Lord. It's awesome that You love us and call us and desire us to know You. Fill our hearts with a longing to seek Your ways. Give us wisdom that we might be filled to overflowing with Your Holy Spirit and be prepared always to give an answer to others about the awesome God that we serve. We pray for Your strength to endure until that glorious day when Jesus appears in all His splendor. Amen.

JULY 17
THE LORD UPHOLDS THE FALLEN

Psalm 145:14: The Lord upholds all those who fall and lifts up all who are bowed down.

Naomi had gone to Moab with her husband, Elimelech, a man from Bethlehem Judah, during a time of famine. Elimelech died and Naomi was left with her two sons, who married Moabite women, Orpah and Ruth. About ten years later, her two sons died, leaving no children. Naomi returned to Bethlehem saying, "I went away full but the Lord has brought me back empty." Her daughter-in-law, Ruth, followed her to Bethlehem. Naomi told her to return to her own people, but Ruth responded, "Don't urge me to leave you or to turn back from you. Where you go, I will go and where you stay I will stay. Your people will be my people and your God my God. Where you die, I will die, and there I will be buried. May the Lord deal with me, be it ever so severely, if anything but death separates you and me." Naomi instructed her to glean the fields of a relative on her husband's side. One day this relative, Boaz, saw Ruth gleaning the fields and instructed his men not to touch her and when she was thirsty to allow her to get a drink of water from jars which the men had filled. Ruth told Naomi all that had happened to her, and she instructed Ruth on the customs of her people and told her what to do. She was obedient in every way and became Boaz's wife. When Ruth became pregnant and had a son, the women of the land said to Naomi, "Praise be to the Lord, who this day has not left you without a kinsman-redeemer. May he become famous throughout Israel." Then Naomi took the child and he was named Obed, who was the father of Jesse, the father of David. Naomi and Ruth tell a story of heartbreak and redemption. When they fell down, the Lord lifted them up. Ruth, a Gentile, is a mother in the lineage of Jesus Christ.

All things are possible with God. Everything precious and dear to us may be taken away, we may feel like we are even being punished, but the Lord upholds the fallen. He did it then and He does it today.

Read Psalm 145:13-21
Ruth 1:1-4 & 4:13-17, 1 Peter 5:10

Lord, at times words fail us when we think of how awesome You are and that You who created all things care so much about everything that happens in our lives. Through prayer and Your word, continually reveal Yourself to us. Draw us into Your presence that we might experience Your glory in our lives and trust You completely. Thank You, Lord. Praise You, Lord. You are worthy! Amen.

JULY 18
WHEN THE SPIRIT OF MAN DEPARTS

Psalm 146:3-4: Do not put your trust in princes, in mortal men, who cannot save. When their spirit departs, they return to the ground; on that very day their plans come to nothing.

When we were young, hopefully our parents were there for us, but then there came a time we were able to take care of ourselves. We go to school. We work. We dream of the future. We go to college perhaps, get a job, get married, have kids, work some more, maybe take a few vacations, work more, take the kids to practice, to school and all the activities they become involved in; plan for college for the kids and then for our own retirement. We grow old in the process. We take very little time to think about and prepare for the real future, the one that is for all eternity, not just a few decades on this earth. All of this is not to be negative towards life and the goals and desires we have, but without the Lord it amounts to nothing, for the day we stop breathing every thought we had and every plan we made comes to an end. In death, though, our eternal hope is to be absent from the body but present with the Lord.

Read Psalm 146
Job 14:10, Ecclesiastes 2:20-23, 2:26 & 9:5-6, 2 Corinthians 5:8

Lord, You have promised us eternal life when we die and leave this earth. Help us put our thoughts towards the things that are everlasting and not those which pass away. You are so vast and infinite, while we are bound by space and time. We rejoice in Your plan of salvation. As we call upon You, help us accept the answers You have for us because You know best. We lift You up and praise Your mighty, holy name. Amen.

JULY 19
ETERNAL HOPE IN HIS UNFAILING LOVE

Psalm 147:11: The Lord delights in those who fear Him; who put their hope in His unfailing love.

To fear our Lord is to be in awe of who He is. Great is our Lord and mighty in power; His understanding has no limit. He determines the number of the stars and calls them by name. He covers the sky with clouds, supplies the earth with rain and makes the grass grow on the hills. There is no man who can do what God can do. We were made to worship Him and Him alone. He has instilled in the hearts of each one of us to seek Him. When we find Him, He gives us His Holy Spirit who guides us in the ways of our God. The fear we have for Him is a reverence for we are humbled in His presence and by the glorious things He has done. By wisdom, the Lord laid the earth's foundations and by understanding He set the heavens in place. So often, we get caught up in our own little world with its drama and heartaches, and also its joys and pleasures, and we forget that this is not all there is; that we have a higher calling and that is to keep our eyes on the ultimate prize of eternity, where there will be no more dying or tears or any of the things that bring heartache to our lives. We are going to a city where the streets are paved with pure gold and its foundation is made of every kind of precious stone. The city does not need the sun or the moon to shine in it for the glory of God gives it light and the Lamb is its lamp.

Read Psalm147
Proverbs 3:19, Jeremiah 10:12 & 32:40, Revelation 21:18-19 & 23

Father, we praise You and worship You for You alone are worthy. There is no God in Heaven or earth like You. Lift us up when we are down. May we never grow weary of serving You for there is no one like our Holy God. Amen.

JULY 20
THE WORD OF GOD

Psalm 148:13: Let them praise the name of the Lord, for His name alone is exalted; His splendor is above the earth and the heavens.

Our psalm today speaks of praise to our God not only by people but by all of His creation, even the sun, the moon and the shining stars, the great sea creatures, lightning and hail, snow and clouds and stormy winds that do His bidding, for He commanded and they were all created. Everything that exists was created by the Word of God. Man, above all, is His most glorious creation. He has given us the ability to reason; to think for ourselves; to have free will. Yet He has instilled in us a desire to know Him. He made us a little lower than the angels and crowned us with glory and honor and put everything under our feet. Jesus too was made a little lower than the angels and is now crowned with glory and honor. He cares about everything He has created. All of His creation depends on Him for their provision, even man, though the Lord has given him the capability to work with his hands to provide food on the table. But if, when we planted, our Lord did not make the plant grow from the seed or cause rain to fall from above to water the ground, there would be no provision. We praise each other for our accomplishments, but we should first and foremost praise our Lord because without Him none of life's pleasures would be possible. He thought of everything that sustains life on this earth. If He were to take it all away, nothing could exist.

Read Psalm 148
John 1:3, 1 Corinthians 3:6, Hebrews 2:6-9

Lord, at times we get so caught up in our own lives we forget that You are the reason we are even here. We need You to guide us in all things in our lives. Without You, life has no real purpose except to gratify the desires of our flesh. Your Word tells us that we have a higher calling than just this life. One day we will fully understand. Until that time, Your grace is sufficient. Thank You for loving us and pouring upon us Your tender mercies. Amen.

JULY 21
THE LORD'S CHOSEN

Psalm 149:4: For the Lord takes delight in His people; He crowns the humble with salvation.

There is coming a time when the Lord will return to earth and take delight in all those whom He has not only chosen but who have chosen Him, and all the earth will praise Him. Until that day comes, our time should be spent seeking and praising Him so that we are prepared for the battles of life. They are not the physical battles that God's chosen people fought in the Old Testament. They are spiritual battles that determine the eternal destiny of our souls. The more time we spend in prayer against the darkness of the evil one, the more powerful we become in the Lord, for He hears and answers our cry. We show God's love and mercy by extending a helping hand to those in need. We are the hands and feet of Jesus Christ in this world and when we remain humble and faithful to Him, we are crowned with His salvation.

Read Psalm 149
Isaiah 45:23-24, Romans 14:11, 2 Corinthians 10:3-4

Heavenly Father, we praise Your Mighty Name. You are the Lord God Almighty worthy of all praise. Help us to seek You and serve You with all of our hearts that we might be humble before You and not desire our own glory. Give us opportunities to show Your love and mercy to others by serving You and them. Life is so very short and we want to store up our treasures in Heaven. Keep us focused on what lies ahead of us in eternal glory with You. Amen.

JULY 22
PRAISE THE LORD!

Psalm 150:6: Let everything that has breath praise the Lord.

We have come to the end of our journey through the Psalms. It has been like a long train ride, making many stops along the way, and we have reached our final destination. But this is not the end. Hopefully it is the beginning of a lifelong fellowship with the Lord. Through the authors of the Psalms, we have learned that our God is powerful, righteous, holy, merciful, and full of love for His creation. There is no other Heavenly Father who so loved the world that He gave His only begotten Son that whoever believes in Him shall not perish but have eternal life. Our God is great and most worthy of praise. He is to be feared above all gods; for all the gods of the nations are idols but the Lord made the heavens. Splendor and majesty are before Him. Strength and joy are in His dwelling place. When we close our eyes and think upon Him, it is as though we are blind to our surroundings and nothing else exists. May we be blind to the things of the world and keep our focus on the ultimate prize of eternal glory with the Father, Son and Holy Spirit where darkness does not dwell and the evils of this world no longer exist. When we put all our attentions towards Him and realize how lovely, how beautiful, and how mighty our Heavenly Father is we can do nothing else but praise Him, for He alone is worthy. Let everything that has breath praise the Lord!

Read Psalm 150
1 Chronicles 16:23-27, Psalm 146:5-6, John 3:16

Father, we lift our voices in praise to You. Let this not be the end of our journey but only the beginning. We lift up Your name and praise You in Your sanctuary, in Your mighty heavens. We praise You for Your acts of power and surpassing greatness. We praise You with the sound of the trumpet, the harp and tambourines. We dance before You and praise You with the strings and flute and the clash of cymbals. Let our voices reach to the heavens as we magnify You, the only true God who was, who is and who is to come! Amen.

JULY 23
THE FEAR OF THE LORD

Proverbs 1:7: The fear of the Lord is the beginning of knowledge, but fools despise wisdom and discipline.

When we are afraid of something, our first instinct is to run and hide in hopes that whatever is frightening us will disappear. When school shootings happen and innocent people are killed, we are afraid and figure out ways to prevent it from happening again. When we fear the Lord, though, we do not run and hide from Him. It is not that kind of fear. It is a reverence for the Almighty because of His majesty, His righteousness and His infinite wisdom. We are to fear the Lord, to walk in all of His ways, to love Him, to serve Him with all of our hearts and souls and to observe the Lord's commands and decrees. When Moses summoned Joshua to lead the people into the Promised Land, he said to him in the presence of all of Israel, "Listen and learn to fear the Lord your God and follow carefully all the words of this law." Nowadays people live as though God is something to flick away by the snap of their fingers. His name is taken in vain so freely, now there is even a saying "OMG." We used to take an oath in His name when testifying to something because we feared Him. We were saying we would not lie because we knew He was listening. The one who despises correction, lacks Godly wisdom and depends upon himself for life's answers is a fool. We learn to fear the Lord by reading His word and seeking Him with all of our hearts. He gives us a glimpse of the everlasting glory of His heavenly kingdom, where He has prepared a place for us when we pass from death to eternal life.

Read Proverbs 1
Deuteronomy 10:12-13 & 20, 31:12, John 14:2

Heavenly Father, thank You for Your precious word that not only gives us instruction on how to live but reveals who You are. We are in reverence and awe of You. Help us to be willing and humble servants so that Your purpose for our lives might be fulfilled. We praise You and thank You for Your many blessings. May we live our lives so that we give honor to You. Amen.

JULY 24
SEEK WISDOM

Proverbs 2:6: For the Lord gives wisdom, and from his mouth comes knowledge and understanding.

Proverbs 2 instructs us to search for wisdom and understanding as if we are searching for a hidden treasure. Wisdom and power are the Lord's. He changes times and seasons. He sets up kings and deposes them. He gives wisdom to the wise and knowledge to the discerning. He reveals deep and hidden things. He knows what lies in darkness, and light dwells with Him. When we have wisdom, we understand what is right and just. When we allow wisdom to enter into our hearts, knowledge will be pleasant to our souls. Discretion will protect us and understanding will guard us. If we ask the Lord for wisdom, He gives it abundantly. Scripture says that victory is in store for the upright and that the Lord is a shield to those who walk blameless before Him. He guards the course of the just and protects the way of His faithful ones. The storms in our lives should make us cry out to Him, for He gives us strength to endure. When we find ourselves in circumstances that we are unsure about, we receive wisdom from the Holy Spirit when we pray. We need to seek the Father, Jesus and the Holy Spirit with all of our hearts and lean not to our own understanding.

Read Proverbs 2
Isaiah 28:29, Daniel 2:20-22

Heavenly Father, we pray for wisdom. As verse 20 says, thus we will walk in the ways of good men and keep to the paths of righteousness. Wisdom is a precious gift that we must seek with all of our hearts so that we may know You and Your ways; that we might walk in paths of righteousness and not veer off into the ways of the world. We love You and praise You. Thank You for life. Help us to be a glory and an honor to You all our days. Amen.

JULY 25
ACKNOWLEDGE THE LORD IN ALL OUR WAYS

Proverbs 3:5-6: Trust in the Lord with all your heart and lean not on your own understanding. In all your ways acknowledge Him, and He will make your paths straight.

Oh, the depth of the riches of the wisdom and knowledge of God. How unsearchable are His judgments and His paths beyond tracing out! Who has known the mind of the Lord or who has been His counselor? The third chapter of Proverbs teaches us more about wisdom. Verse 13 says, blessed is the man who finds wisdom, the man who gains understanding, for she is more profitable than silver and yields better returns than gold. She is more precious than rubies; nothing we desire can compare to her. Long life is in her right hand; in her left hand are riches and honor. Her ways are pleasant ways and all her paths are peace. She is a tree of life to those who embrace her; those who lay hold of her will be blessed. By wisdom, the Lord laid the earth's foundations, by understanding He set the Heavens in place; by His knowledge the deeps were divided and the clouds let drop the dew. These things may be difficult to grasp, yet our Lord is all of these things and much, much more.

Read Proverbs 3
Job 34:21, Romans 11:33-36

Heavenly Father, thank You for Your promises. Give us hearts and minds to follow Your precepts, to yield ourselves to Your Spirit and seek wisdom that we might know her. Help us in our weakness. Give us Your strength. Help us to yield to Your Spirit so that our prayers reach Your throne and Your will is accomplished, not only in our lives but in this world that You have created. Remember our nation, and our troops as they serve selflessly. Protect each and every one of them. Amen.

JULY 26
THE VIRTUE OF WISDOM

Proverbs 4:7-9: Wisdom is supreme; therefore get wisdom. Though it cost all you have, get understanding. Esteem her, and she will exalt you; embrace her, and she will honor you. She will set a garland of grace on your head and present you with a crown of splendor.

Proverbs might also be called the Book of Wisdom. It gives insight into who she is and what our lives will be like when we pursue wisdom as we would a hidden treasure that yields a multitude of riches. Wisdom is health to our bodies and our minds. When we seek her, we find the ways of the Lord. King Solomon asked the Lord for wisdom to govern the people. God said to him, "Since this is your heart's desire and you have not asked for wealth, riches or honor, nor for the death of your enemies, and since you have not asked for a long life but for wisdom and knowledge. . .therefore wisdom and knowledge will be given you." The whole world sought audience with Solomon to hear the wisdom God had put in his heart. There are follies in not seeking wisdom. Verse 19 tells us: But the way of the wicked is like deep darkness; they do not know what makes them stumble. People are seeking answers, seeking to know what life is all about, when all we have to do is seek wisdom. A wise person has great power and a person of knowledge increases strength. If we do nothing else in our lifetime but follow His instructions, we have done His will and found wisdom.

Read Proverbs 4
1 Kings 10:24, 2 Chronicles 1:11-12, Proverbs 24:5

Heavenly Father, open our hearts and our minds to seek wisdom, to yearn for understanding. for we know this pleases You. Melt our hardened hearts that allow us to let the things of this world interfere with our walk with You. Fill each of us anew in the power of the Holy Spirit so that we may pray with fervency. There are times when we do not understand what is happening. Help us to trust You and know that understanding follows in Your timing. We praise You and love You. Amen.

JULY 27
COMMITMENT

Proverbs 5:3-6: For the lips of an adulteress drip honey, and her speech is smoother than oil; but in the end she is bitter as gall, sharp as a double-edged sword. Her feet go down to death; her steps lead straight to the grave. She gives no thought to the way of life; her paths are crooked, but she knows it not.

Commitment is a word that many of us are afraid of. We want freedom to do what we want when we want to do it. If it feels good, do it, is one saying. Or how about the lyrics of a song which tell us: "If you can't be with the one you love, love the one you're with." Deep inside our souls we all long for commitment. That is something that the marriage vows are supposed to bring: till death do us part. Once that commitment is made, it should be kept. But everywhere we turn, there's temptation. And, hey, who's going to know if we just have a little fun once in a while anyway. Today's scripture leaves no question where this path leads. The grass is not always greener on the other side. All that we've worked a lifetime for can be destroyed by one act of adultery. As tempting as the adulteress can make it look, it ends in bitterness and death. We are tempted many times throughout our life, but there is always a way of escape when we keep our eyes on Jesus. It's when we wander away little by little and allow our protective armor to be cracked that we fall into sin, which leads to death if we do not repent.

Read Proverbs 5
1 Corinthians 10:13, Ephesians 6:13, James 1:13-15

Heavenly Father, who sits on Your throne and the clouds are the dust of Your feet, we praise and lift up Your Holy Name. Give us strength so we do not fall into temptation. Touch our hearts so we might live for You and You alone. Amen.

JULY 28
THINGS THE LORD HATES

Proverbs 6:16-19: There are six things the Lord hates, seven that are detestable to him: haughty eyes, a lying tongue, hands that shed innocent blood, a heart that devises wicked schemes, feet that are quick to rush into evil, a false witness who pours out lies and a man who stirs up dissension among brothers.

Chapter 6 is a similar theme to the previous chapter, how the ways of wickedness lead to destruction but the ways of righteousness give life. There are very few times in the Bible where it says that the Lord hates something so when we read the verses today, let us bind them to our hearts so that we do not find ourselves guilty of such things. Haughty eyes mean to exalt one's self or to look down on another as though we are superior to them. A lying tongue needs no explanation; nor do hands that shed innocent blood. When we guard our hearts, it is the wellspring of life and our desire will not be to partake in evil. If there's any question in our minds about doing something or going somewhere or being with someone, then we need to consider whether it would please the Lord. A false witness who pours out lies and a man who stirs up dissension among brothers also needs no explanation. These should not be difficult things to stay away from, and it pleases our Heavenly Father if we do.

Read Proverbs 6
Psalm 34:13, Proverbs 4:23

Heavenly Father, we lift up Your name above all names. You are holy. Help us to honor and keep Your ways in our hearts that we do not veer away from them. Fill our minds with Your word, presence and holiness, that we might live for You. Help us to know that You love us unconditionally and all You ask in return is that we trust and obey You. We lift up our nation, that the complacency that has swept over us will be lifted, that our eyes will be open and that we will be on our knees before You, praying for a return to righteousness. Amen.

JULY 29
MAKE WISDOM OUR SISTER

Proverbs 7:4: Say to wisdom, you are my sister; and call understanding your kinsman.

A sister is someone who has the same parents as another person. Sisters enjoy a special bond that no one else can share. Twin sisters usually are very close, especially if they are identical. They might enjoy looking exactly alike, wearing the same clothes and trying to trick people as to their identity. It is a bond that is not easily broken, though can be. In this proverb we are instructed to make wisdom our sister. If we have a really special relationship with our sister, we might talk every single day and know every little detail about each other's lives. This is how we can grow in wisdom by treating her as that kind of sister. If we look to the Lord and ask for wisdom, He gives generously to all who ask. One dictionary definition says wisdom is the quality of being wise; ability to judge soundly and deal sagaciously with facts, especially as they relate to life and conduct; knowledge, with the capacity to make due use of it; discernment and judgment. The definitions in this dictionary also have spiritual connotations, and end with: Behold, the fear of the Lord, that is wisdom.

Read Proverbs 7
Job 9:2, 1 Corinthians 1:30, James 1:5

Lord, You know all things. When we ask, You answer. We pray for an abundance of Your wisdom. The things of this world can be so overwhelming at times that we get caught up in what is around us and lose sight of our salvation. Keep us focused. Give us Your strength to endure to the end. We continue to hold our nation up in prayer. Help Your people who are called by Your name to humble themselves and pray so that the land may be healed. Amen.

JULY 30
THE LORD LOVES THOSE WHO LOVE HIM

Proverbs 8:17: I love them that love me; and those that seek me early shall find me. (KJV)

We find it easy to love those who love us. We want to talk with them, share our lives with them and be with them as much as possible. This is the type of love our Father has for those who seek Him with all of their heart and soul. He loves all of His creation, and He especially loves those who love Him. When we walk in obedience to His commands, this is love.

When we love the world or anything in it, the love of the Father is not in us because the cravings of sinful man, the lust of his eyes and the boastings of what he has and does comes not from the Father but from the world. Our desire should be to seek the Father's love, and just as Jesus Christ laid down His life for us we should be so filled with His love that we ought to lay down our lives for our brothers. This is perfect love.

Read Proverbs 8
Deuteronomy 4:29, 1 John 2:15-17 & 3:16, 2 John 6

Father, Your love is everlasting. Help us to see and love others as You do, for we are all Your children and we are made in Your image. When we seek You in love, we find You. May our hearts and souls be full of this love. In Jesus' precious name, we pray. Amen.

JULY 31
REBUKE NOT A MOCKER

Proverbs 9:8: Do not rebuke a mocker or he will hate you; rebuke a wise man and he will love you.

In our zeal to serve the Lord, we try to "convert" those who do not understand His ways and we forget that it is the Holy Spirit who does the converting. No one comes to Jesus unless the Father draws Him. We will encounter those who mock, but we have to know when to keep our mouth shut because when we try bringing someone to the Lord without the help of the Holy Spirit it can result in their hearts being even more hardened against the things of God. Without the Holy Spirit, they cannot understand spiritual things; therefore, our verse today, "Do not rebuke a mocker." Someone who is wise in spiritual things, if the Holy Spirit quickens their heart to speak a word to that person who may be struggling or who has for one reason or another gone astray, they will gladly receive the word of God. With a word of encouragement and love, the Holy Spirit quickens their spirit and they will once again seek Him with all of their heart.

Read Proverbs 9
John 6:44, Ephesians 3:4

Heavenly Father, reach down into our hearts and souls. Mold us into the men and women You want us to be so that we may be used for the glory of Jesus in all we say and do. Touch those who receive this word. Help us to bind it upon our hearts and go through this day knowing You are with us and You guide and keep our every footstep. Amen.

AUGUST 1
SWEET SMELLING AROMA

Proverbs 10:12: Hatred stirs up dissension, but love covers over all wrong.

Proverbs 10 talks about the joy and grief a wise or foolish son can bring to his parents. It tells us that lazy hands make a man poor but diligent hands bring wealth; that the tongue of the righteous is choice silver, but the heart of the wicked is of little value. Today's passage talks about hate and love, two very strong emotions that motivate the hearts of mankind. We can't see or touch them but they are very real. Hate leads people to do horrible things to themselves and others. It is like a cancer that at first may be undetected but when left untreated it continues to grow until the whole body is consumed with it. Love is just the opposite. It motivates people to share and give. It brings peace and contentment and fills the air with a sweet smelling aroma that people want to be around. It's like walking into a house with the smell of fresh baked cookies, and we want them! For we are to God the aroma of Christ among those who are being saved and those who are perishing.

Read Proverbs 10
Psalm 119:125, Song of Songs 4:10, Romans 1:20, 2 Corinthians 2:15

The devotional Streams in the Desert talks about the cross of sacrifice and asks the reader to bind him or herself to the altar of sacrifice, to the cross of Jesus, and in good and bad times to never stray from it. Let that be our prayer today, that we bind ourselves to the cross, the altar of sacrifice, and be a living sacrifice for our Lord and Savior Jesus Christ. May everything we think and do be a glory and honor to You. Thank You, Lord, for loving us more than anyone ever could. Amen.

AUGUST 2
HE WHO WINS SOULS IS WISE

Proverbs 11:30: The fruit of the righteous is a tree of life, and he who wins souls is wise.

Just as in Chapter 10, this entire chapter compares righteousness with wickedness and the rewards of both. One leads to pleasing God and eternal life; the other does not. As we travel through the day, let's ask Him to give us the opportunity to share our faith with someone. We may not see the fruit of the seeds we plant until eternity, but words of encouragement can lift someone up. Peter said to always be prepared to give an answer to everyone who asks so we can give the reason for the hope that we have, but we are to do this with gentleness and respect. We have probably missed opportunities to share our faith, perhaps because we forgot that we once were sinners who need a Savior and we looked to ourselves rather than Jesus. Our Lord is merciful and gives us other opportunities. During those times of seeming failure, let's pray the Lord sends someone else to minister to that person, for each soul is precious in the sight of the Lord.

Read Proverbs 11
Acts 15:11, Ephesians 2:4-5, 1 Peter 3:15

Lord, we pray that You use us in a way that glorifies You. Bring people into our path who are searching for You, just as we once were. Give us the words to speak so that the seeds we sow will grow into a desire to seek the Living God who gives generously to all who ask. Use us to fulfill Your plan and Your purposes, that our souls may rejoice with the knowledge You walk with us each step of the way. Amen.

AUGUST 3
RIGHTEOUSNESS LEADS TO LIFE EVERLASTING

Proverbs 12:28: In the way of righteousness there is life; along that path is immortality.

As we begin to age, we realize our mortality and start looking for ways to keep young. Everywhere we turn these days, there are ads to help make us look younger. Dr. Oz has daily programs telling us which foods are beneficial to keep us younger longer, and which foods to avoid. There's a billion dollar industry that thrives because people are looking for ways to stay young. Legend has it that Ponce de Leon discovered the fountain of youth in Florida and people traveled from all over the world to find it. Youth is vibrant. It is filled with energy and excitement and hope for the future. There is adventure in being young. There's a whole world to be explored and when we are young we have dreams of conquering it. In our youth, we are often rebellious and feel indestructible and think we are going to live forever. The preacher says in Ecclesiastes to remember our Creator in the days of our youth, before the days of trouble come and the years approach when we will say, "I find no pleasure in them." Life is about more than trying to stay young. We find its purpose in Jesus Christ. He is the only path that leads to immortality. If Christ is in us, although our bodies are dead because of sin, our spirit is alive because of His righteousness, and the reward of righteousness in Jesus Christ is eternal life; thereby passing from death in this earthly body to life everlasting.

Read Proverbs 12
Ecclesiastes 12:1, Isaiah 40:30, Jeremiah 31:19, Romans 8:10,
1 Peter 1:18-19

Lord, help us to put away the follies of our youth which is so fleeting. We pray for the power of the Holy Spirit to infuse us so that the desire of what we see does not take us away from keeping focused on You. We pray for Your wisdom that guides us into all truth. Thank you for Your love and protection throughout this day's journey. Help us touch someone else with the love of Jesus. Amen.

AUGUST 4
BE CAREFUL WHERE WE WALK

Proverbs 13:20: He who walks with the wise grows wise; but a companion of fools suffers harm.

Today's verse instructs us to be very careful about the company we keep, because the enemy of our souls is very subtle. We may go places or be with someone who does not believe in Christ as their Savior, and we may think: Oh, this isn't so bad; what's the big deal? It goes one step at a time until we have gotten ourselves so far away from the things of God we don't even know how it happened. Keeping company with fellow believers lifts us up and helps us grow stronger in our faith. The things of God that we strive for with all of our hearts last forever in eternity. Religion that the Father accepts as pure and faultless is this: to look after orphans and widows in their distress and to keep one's self from being polluted by the world. It is one thing to try and bring someone into the kingdom when the Holy Spirit guides us, but it is another to keep constant company with unbelievers because it may cause us to walk away from our first love and forsake faith in Christ.

Read Proverbs 13
2 Corinthians 6:14, 2 Thessalonians 3:2-3, James 1:27, 1 John 1:5-6,
Revelation 2:4

Father, we lift our hearts, minds and souls to You. We praise and glorify You for You alone are worthy. Give us a measure of faith this day so we might walk boldly and in the assurance that we have Jesus as our Savior, the one who sacrificed His life on the cross and redeemed us from eternal death. Thank You for His precious blood that wipes away all of our sins. Bring us into Your presence by the power of Your Spirit and help us daily to walk with You. Amen.

AUGUST 5
THE WAYS OF THE LORD ARE RIGHTEOUSNESS

Proverbs 14:12: There is a way that seems right to a man, but in the end it leads to death.

The result of going our own way is death, not only in this life but in the life to come. The second death is not only of the body but of our eternal soul in hell without God, forever in outer darkness. We can't even imagine total darkness. Our lives on this earth, even in sin, are filled with light: the sun by day and the moon and stars by night. The thought of total and absolute darkness for all eternity is such a frightening thought that that alone should make us stop in our tracks and consider our ways. For if God did not spare angels when they sinned but sent them to hell, putting them into gloomy dungeons to be held for judgment, if he did not spare the ancient world when he brought the flood on its ungodly people, if this is so then the Lord knows how to rescue godly men from trials and to hold the unrighteous for the day of judgment. The Holy Spirit checks our spirits when we begin to wander. We should ask Him to keep Jesus uppermost in our minds, hearts and souls so that in all circumstances we know the right way to go. If there's any question, we need to stop, look and listen, until we know which direction to take.

Read Proverbs 14
Luke 13:28, 2 Peter 2:4-10, Revelation 2:11 & 21:8

Heavenly Father, help us to keep our hearts, minds and souls directed toward You so we find favor before You and You would bless us beyond anything we could imagine. We know we will be amazed at Your blessings. This is such a hard time for so many of Your people. May we always remember that You are with us and never forsake us. Help us to see You in all of our circumstances, no matter what they are. Teach us Your ways so that we will never forsake You. Amen.

AUGUST 6
EYES OF THE LORD

Proverbs 15:3: The eyes of the Lord are everywhere, keeping watch on the wicked and the good.

In the Old Testament, the Lord gave the children of Israel instructions concerning the land they were about to enter. He said it was not like the land of Egypt from which they had come but it is a land of mountains and valleys that drinks rain from Heaven. He said it was a land that the eyes of the Lord God are continually on from the beginning of the year to its end. If the people were faithful to Him He said He would send rain on the land in its season and they would gather in the grain, new wine and oil. But they soon began serving other gods. Amos tells us the eyes of the Sovereign Lord were on the sinful kingdom to destroy it from the face of the earth, yet He would not totally destroy the house of Jacob. The eyes of the Lord range throughout the earth to strengthen those whose hearts are fully committed to Him. He is on his heavenly throne and He observes the sons of men. His eyes are on those who fear Him, on those whose hope is in His unfailing love. We can hide our secrets from others but never from the One who sits on His throne in the heavens. The eyes of the Lord are on the righteous and His ears are attentive to their prayer.

Read Proverbs 15
Deuteronomy 11:10-15, 2 Chronicles 16:9, Psalm 11:4, 33:18, 34:15, Proverbs 22:12, 1 Peter 3:12

Lord, Your holiness is awesome. You and You alone are worthy of our praises. Tug at our hearts when we begin to stray and bring us back to You, our first love and the Savior of our souls. We thank You that in Jesus are hidden all the treasures of wisdom and knowledge and that we have access to those treasures when we follow and trust Him with all our hearts. We pray to be more like Him who has given us eternal life. Amen.

AUGUST 7
THROUGH LOVE AND FAITHFULNESS

Proverbs 16:6: Through love and faithfulness sin is atoned for, through the fear of the Lord a man avoids evil.

Pride goes before destruction, a haughty spirit before a fall. We admire men and women who attain fame and great wealth but if we were to know the intimate details of their lives we would find most of them are prideful and their lives are full of sorrow and heartaches. In the end, they lose it all. A perverse man stirs up dissension, and a gossip separates close friends. But the Lord detests all the proud of heart, and unless they repent they will not go unpunished. Whoever gives heed to instruction, though, prospers and those who trust in the Lord are blessed. Our Heavenly Father created man and woman to be in harmony with nature and communion with Him. He does not want us to flounder in life. Our tendency is to think we do not need help; we can do it ourselves. Through the centuries, this has been the way of many, but our Lord has a greater plan. He sent Jesus. His purpose for coming was foretold centuries before it happened. It was the Lord's will to crush Him and cause Him to suffer. His righteous servant justified many, and He bore their iniquities. We are a generation blessed not only to have this knowledge but to have His Holy Word to guide us. We have the hope of eternal glory with our Heavenly Father, Jesus and the Holy Spirit.

Read Proverbs 16
Psalm 50:10, Isaiah 53:10-11, 1 Peter 2:24

Almighty Father, You were before all things and in You all things exist. Help us to wrap our minds around this concept. We are so limited by and we get so caught up in our own trials and tribulations that many times we forget that You are right beside us waiting for us to call upon You for help. You own the cattle on a thousand hills, which is only a small measure of your limitless bounty. In other words, it's all Yours. So help us to not worry about our needs. Help us to remember that You have a vast supply and all we need do is ask. Amen.

AUGUST 8
PURIFICATION

Proverbs 17:3: The crucible for silver and the furnace for gold, but the Lord tests the heart.

The process of refining silver and gold involves dangerous chemicals and temperatures over 1,000 degrees in order to separate the impurities mixed in with these metals. Once the process is complete, the end result is something beautiful and useful. It is this way with the heart of man, although we do not go through a chemical process of refinement in order to be made pure. Even if we did, we could never be good enough to see God, which is why Jesus came. He suffered pain more than most of us could ever bear, to the point of sweating drops of blood. He hung for hours on a cross. He gave up His life and then went into the grave for three days. He went through the refining process for us. Because He rose again, we know He overcame death. When we believe this, we have the promise of life after death. We are tried and tested many times. Our Heavenly Father desires a people who are pure in their thoughts and words. He constantly searches us so see whether there is anything hidden within us. We harbor many things in our heart, such hatred, rebellion, and unforgiveness. Just as gold and silver need refining to become pure, so do we. This is possible only when we believe in Jesus Christ as our Savior.

Read Proverbs 17
1 Kings 8:39, Jeremiah 17:9-10, Luke 22:44, 1 Peter 1:22

Heavenly Father, we rejoice that You have called us to be Your children and that we have answered the call. We pray that You continually search our hearts and reveal the deep hidden secrets that reside there. Help us to be honest with You and with ourselves so that we can be set free from the sins that separate us from You. Also help us to know that the results of this process are glorious and that You want to do this not to condemn us but to bless us. Amen.

AUGUST 9
ARE WE WHO WE SAY WE ARE?

Proverbs 18:17: The first to present his case seems right, til another comes forward and questions him.

There are times we have been told something as fact by our children, friends, or anyone for that matter, and took it for the absolute truth, only to learn that it is not in fact true, or only partially true. We all have a tendency to jade things in our favor, even when it means twisting it around a little bit in a way that a lie is made to appear as the truth, but when we are questioned about it the truth eventually comes out. This is all sort of generic but it fits in with our proverb today which continues down the path of the consequences of our actions. The Lord knows what is going on on the inside of us. Outward appearances are often deceitful, which is why when someone first presents their case we cannot always take it at face value. What we see with our eyes is not what is always happening on the inside. This is why when we come to know Jesus as our Savior, it is important to begin reading the Scriptures and praying. It is through life's journey with Him that He teaches us the meaning of honesty with ourselves and others. He completely heals us so that our outward appearance is a true reflection of the person we are on the inside. He is the only one we can trust to do this because He never uses any of our faults against us. He forgives us and gives us wisdom to be more like Him.

Read Proverbs 18
Isaiah 11:3, Mark 7:20-23, Ephesians 3:16-19, James 3:13-16

Precious Lord, we thank You for Your word that reveals who You are, what You desire for us and the unconditional love that You pour out on us. We pray You continually search our hearts and minds. If we are displeasing to You in any way, reveal this so that we change our ways, for Your ways lead to life everlasting. Amen.

AUGUST 10
A LIE

Proverbs 19:9: A false witness will not go unpunished, and he who pours out lies will perish.

From the time that one man chose to rebel against God and sin entered the world, we have all been influenced by the lies of Satan who was a murderer from the beginning and did not hold to the truth. It does not please our Heavenly Father when we lie, even a so-called white lie. God is not a man that He should lie. He sent Jesus to show us the truth. It is the truth that sets us free, not a lie. When we lie, it usually is followed by another lie to cover up the first. It is impossible for us to fool the Lord, and we will be held accountable for every careless and idle word that we speak. The plan which the Father has set before us brings redemption for all sin, including lies. He has rescued us from the dominion of darkness and brought us into the kingdom of the Son He loves. We are redeemed by the precious blood of Jesus and our sins are forgiven. We can never be perfect in this lifetime but we can know the One who is perfect. In this we can rejoice for we are set free by the truth of Jesus, the Son of God and Savior of the world.

Read Proverbs 19
Matthew 12:36-37, John 8:44, Colossians 1:13-14

Jesus, thank You for setting us free from the lies of this world. Search our hearts and minds and reveal Your truth to us so that we will not lie and will not believe a lie. You tell us in Scripture that You are the way, the truth, and the life and no man comes to the Father but by You. Draw us by the Holy Spirit into the light of Your presence so that our lives will be a reflection of You so when others see Your light in us they will desire the truth of God that sets all men free. Amen.

AUGUST 11
THE SLUGGARD FINDS NOTHING AT HARVESTIME

Proverbs 20:4: A sluggard does not plow in season so at harvest time he looks but finds nothing.

Sluggard is mentioned 11 times in Proverbs and it is never flattering. He or she is someone who sits back and watches idly while others do the work. They hope to benefit off of what others do because they're too lazy to do anything themselves. But if a man is lazy, the rafters sag; and if his hands are idle, the house leaks. If a believer in Christ falls into this category, he or she is worse than an unbeliever for they do not provide for their own family and have denied the faith. We must take some sort of action in order to receive a benefit from it. A woman whose husband had died said to Elisha that creditors were coming to take her two sons because of the debt her late husband owed because she had no means to pay the debt. Elisha told her to go around and ask all of her neighbors for empty jars. She had just a little oil and Elisha instructed her to pour the oil into the jars and keep pouring. When there was not a jar left, the oil stopped flowing. She had such an abundance she sold the oil to pay her debts and had enough remaining for her and her sons to live on. She didn't sit by feeling sorry for herself because of the circumstances she was in. She took action and got results. The Lord provides all of our needs but we must act in order to receive, and not be lazy.

Read Proverbs 20
2 Kings 4:1-7, Ecclesiastes 10:18, 1 Timothy 5:8

Heavenly Father, help us not to be lazy about life. There are times we just sit back and do nothing, saying that You will take care of everything for us. We know life doesn't work that way. Help us to set an example for others by getting up out of our chairs, planting the seed and reaping the harvest. We pray for wisdom in order to do all You intend for us to accomplish during our lives. Thank you for calling us to serve You. May we never lose sight of the promise of eternal life with You where death no longer exists and the light of God continually shines. Amen.

AUGUST 12
RESULTS OF OUR ACTIONS

Proverbs 21:13: If a man shuts his ear to the cry of the poor, he too will cry out and not be answered.

Had those who were personally unaffected by the atrocities committed by Adolf Hitler not turned a blind eye to what was going on, the Holocaust may never have happened. That may be a stretch when talking about a madman bent on the destruction of a race or races of people, but it's within the realm of possibilities. Just because something horrible is not happening to us doesn't mean we shouldn't care about it, because we may be the next to suffer. Jesus tells the story of a man of noble birth who went to a distant country to have himself appointed king and then to return. He called ten of his servants and instructed them to take mina (money) and put it to work until he came back. When he returned, he called the first servant who had earned ten mina for the ones he had been given. The second servant had earned five for his. The king said that because they were trustworthy in a very small matter he would give them authority over ten and five cities. Then another servant came and gave back the mina which the king had given him. He said he was afraid because he knew his master was a hard man; he took out what he did not put in and reaped what he did not sow. His master called him a wicked servant and instructed those standing by to take his mina and give it to the one who had ten minas. The last servant left to others what he himself should have done. The master of the servant said that everyone who has will be given more but the one who has nothing, even what he has will be taken away. When we see a need, we must help when possible and do it with all of our heart; not turn the other way hoping someone else will take care of it. If we sow for ourselves righteousness, we reap the fruit of unfailing love but if we have planted wickedness, we reap the same.

Read Proverbs 21
Hosea 10:12-13, Luke 19:12-26

Precious Lord, help us not to look the other way when we hear cries for help. We so often turn a blind eye if we are not personally involved. Help us to be patient, to listen, to consider our surroundings and to pray. We don't always know why things happen the way they do but when we listen before speaking, we gain understanding. Lord, give us the ability to do this in our lives that we might be the hands and feet of Jesus and treat everyone the way He would treat them. Amen.

AUGUST 13
TRAIN A CHILD

Proverbs 22:6: Train a child in the way he should go and when he is old he will not turn from it.

Having children is a lifetime responsibility, full of joy and sorrows. Just as our parents did, we pass on to our children what we have learned. As believers in Christ, we should not only talk about the things of God but, more importantly, our lives should be an example of who we are in Christ What does it tell a child when we go to church on Sunday, praise the Lord, listen to the sermon and then go home and take the name of the Lord in vain, gossip or speak poorly of others, drink alcohol or smoke? Our actions speak louder than any words we utter. When we believe in Christ as our Savior, when we profess that He is Lord of our lives and put into practice His teachings, our lives are the same in public and in private. Our children learn by the example we set. We should not live only to please ourselves but in humility we should consider others better than ourselves. This is the example that Christ gave us when He walked on the earth, and this is how we should teach and train our children so that when they are old they will not turn from their training but pass down through the generations the redeeming power of Christ unto eternal life.

Read Proverbs 22
Job 27:3-4, Philippians 2:3, 1 John 5:11-12

Heavenly Father, we pray for wisdom to train our children in the way they should go. As they journey through life, draw them to You. Watch over them and protect them. Surround them with Your eternal love so that they will come to know You, the Giver of life everlasting. Help us to be people who live godly lives, teaching our children the ways of the Savior, not only with words but by example. Amen.

AUGUST 14
DECEIT OF RICHES

Proverbs 23:5: Cast but a glance at riches and they are gone; for they will surely sprout wings and fly off to the sky like an eagle.

The ways of this world tell us if we attain wealth we will have all we need and live healthy and happy lives. The funny thing is, it is never enough. Great riches bring unhappiness and loneliness. We can't trust others to be true friends for how do we do if their friendship is real or based only on wanting to share in our riches. Disaster can strike suddenly and all that we worked so hard for can be gone in an instant. Let us not boast in riches but let us boast that we understand the way of the Lord and know Him, for He is the One who exercises kindness and justice in all the earth. By Him we receive abundant provision of grace and the gift of righteousness through Jesus Christ. Our lives do not consist in the abundance of our possessions. Those who want to get rich fall into temptation and a trap. Many foolish and harmful desires plunge them into ruin and destruction. Those who do attain great wealth in this life are commanded not to be arrogant and put their hope in it, but to put their hope in God, who richly provides us with everything for our enjoyment. We don't have to strive for riches for our Father in Heaven owns it all. He gives freely to those who ask. We may not have wealth and possessions by the standards of this world but we have eternal riches in Heaven where eye has not seen nor ear heard the things that the Lord has prepared for those who love Him.

Read Proverbs 23
Jeremiah 9:23-24, 1 Corinthians 2:9, 1 Timothy 6:9-10 & 17-19

Lord of all creation, help us keep our eye on the prize that awaits us in eternity so that we do not fall into the trap of desiring more and more things in this world, all of which will be left behind when You call us home to be with You. Fill us to overflowing with Your love and help us to give that love to others so they will desire to know and serve You. Life's mysteries will one day be revealed by You. Until that time, we pray that You continually increase our faith so that no matter what happens in life we trust You in all things. Amen.

AUGUST 15
VENGEANCE IS MINE, SAYS THE LORD

Proverbs 24:28-29: Do not testify against your neighbor without cause, or use your lips to deceive. Do not say, "I'll do to him as he has done to me; I'll pay that man back for what he did."

An expert in the law asked Jesus, "And who is my neighbor," to which He replied by telling the story of the Good Samaritan. Our neighbor can be anyone, not just the person living next door, which means we must be careful when we speak that we do not gossip about or betray a confidence. We must know what we are doing before we take any action that could be detrimental to another. This is not always easy to do, especially if we have been on the receiving end of lies or dishonesty. If this happens, we are not to be vengeful or spiteful. Jesus tells us to love our enemies, to pray for those who persecute us. If we don't, we are no different than pagans, for the Lord causes the sun to rise on the evil and the good and He sends rain on the righteous and unrighteous. He alone is the judge for He judges by the heart. As followers of Christ, we are to read the Holy Bible, pray for guidance and love others as Jesus loves them. We are not put here to be gossips and slanderers or to take retribution against those who have done wrong. Our responsibility is to let the light of Christ shine before men so that they may see our good deeds and praise our Heavenly Father.

Read Proverbs 24
Proverbs 25:18, Matthew 5:16 & 44-48, Luke 10:29-37, Romans 12:19

Lord, Your Word tells us that You are not willing that anyone should perish but that all would come to eternal life. Search our hearts, and if we harbor any ill will towards another, reveal it to us that we might humble ourselves before You and ask forgiveness. We must forgive others before we ourselves can be forgiven. We pray to be set free from anything that would separate us from You so that when we pray we may come boldly before Your throne of grace with our petitions, and You will hear and answer according to Your perfect will. Amen.

AUGUST 16
LOVE YOUR ENEMY

Proverbs 25:21-22: If your enemy is hungry, give him food to eat; if he is thirsty, give him water to drink. In doing this you will heap burning coals on his head and the Lord will reward you.

Every single person who has been, who is and who will be is precious and special to our Heavenly Father. It is we who are created who do not look at each other in the way God looks at us. When we look at others, we see their faults; yet we cannot see our own. We are quick to judge, yet don't want to be judged. When someone hurts us or becomes our enemy, we devise ways to get even in some way. The Lord tells us when we have enemies, and we all do at some point, we are not to look at them with disdain and disgust or devise ways to get back at them. Love begets love and when we love our enemies, it is difficult for them to fight against us. If we don't give them fuel for the fire, it eventually is extinguished. The love of Christ transcends all human understanding but it is a love He freely gave and gives to all, for Christ loved us and gave Himself up as a fragrant offering and sacrifice to God. This is the life of a Christian, to proclaim the love of Christ by having mercy on all and not harboring hatred in our hearts. By sharing all the Lord has provided, perhaps even God's enemies will turn to Christ and also inherit the promise of His love and everlasting life.

Read Proverbs 25
Isaiah 40:28, Luke 6:27-36, Ephesians 5:2

Jesus, thank You for loving all of Your creation. Help us to love others as You love them. We call ourselves Christian but we don't always live up to it. Pour Your love into our hearts and minds that we might be the vessels You want us to be. Amen.

AUGUST 17
OUR CHOICES

Proverbs 26:27: If a man digs a pit, he will fall into it; if a man rolls a stone, it will roll back on him.

Our proverb today speaks of those who are wise in their own eyes and do not allow the Spirit of God to come into their heart to guide them through this life to eternal life. Stay clear of the fool who depends on himself for instruction; the sluggard who is too lazy to even feed himself if it takes too much effort; the mischief-maker who says and does hurtful things to others but when called on the carpet says he's only joking; the slanderer who intentionally speaks ill of others and keeps the fires burning as long as gossip continues, to the detriment of all who participate; the one with evil intentions who covers up what he really wants to do with smooth talking. If we participate in or approve of these things, we are dragged down and may even become guilty of adding fuel to the fire which allows the wood to keep burning. We are responsible for the choices we make, and if we choose to believe in Jesus Christ, He blots out our transgressions for His own sake and remembers our sins no more.

Read Proverbs 26
Isaiah 43:25, Revelation 20:15

Heavenly Father, we humbly come before You this day asking that You search our hearts. When we fail You, help us to be quick to ask forgiveness and cleansing by the blood of Jesus. Thank You that when we do this, our sins are thrown into the sea of forgetfulness and we are reconciled to You. Amen.

AUGUST 18
BOAST IN THE LORD

Proverbs 27:1: Do not boast about tomorrow, for you do not know what a day may bring.

At times we become self-reliant and may even feel like the world is ours, putting aside any knowledge of the Creator of all things. This is folly, for as we have no say in our birth we have no say in our death. Each day is a gift from God. That is why we should live in the present, where He is. Our past is behind us and, if we have failed, we should learn from our mistakes and ask forgiveness. Every moment of every day matters because that too becomes our past. It is a prideful thing as Christians to boast about ourselves. Our lives were headed the way of death until we came to know Christ as our Savior. When that happened, our only boasting became the cross of our Lord Jesus Christ, to whom belongs all glory and praise. We can plan for tomorrow but we should not worry about it, for tomorrow will worry about itself. Each day has enough trouble of its own. When we live every moment with the Lord, we are storing up riches in Heaven that will last for all eternity, unlike the things that we acquire in life and the plans that we make, all of which will pass away. All men and women are like grass and all their glory is like the flowers of the field. The grass withers and the flowers fall but the word of the Lord stands forever. We have been born again, not of perishable seed but of imperishable, through the living and enduring word of God.

Read Proverbs 27
Jeremiah 10:16, Matthew 6:34, Galatians 6:14, 1 Peter 1:23-25

Lord, may we never boast of ourselves for today we are but who knows what tomorrow brings. Our flesh will one day pass away and we will take nothing of earthly value with us; only that which we have done for Christ. Help us live each moment for You knowing that You know us best and guide us in the ways of everlasting life. Amen.

AUGUST 19
WALK IN WISDOM AND KEEP SAFE

Proverbs 28:26: He who trusts in himself is a fool, but he who walks in wisdom is kept safe.

Men and women become wise in this world through much study and life experience, but God has made foolish the wisdom of the world. God's ultimate wisdom is salvation through His Son Jesus Christ. No one has devised such a plan of mercy and love. No one has given us understanding and revelation of the true things of God except Jesus. The wisest man on earth was Solomon, King of Israel, but he followed strange women, worshiped their gods and forsook the God of his fathers. He wrote the Book of Proverbs, the Book of Ecclesiastes, as well as the Song of Solomon. All three books are almost cynical at times and when taken as a whole they may leave the reader questioning what it all means, for the wisest man on earth could not grasp the true wisdom of God. It is because he trusted in himself and those with whom he surrounded himself, instead of seeking his Creator, the One who knew him and what he was capable of. The Lord declares that His thoughts and ways are not our thoughts and ways. We struggle with the flesh and our own sinful desires, but when the Lord calls us to Him we can overcome our ways by trusting Him. We do this by spending time alone with Him, pouring out our innermost secrets to Him, reading His word and, by faith, believing all that He reveals to us, even if we don't always understand. True wisdom comes from the Lord and brings eternal life to those who seek it.

Read Proverbs 28
Psalm 111:10, Isaiah 55:8, 1 Corinthians 1:20-25, James 3:17

Heavenly Father, thank You for giving us the Bible. Through it, we come to know You when we have faith that by Your Spirit the words were penned. You have revealed the eternal consequences of trusting in ourselves or trusting in You. You have set before us words of wisdom and knowledge. Take us by the hand and show us the way that leads to life everlasting in Your kingdom. Amen.

AUGUST 20
PRIDE BRINGS A MAN LOW

Proverbs 29:23: A man's pride brings him low, but a man of lowly spirit gains honor.

One thing that gets in our way of trusting the Lord completely is pride. We say, "Oh, we can do that. It's not necessary to bother the Lord with these mundane, trivial things." This is the opposite of what Scripture teaches us. The Lord God Almighty wants us to ask for guidance in everything we do. This is how we come to know Him. When we learn to talk to Him about the small things, it is much easier to trust Him with the major things. When our pride gets in the way of our relationship with Him, it's time to acknowledge our sin, ask forgiveness and be humble before Him. With ourselves out of the way, the Lord shines the brightest for we are not then looking for our own glory but for His. This is opposite of how the world looks at things. When a man or woman accomplishes great things, it is easy to praise and honor them, forgetting that it is the Lord who gives talents and gifts to achieve those accomplishments. All glory, honor and praise belong to Him and Him alone.

Read Proverbs 29
Isaiah 66:2, 1Timothy 6:3-4, James 4:10

Heavenly Father, thank You for another day. Fill us anew with Your Spirit and keep us ever humble in Your sight. You know that our human tendency is to lift ourselves up. We ask that You remove pride from our lives and humble us in Your presence. When we honor and glorify You is when we are lifted up, not of ourselves but by Your grace and mercy. Amen.

AUGUST 21
THE LORD PROVIDES OUR NEEDS

Proverbs 30:8-9: Keep falsehood and lies far from me. Give me neither poverty nor riches but give me only my daily bread. Otherwise I may have too much and disown You and say, "Who is the Lord?" Or I may become poor and steal and so dishonor the name of the Lord

Up until this chapter, King Solomon has been the author of the Book of Proverbs. The sayings of Agur continue with the same theme: human nature and the consequences of our choices. When we have too much of everything, we tend to think we don't need God because all is well. When we are poor and unable to meet our needs, our lives can be consumed with thoughts of one day being in a better place but in the meantime doing things out of desperation because we feel forsaken. Human nature is often reactive. Left to our own devices, we panic, become fearful and, at times, prideful. If we know the Lord, our reaction should be different, for we have learned the secret of being content in any and every situation, whether well fed or hungry, whether living in plenty or in want, for we can do everything through Him who gives us strength. We know our abundance is a gift from God and we should freely share with others. When we are poor, we know He provides. He is a faithful God who does no wrong. Upright and just is He.

Read Proverbs 30
Deuteronomy 32:3-4, Psalm 37:25, Philippians 4:11

Father, You know how much we need You. May we be satisfied whatever our situation and know that You provide our every need. When we are blessed, give us opportunities to share those blessings with others. We thank You for Your wonderful provision. Amen.

AUGUST 22
REWARDS OF VIRTUE

Proverbs 31:30: Charm is deceptive and beauty is fleeting but a woman who fears the Lord is to be praised.

Throughout Proverbs, King Solomon has written instructions to his son about life. Our last Proverb is somewhat different. It is from King Lemuel's mother to her son. It is not certain who King Lemuel is but there is speculation it is a poetic name for Solomon. She tells him how important it is to be focused on his duties, not to spend his strength on strange women. Solomon had many wives and concubines, which ultimately lead to his falling away from serving the Lord. He was instructed by his mother not to partake in strong drink. He was to speak up for those who could not speak for themselves and defend the rights of the poor and needy. His mother tells him the benefits of having a virtuous wife who tends to the needs of her family; that if she is of noble character she would be worth far more than rubies. Not only would he be blessed and respected because of this but so would she and their children. As we grow older, we should realize life is not only about ourselves and what we think will satisfy our longings. Time is fleeting and as we look back on our lives, it is obvious that the beauty and charm of youth is deceptive because it does not last. The years go quickly and that which was used unworthily brings regret and sorrow, but a woman who fears the Lord is rewarded for her works. When we live only for our selfish desires and give no thought to the needs of others, we end up lonely, without hope. When we live for the things of God, virtue comes naturally and we can spread that virtue to others.

Read Proverbs 31
1 Kings 11:3-4, 2 Timothy 2:22

Lord, thank You for the Book of Proverbs with its wisdom and instruction. King Solomon had much wisdom, yet he allowed himself to be taken away from You by the women he chose to marry. Help us to keep our eyes on You and seek virtue so that we may follow You with all of our hearts and not be caught up in things that take us away from You. Amen.

AUGUST 23
TRUE OBEDIENCE

Matthew 1:19: Because Joseph her husband was a righteous man and did not want to expose her to public disgrace, he had in mind to divorce her quietly.

When Mary and Joseph were betrothed, it was as though they were already married, even though the marriage had not yet been consummated. When Joseph learned that Mary was pregnant, he wanted to quietly put her away because the custom in those days would most likely have been death for Mary because of her "illegitimate" pregnancy. When the Angel Gabriel appeared to Joseph, he was obedient and did what he was told to do. God's plans were fulfilled. Jesus, the Savior, was born. From the time of His birth, Joseph obeyed God's direction, taking his family away from harm when the angel directed him. May we be so in tune with God's Spirit that when He speaks to us, we are obedient to His direction so that His will for our lives is fulfilled.

Read Matthew 1 & 2

Heavenly Father, we thank You for Your wonderful plan of salvation. We ask that you prepare us for what we believe are the end days, and that soon Jesus will appear and set up His kingdom upon this earth. Help us be obedient to You, to pray and seek Your face and to recognize the ever gentle nudging of the Holy Spirit in our lives. We ask this in the precious name of Jesus, our Savior. Amen.

AUGUST 24
THE SAVIOR OF THE WORLD

Matthew 3:16-17: As soon as Jesus was baptized, He went up out of the water. At that moment Heaven was opened, and he saw the Spirit of God descending like a dove and lighting on Him. And a voice from Heaven said, This is my Son, whom I love; with Him I am well pleased.

God's promises of old are fulfilled in the New Testament. After 400 years of silence to His people because of their continual disobedience, the Savior of the world was born. Matthew writes of Jesus' genealogy, His birth and the obedience of both Mary and Joseph, as the Son of God was brought into the world. Today's verse tells us about the beginning of Jesus' public appearance and the ministry that followed. Until this time, we knew very little about Jesus' life. We can assume he had a normal and fairly quiet childhood, but when He came to be baptized by John the Baptist, the heavens opened wide and the voice of the Father said, "This is my Son, in whom I am well pleased." He anointed Jesus, and His earthly ministry began. It must have been awesome to see the Spirit of God descend on Jesus as a dove and hear the Father's voice. As we begin our journey through the New Testament, we will come to know Jesus in a way that transforms our lives and draws us closer to Him.

Read Matthew 3

Heavenly Father, we lift You up and thank You for Your plan of salvation, for the precious blood of Jesus that washes away the sins of the world. As we go through the New Testament, as we read Your Holy Word, let it penetrate our minds and hearts so we may know Jesus as we have never known Him before. Give us boldness to share our faith with others in humbleness and in love, that they too might know You and have the gift of eternal life, through Christ Jesus. We love You, Lord. In Jesus' precious name we pray. Amen.

AUGUST 25
JESUS SAID, FOLLOW ME

Matthew 4:19-20: "Come follow me," Jesus said, "and I will make you fishers of men." At once, they left their nets and followed Him.

As a child, the prophet Samuel ministered before the Lord under Eli, the priest. One night, Samuel was lying down in the temple of the Lord where the ark of God was and the Lord called Samuel. Samuel ran to Eli thinking it was he who was calling but Eli said, "I did not call you. Go back and lie down." This happened two more times because Samuel did not yet know the Lord's voice. The third time, Eli instructed Samuel to go back and lie down and if he heard the voice again to respond by saying, "Speak, Lord, your servant is listening." This may be the way we live our lives at times. The Lord calls us but we go to another because we do not recognize His voice. But when we lay still and listen, we can respond by saying, "Speak, Lord, for your servant is listening." After 40 days of fasting and being tempted of the devil, Jesus came out of the wilderness and began to choose His disciples. As He spoke to each one of them, they left what they were doing to follow Him. It should be this way with us, for we are also His disciples. He has a purpose and a calling for each of our lives. We don't need to be puzzled about this but only answer when He calls. His intentions are good toward us because He loves us. Through us, He wants to show the world who He is so they will see His light and follow Him.

Read Matthew 4

Jesus, we thank You for another glorious day. Thank You for calling each and every one of us to follow You. Give us a heart to be true to that calling, to look to You in all we do and to not lean to our own understanding. Help us to continually look Heaven-ward and know that this is where our ultimate destination is. Give us each the opportunity today to touch the life of another in deed or word and do it as unto You. In Your precious name we pray. Amen.

AUGUST 26
LET OUR LIGHT SHINE

Matthew 5:14-16: You are the light of the world. A city on a hill cannot be hidden. Neither do people light a lamp and put it under a bowl. Instead, they put it on its stand and it gives light to everyone in the house. In the same way, let your light shine before men, that they may see your good deeds and praise your Father in heaven.

Chapters 5-7 are known as the Sermon on the Mount. Jesus taught about the fulfillment of the law under the Old Testament, about murder, adultery, divorce, loving your enemies, giving to the needy, prayer and fasting. He said that His followers are blessed when people insult them and persecute them and falsely say all kinds of evil against them because of Him. He said to rejoice and be glad because great is their reward in Heaven. He spoke of being the salt and light of the earth. Salt acts as a preservative. Countries without refrigeration use it to keep meat from rotting sooner than it otherwise would. Salt causes pain when poured into a wound. It also gives flavor to food. To be salt means to be different than the world, for if salt loses its saltiness it is no longer good for anything. Light causes things to be brought out in the open. Without light, darkness abounds. When Jesus finished speaking, the crowds were amazed at His teaching, because He taught as one who had authority and not as the teachers of the law. By following Jesus' teachings, Christians are salt and light to a fallen world.

Read Matthew 5-7

Precious Jesus, thank You for Your life and the example it gave to us. Thank You for Your teachings and the words of the Sermon on the Mount that give us guidance as to how we should live. Give us boldness to proclaim who You are and wisdom to know when to be quiet. We know we must speak the Word, but help us to remember that it is the Holy Spirit who does the work of bringing people to You. Help us to trust You and know that we are safe in Your hands from now until the time You return again. We love You. In Your wonderful name we pray. Amen.

AUGUST 27
CALMING THE STORMS OF LIFE

Matthew 8:26-27: He replied, "You of little faith, why are you so afraid?" Then he got up and rebuked the winds and the waves and it was completely calm. The men were amazed and asked, "What kind of man is this? Even the winds and the waves obey him!"

After the Sermon on the Mount, Jesus came down from the mountain and great multitudes followed Him. He healed all who asked Him. His disciples had witnessed and experienced Jesus' miracles but they panicked when they were on a boat and a violent storm arose. They thought they would all die as Jesus slept soundly through it all. Fearing they would perish, they woke Him. He was amazed at their unbelief. They had been with Him the entire time, saw all the miracles that had been performed, yet in their storm they were helpless. When He rebuked the waves and the wind, the storm ceased at once. So it is in our lives. We know Jesus, we love Him, yet at times we think He is not there to answer our prayers and we question our faith. Through the storms of life, He calms the waves that at times seem to overtake us. We must trust Him even when the answer to prayer does not come when we think it should. He is faithful and He always calms the storms of our lives.

Read Matthew 8 & 9

Jesus, thank You so much for Your word and for Your faithfulness. Through the storms of life, increase our faith and draw us closer to you. Help us to know that the storms are what strengthen us and give us the ability to see Your mighty hand at work. May we be faithful followers of You and trust You with all our hearts, souls and minds. Amen.

AUGUST 28
SHREWD AS SNAKES, INNOCENT AS DOVES

Matthew 10:16: I am sending you out like sheep among wolves. Therefore, be as shrewd as snakes and innocent as doves.

We might wonder what Jesus was talking about when He spoke these words. When we think of snakes, it's not the most pleasant thing. If someone says, "He's a snake," it's not a compliment. A rattlesnake can curl up and strike a poisonous blow to its victim, but it only does this to protect itself from danger. Probably more times than not, a snake quietly slithers away because it isn't worth a strike. A dove, on the other hand, is a docile bird that even makes a good pet. When Jesus tells his disciples he is sending them out like sheep among wolves, he is also telling them how to protect themselves. The Holy Spirit is our guide and lets us know when to speak and when to be quiet and listen. When we speak, we should do it in gentleness and love, not in condemnation of another. In Chapter 10, Jesus tells us the things we must do to follow Him. To our natural minds, it may seem harsh but when we look at the cross that He hung on and His sacrifice for us, we can do all things through Him who strengthens us. If we love Him, serve Him and yield to Him, there is nothing to fear.

Read Matthew 10

Jesus, we thank You for this new day. Fill our hearts with Your love. Let us not lean to our own understanding because apart from You we can do nothing that satisfies our souls. Help us to be empty vessels, quiet before You and yielded to the precious Holy Spirit. Thank You for Your blood that was shed upon the cross for the forgiveness of our sins. It is so marvelous! Amen.

AUGUST 29
I WILL GIVE YOU REST

Matthew 11:28-30: Come to me, all you who are weary and burdened, and I will give you rest. Take my yoke upon you and learn from Me, for I am gentle and humble in heart, and you will find rest for your souls, for My yoke is easy and My burden is light.

A yoke is an oppressive agency reducing to subjection, submission, humiliation or servitude; hence, servitude, slavery, bondage, service. This was and is a constant problem in the world. Those in authority often think they know better than their "subjects" and they continually impose heavy burdens upon the people; yet they do not adhere to those same burdens. Jesus is just the opposite. His yoke is not heavy, for He carries us when the burden seems more than we can bear. He asks that we submit and trust in Him and our burdens will be light. We do not have to figure out who Jesus is because all His words reveal who He is. He is the truth. With Jesus, there is no hidden agenda. We never have to question His motives. He was born a man but He is also the Son of God. He came to show us who the Father is so we can know Him and have peace within ourselves.

Read Matthew 11 & 12

Heavenly Father, we rejoice in Your plan of salvation. We thank You that we have Your Holy Word so we can know You. We thank You for Jesus, for His teachings, for His ultimate sacrifice on the cross, and His resurrection. Help us to continually look to You and not ourselves. Let us not question the path You have laid out for us. Give us wisdom by Your Holy Spirit to recognize His voice and follow without hesitation. We praise You, Lord, and thank You for the gift of life. Help us use it for Your glory and honor. Amen.

AUGUST 30
FAITH

Matthew 13:58: And He did not do many miracles there because of their lack of faith.

Everywhere Jesus went during His ministry, He healed the sick, opened blind eyes and taught of the Kingdom of God. Many people followed Him. More than once, He fed crowds of over 5,000 with a few small loaves and fishes. Those who thought they knew Him best doubted that He was the Son of God. Because of their unbelief, He was unable to perform any miracles. When we look around us, we can see with our eyes the existence of a Supreme Being if we want to, or we can just believe that the world came out of some great explosion or big bang, and we just evolved to the state we are in now. It also takes a measure of faith to believe these things and it leaves us to dangle on our own to figure out what we are really doing here. Faith in Jesus Christ gives us the answers and the knowledge that we are not just floundering by ourselves. Because of what He did on the cross we are now joined with our Father in Heaven. He loves us and wants to share with us all that is His. That thought is mind-boggling, but with faith all of this is possible. If we believe this, He also does miracles in our lives.

Read Matthew 13 & 14

Heavenly Father, we thank You for this new and glorious day and all You have planned for us. Help us to reach the height of what You want us to be in this life. Give us a measure of faith that surpasses even our own understanding so that we never doubt what You are doing in our lives. We love you and we thank You for Your plan of salvation. The fact that You love us so much is almost too much to comprehend, but our faith allows us to believe that it is true. In Jesus' name we pray. Amen.

AUGUST 31
LIP SERVICE

Matthew 15:8-9: These people honor me with their lips but their hearts are far from me. They worship me in vain; their teachings are but rules taught by men.

If we claim to love God, yet hate a brother or sister, we are a liar. This is giving lip service to God because whoever does not love their brother or sister whom they have seen cannot love God whom they have not seen. Not everyone who says, Lord, Lord, will enter the kingdom of Heaven, but only the one who does the will of the Father who is in Heaven. On the day of judgment, many will say, "Did we not prophesy in Your name and drive out demons and perform miracles?" Then the Lord will say to them, "I never knew you. Away from me you evildoers." We are known by our fruits, for a good tree cannot bear bad fruit, nor a bad tree good fruit. (Matthew 7:16-23) We cannot lie to anyone and get away with it. Eventually, the truth comes out. Lies are never justified. He who is the glory of Israel does not lie or change His mind, for He is not a human being that He should change His mind (1 Samuel 15:29). This is why we can trust the Word of God.

Read Matthew 15

Jesus, heal the wounds of our lives. Break down the walls that we have built as a barrier of protection because of past hurts. We are all wounded, but when we consider the wounds You suffered and the pain You bore on the cross we realize that when we come to You, You set us free. When we allow You to come into our hearts and lives, You fill us with Your love so that we in turn are able to love others. Amen.

SEPTEMBER 1
DENYING SELF

Matthew 16:24-26: Then Jesus said to his disciples, If anyone would come after me, he must deny himself and take up his cross and follow me. For whoever wants to save his life will lose it, but whoever loses his life for me will find it. What good will it be for a man if he gains the whole world, yet forfeits his soul? Or what can a man give in exchange for his soul?

For the first time in His ministry, Jesus asks his disciples who they say He is. When they respond, "You are the Christ, the Son of the Living God," He tells them it has been revealed to them by the Father but that they are to tell no one. He continues teaching them what it means to be His followers. They are to deny themselves and follow Him. What does it mean to deny ourselves and follow Jesus? When we meet the person of our dreams and fall madly in love, we give all of our time and attention to that person. We want to please them. We think of them continually and look forward to the times when we will be together. In a way, we are giving up ourselves to be everything to that other person. This is how we should be when we give our hearts to Jesus, only more so because He is the one who never leaves us. He is with us in times of trouble and in times of rejoicing. We never have to be anything but ourselves with Jesus because He already knows us. We don't have to pretend with Him. We give ourselves to Him so that we may truly live, not only in this life but in eternity. We have no reason to hesitate giving our life to follow Him. He has all the answers and He wants to share them with us. Anything this world has to offer is nothing compared to the glorious riches He has planned for us. His teaching is that we should not put all of our efforts into gaining worldly things, but have our sights on doing His will.

Read Matthew 16

Jesus, we thank You for Your wisdom, for teaching us the ways of the Father, for giving us life everlasting. May we die to ourselves and continually yield to You, to be all that You want us to be. When we follow You with all our hearts, there is such satisfaction and joy. Show us how to pray so we might please the Father. Thank You for Your sacrifice and the knowledge that when we die, we will be with You in eternity! In Your precious name we pray. Amen.

SEPTEMBER 2
FAITH AS SMALL AS A MUSTARD SEED

Matthew 17:20-21: He replied, Because you have so little faith. I tell you the truth, if you have faith as small as a mustard seed, you can say to this mountain, Move from here to there, and it will move. Nothing will be impossible for you.

A mustard seed is very, very small, which means it doesn't take much faith to do the things Jesus says we can do. This verse refers to the time when His disciples were asked to cast out a devil from a boy who had seizures. Demons threw him into the fire and the disciples could not cast him out because of their lack of faith in the power of Jesus. We try so hard to do things on our own but fail because we do not look to Jesus. Sometimes the Father's will may not be the way we want it. This is not meant as a rebuke. Jesus is teaching us to trust Him because He is the one who removes the obstacles in our lives if we have faith in Him. Chapters 17 and 18 are full of Jesus' teachings on how we are to live for Him. We are to come to Him as children and trust Him with all our hearts; when two or three believers gather together in His name and ask anything according to His will, He hears and answers our prayers. We are to forgive others unconditionally and harbor no ill feelings in our hearts toward them. Each time we do this, our faith grows and we have peace in our hearts.

Read Matthew 17 & 18

Heavenly Father, we thank You for Your unconditional love for us. We thank You that all You ask of us is to trust and love You with all of our hearts. Thank You for guiding us through life's trials and triumphs. We ask that You give each of us a measure of faith so we can walk with You hand in hand in the knowledge that Your word is true and You mean what You say. As we go through this day, show us how to use our faith for Your glory. In Jesus' name we pray. Amen.

SEPTEMBER 3
SERVING JESUS AND OTHERS

Matthew 20:26-28: Not so with you. Instead, whoever wants to become great among you must be your servant, and whoever wants to be first must be your slave—just as the Son of Man did not come to be served, but to serve, and to give his life as a ransom for many.

The mother of two of Jesus' disciples came to Him. She wanted her sons to sit on the left and right hands of Jesus when He ascended to

His throne, which made the remaining disciples angry. Jesus rebuked them all, saying it was not His decision where the disciples would sit but His Father's, and that it should not be a concern of theirs anyway; that their real goal should be to serve each other as He came to serve us. The teachings of Jesus are not complicated. They go against our human nature, and that is His point. We are to die to ourselves and follow Him with all of our hearts. When we follow Him, it gives us richness of life. We don't have to wear ourselves out by continually planning and figuring. We must look to Him and think of Him in all we say and do. If we trust Him, we are satisfied. We will not only please Jesus but our Father in Heaven.

Read Matthew 19 & 20

We thank You so much, Lord, for Your wonderful teachings. Humble us in Your presence so we serve You unquestionably and with all of our hearts. Help us to take time each day to serve others. We love You and thank You so much for Your sacrifice. In Your precious name we pray. Amen.

SEPTEMBER 4
LOVE THE LORD OUR GOD

Matthew 22:37-39: Jesus replied, "Love the Lord your God with all your heart and with all your soul and with all your mind. This is the first and greatest commandment. And the second is like it: Love your neighbor as yourself."

Throughout Chapters 21 to 23, the Pharisees and Sadducees, the political parties of those days, were continually bombarding Jesus with all kinds of questions concerning the Kingdom of God. They were not doing it to learn anything but to try and trap Jesus in His words so they could prove Him to be a heretic or a false prophet. Jesus knew their intent and rebuked them because of their deceitfulness. We cannot pretend with the Lord because He knows our every thought, including our heart's desire. When we are honest, we have confidence in our walk with Him because we are hiding nothing. It should be our desire to love the Lord our God with all our heart, soul and mind.

Read Matthew 21-23

Heavenly Father, thank You for this day. Help us to give our entire thoughts to You and be still so that we might hear Your voice and know the desire of Your heart for us. Give us renewed strength and guide us continually, for Your glory and honor. In the precious name of Jesus we pray. Amen.

SEPTEMBER 5
VIGILANCE

Matthew 24:10-14: At that time, many will turn away from the faith and will betray and hate each other, and many false prophets will appear and deceive many people. Because of the increase of wickedness, the love of most will grow cold, but he who stands firm to the end will be saved. And this gospel of the kingdom will be preached in the whole world as a testimony to all nations, and then the end will come.

Jesus speaks in detail about the end times and what to expect. He tells us to be vigilant, to flee from those who claim another way to salvation or who preach another gospel other than Christ crucified. He tells us that times will be very difficult, that there will be great wickedness and people's hearts will turn cold, but that in the end those who remain faithful to Him will be rewarded. Through life's trials, it sometimes seems easier to give up on our faith and say it isn't worth it. That is a trick of Satan because the truth is just the opposite. No man knows the hour or the day when Jesus will return and the point He is making is to always be prepared because we don't know, but it will be as a thief in the night, at a time when we least expect it. So we are to draw close to Jesus, keep Him uppermost in our thoughts throughout the day, pray without ceasing and, no matter what the circumstances, know that He is with us.

Read Matthew 24 & 25

Heavenly Father, we rejoice in Your plan of salvation. Draw us closer to You. Keep us in Your care and help us never to be sidetracked by the temptations in this world. Help us to lift up everything in prayer to You and know that You are the one who knows all things and why they happen. Help us to trust You and never doubt. We pray this in the precious name of Jesus. Amen.

SEPTEMBER 6
THE BODY AND THE BLOOD

Matthew 26:26-28: While they were eating, Jesus took bread, gave thanks and broke it, and gave it to his disciples, saying, Take and eat; this is my body. Then he took the cup, gave thanks and offered it to them, saying, Drink from it, all of you. This is my blood of the covenant, which is poured out for many for the forgiveness of sins.

Jesus loves us so much that He left His place in glory. He came to earth, had an incredible ministry of healing, died for the sins of the world and was raised from the dead. He led a life of example, teaching God's love and letting us unquestionably know that a glorious life with Him awaits us. He gave us bread and wine by which to remember Him. Each time we partake in the sacraments, it is reliving His sacrifice for us. It is somber, it is holy, it is unimaginable, yet wonderful in its simplicity. It reminds us that, yes, He did sacrifice all; He did give His life and shed His blood for our sins; and, yes, He is sitting on the right hand of God Almighty waiting to once again return. When we have the opportunity to take Holy Communion, we should do it in reverence, to remind us who Jesus is. It is indeed the greatest story ever told.

Read Matthew 26

Jesus, there are no words to express our thankfulness for what You did for us. May we never forget the sacrifice that You made upon the cross to make all of this possible. We thank You that because of that sacrifice we will not die in our sins. One day, the things of this world will pass away. There will be no more sorrow, no more tears, no more dying. We praise You. We love You and we thank You. In Your precious name, we pray. Amen.

SEPTEMBER 7
THE VEIL IS TORN

Matthew 27:51-53: At that moment the curtain of the temple was torn in two from top to bottom. The earth shook and the rocks split. The tombs broke open and the bodies of many holy people who had died were raised to life. They came out of the tombs, and after Jesus' resurrection they went into the holy city and appeared to many people.

The tearing of the temple curtain was so significant. It indicated an end to the veil over God's people. They would no longer have to rely on the priests to go into the Holy of Holies to ask forgiveness for their sins but the kingdom was and is now available to all who believe in Christ as Savior of the world. The Bible does not expound on the people who rose from the dead except to say that after Jesus' resurrection they went to the Holy City and appeared to many people. Imagine the amazement of those who knew them! What a sign that was. The life, death and resurrection of the Savior is a story of true and holy love. It should make our hearts full to overflowing with the knowledge that it is the answer to life. The Book of Matthew ends with the words of Jesus, "And surely I am with you always, to the very end of the age." The King James Version says, "Lo, I am with you alway, even unto the end of the world," and surely He is.

Read Matthew 27 & 28

Thank You, Father, for all things, especially for Your overwhelming love for Your creation. Thank You for Your plan of redemption that we might boldly come to the throne of grace and worship You. Thank You that You are with us always and You will never leave us. Open our eyes to Your will for our lives and help us to follow the Holy Spirit and go unquestionably where He leads us. In Jesus' precious name we pray. Amen.

SEPTEMBER 8
PRAYER AND FASTING

Mark 1:12-13: At once the Spirit sent him out into the desert, and he was in the desert forty days, being tempted by Satan. He was with the wild animals, and angels attended him.

Mark's gospel begins with Jesus' public ministry rather than the stories of his birth and childhood. A large section of this gospel is devoted to the last week of Jesus' life. Jesus was tempted by Satan, who was arrogant enough to say, If You are the Son of God, do what I tell you to do. Jesus always answered with the Word of God. In the Old Testament, Ezra went back to Jerusalem after the second exodus and called for a fast. They fasted and petitioned the Lord about their request and He answered their prayer (Ezra 8:23). Jesus fasted for 40 days before beginning his public ministry. Later in the gospels, when some of Jesus' disciples were trying to cast out demons but could not, Jesus said to them that this kind goes forth by prayer and fasting. Forty days is a long time to fast and something that should be done only by a true leading of the Holy Spirit, but it is an example of self-denial, a time alone with the Lord to seek His will and be filled with the power of the Spirit. After Jesus' time in the desert, He began teaching about the kingdom of God, casting out devils and healing people.

Read Mark 1 & 2

Heavenly Father, thank You for this new and glorious day. Help us to take to heart what Jesus taught us. He is Your son, yet He walked among us, teaching us who You are and telling us that we can be in relationship with You. Help us to walk humbly before You and seek Your will. Show us how to draw closer to You, in fasting, in prayer, or however the Spirit leads us, so we may know You in Your fullness. We love You, Lord. In Jesus' name we pray. Amen.

SEPTEMBER 9
DIVIDED WE FALL

Mark 3:23-26: So Jesus called them and spoke to them in parables: How can Satan drive out Satan? If a kingdom is divided against itself, that kingdom cannot stand. If a house is divided against itself, that house cannot stand. And if Satan opposes himself and is divided, he cannot stand; his end has come.

Wherever there is dissension, there is division. There is no foundation upon which anything can be built because there is no unity. This is what Jesus is saying to those who accused Him of being Satan when He was healing people and setting them free of demons. He told those who accused Him that there was no way even Satan's kingdom could stand if it was divided against itself. When we are in unity with God, there is no need to fear because there is no way we can fail. Even at times when it seems impossible to do what He asks us to do, it can be done because He is the sovereign God. Our trouble comes in dividing ourselves from Him, in going our own way and doing our own thing. That is when things fall apart. When we come together as two or more in order to accomplish a certain goal but then don't have the same objective, there is bitterness and division and the goal can never be accomplished. It is so important to pray and seek the Lord's will, to bind the powers of darkness that would interfere in any way, and to quietly wait until there is unity of mind and purpose. That is when the Lord works and His will is accomplished.

Read Mark 3 & 4

Heavenly Father, we thank You for a new day, a new beginning. Keep us so close to You so that we are in perfect unity with You and in no way divide ourselves from You and walk alone. It is an awesome thing that You have called us to be in fellowship with You and that You have nothing but goodness and mercy stored up for those who follow You with all their hearts. Help us not to wander but to wait upon You. Lead and guide us in life's decisions. In Jesus' precious name we pray. Amen.

SEPTEMBER 10
UNCLEAN

Mark 7:15: Nothing outside a man can make him unclean by going into him. Rather, it is what comes out of a man that makes him unclean.

After the Pharisees rebuked Jesus because some of his disciples were eating without first washing their hands, Jesus spoke the words in

A Daily Devotional of God's Unending Love

today's verse. He then expounded and said that nothing that enters a man from the outside makes him unclean, it is what comes out of a man that makes him unclean, for from within, out of man's hearts, come evil thoughts, theft, murder, adultery, greed, malice, deceit, lewdness, envy, slander, arrogance and folly. We must be mindful of what we put into our minds, what programs we watch on TV, what movies we go to, what books or magazines we read. The things that we put our thoughts on are the things that we let into our heart and those are the things that proceed out of our mouths. The Lord says to love Him with all our hearts, minds and souls. When we do, our thoughts and our hearts will be pure as He is pure. He wants us to love Him, to desire to be with Him, not to let the things of this world grab us and take hold in our hearts so that when we speak or act we do things that are unclean. If we are full of Him and His mercy, we speak and do that which gives glory and honor to our Father in Heaven.

Read Mark 5-7

Heavenly Father, cleanse us daily by the precious blood of Jesus. Keep us whole and holy before You. Help us to keep our minds continually on You so that we don't let the things of this world influence our thoughts and hearts in any way. Help us to be a witness for Your eternal Kingdom, to spread the gospel of the good news of Jesus our Savior and to rejoice in our salvation. In Jesus' name we pray. Amen.

SEPTEMBER 11
BE NOT ASHAMED OF OUR FAITH

Mark 8:38: If anyone is ashamed of me and my words in this adulterous and sinful generation, the Son of Man will be ashamed of him when he comes in his Father's glory with the holy angels.

Our faith in Jesus is nothing to be ashamed of. When opportunities arise to share our faith, we should not be shy about it. We are to be bold in the knowledge that there is a Savior who has redeemed us from our sins; that He died not only for our sins but for the sins of the entire world. He then rose from the dead, ascended into heaven and now sits at the right hand of the Father. He is our continual intercessor and He has sent us His Holy Spirit to dwell within us. We should not be intimidated by unbelievers. We should respond in the love and compassion of Jesus in the hope that they will come to know Him as their Savior. We need to see others as He sees them and remember that we are sinners saved by grace.

Read Mark 8 & 9

Heavenly Father, thank You for Sunday, a special day of rest, not only physically but spiritually, a time to be quiet before You and renew our strength. Help us to never, ever be ashamed of Jesus and who He is in our lives. We cannot thank You enough for loving us, wrapping Your arms around us and protecting us. We praise You and we love You. In Jesus' precious name we pray. Amen.

SEPTEMBER 12
BEING A SERVANT

Mark 10:42-45: Jesus called them together and said, You know that those who are regarded as rulers of the Gentiles lord it over them, and their high officials exercise authority over them. Not so with you. Instead, whoever wants to become great among you must be your servant, and whoever wants to be first must be slave of all. For even the Son of Man did not come to be served, but to serve, and to give his life as a ransom for many.

Jesus does not want us to have power or control over others. We are all individuals who should look solely to the Lord for authority. If everyone lived that way, there would be peace on earth. In this regard, Jesus gave us the perfect example of what it means to be a servant. At the last supper, He wrapped a cloth around His loins, took a bowl of water and began to wash the disciples' feet. The custom of those days was to have the servant of the house, not the master, wash the feet of those who entered. He who created the world humbled himself by this act of servanthood. The Lord uses us to speak words of encouragement and knowledge, not as a master with authority but as humble servants. This is something that is in contrast to the way of the world. Let's keep our eyes on Him with a spirit of servitude, and give glory and honor to the Lord of all.

Read Mark 10 & 11

Jesus, we thank You so much that when You walked upon this earth You taught us to live not only by Your words but by Your actions. Give us continual insight into Your will for us. Help us to not look to worldly gain but to know that our riches are stored in Heaven and that as we continue in this journey called life, that we will be humble and not seek greatness but be a servant as You were a servant. We love You and thank You once again for Your sacrifice upon the cross. In Your precious name we pray. Amen.

SEPTEMBER 13
SIGNS OF THE END

Mark 13:5-8: Jesus said to them (the disciples), "Watch out that no one deceives you. Many will come in my name claiming, I am he, and will deceive many. When you hear of wars and rumors of wars, do not be alarmed. Such things must happen, but the end is still to come. Nation will rise against nation, and kingdom against kingdom. There will be earthquakes in various places, and famines. These are the beginning of birth pains."

Jesus is responding to his disciples' inquires about when the end of the world will come. He explained to them that these are some of the signs. He also tells us that no one knows the time of His return, not even the angels in Heaven, but only the Father and that this gospel must be preached to all nations and then the end will come. The Word of God is clear about who Jesus is, why He came and the Father's purpose for our lives. We need to be prepared for His return at any moment because surely it will come as a thief in the night and we don't want to be caught unawares. We have nothing to fear when the end is near because He guides and protects us. The end is coming and Jesus will soon return. He wants us to live each moment with Him, to watch and pray and be prepared for that glorious day when we look up into the sky and see Him on His white horse with all the saints and angels.

Read Mark 12 & 13

Heavenly Father, we thank You for giving us the Holy Scriptures so that we can truly know You. Thank You for Your wonderful plan of salvation and that we have nothing to fear in Christ Jesus. We know that no matter what our situation He is walking beside us. All we have to do is believe and follow the Spirit's leading. Give us wisdom to do so. We ask all of this in Jesus' precious name. Amen.

SEPTEMBER 14
WATCH AND PRAY

Mark 14:38: Watch and pray that you will not fall into temptation. The spirit is willing but the body is weak.

Before His crucifixion, Jesus and His disciples went alone to pray in the Garden of Gethsemane. He asked them to watch and pray for Him, but when He returned they were sleeping. This chapter is power packed with the last days of Jesus. He was anointed with perfume for His burial. He told His disciples where to go to prepare for the Passover. He served the first communion. He foretold of His betrayal by Judas; that the disciples would forsake Him; that He would die but then rise from the dead. This verse is so apropos to life. We can find time for any and everything but when it comes time to be quiet before the Lord, to watch and pray so we don't fall into temptation, the spirit is willing but the body is weak. We often let "time robbers" interfere with our prayer time. It is a trick of the devil, for sure. We need to be with our Lord, to love Him with all our heart. When we do, we want to pray and be in His presence. We cherish every moment and long for the times when we can be quiet with Him. Jesus is the best friend we could ever have. He asks only that we love Him. When we consider His sacrifice, His resurrection and His soon return, we can do nothing but love Him.

Read Mark 14

Jesus, we are thankful that when we were separated from the Father because of sin You came to this earth and died for us; You rose from the dead and are now sitting at the right hand of the Father as our intercessor. Help us yield to the Spirit so we die daily to our flesh. Each moment with You is the sweetness of life. As we grow closer to You, we know we will be able to share You with others so they too can rejoice in their salvation. In Your precious name we pray. Amen.

SEPTEMBER 15
PREACH THE GOOD NEWS

Mark 16:15-16: He said, Go into all the world and preach the good news to all creation. Whoever believes and is baptized will be saved, but whoever does not believe will be condemned.

These are the words of Jesus after His resurrection and they are the sum total of what we, as his disciples, are to do until He returns. We don't have to shout it from the rooftops but we must earnestly pray that when the opportunity arises to share our faith with someone that the Holy Spirit guides us in the words we should use. Sometimes it may not even be words. Someone may just need a reassuring hug to let them know they are cared for. Sometimes the word that we speak may seem to have no effect, but His word never comes back void and it may take other events or others speaking a word of encouragement as well. The important thing is to be yielded to the Spirit so that when the time comes to share our faith we are not shy about it.

Read Mark 15 & 16

Heavenly Father, we thank You for a new and glorious day. We thank You that Jesus came into the world to die for our sins. We thank you especially that He rose again from the grave and will soon return. Lord, give us boldness and discernment to know when to speak and when not to. Help us to be true witnesses for You so others might see the light of Jesus shining through us and they will desire it for themselves. We pray this in Jesus' name. Amen.

SEPTEMBER 16
OBEDIENCE

Luke 1:19-20: The angel answered, I am Gabriel. I stand in the presence of God, and I have been sent to speak to you and to tell you this good news. And now you will be silent and not able to speak until the day this happens, because you did not believe my words, which will come true at their proper time.

The first chapter of Luke is an accounting of the coming births of John the Baptist and Jesus by the Archangel Gabriel. When Gabriel appeared to Zechariah, the priest, to tell him that he would have a son and that his name would be John, Zechariah questioned Gabriel. Because of his unbelief, he became mute until the time that John was born. When Gabriel appeared to Mary, she had no doubts as to what he said to her. When he said this will be accomplished by the Holy Spirit overshadowing her, without any hesitation she said, "May it be unto me as you have said." In our lives, we may not have the Archangel Gabriel appear and tell us what the Lord's plan is, but we can believe His word and know that He is the same God today, yesterday and forever. His word does not change and He does not change. The things that He has planned for us will be accomplished. If we harden our hearts or are disobedient, they may not be accomplished through us, which is our loss, but they will be accomplished. If we never hear His voice as Zechariah and Mary did, we have His word. When we live by His word, we are His obedient servants.

Read Luke 1

Heavenly Father, help us to seek You and know You and be open to the leading of the Holy Spirit. Help our unbelief that we may not question His leading. We want so much to please You and to honor You with our lives because we know that we are here for a purpose and we know what lies ahead of us in Your kingdom. May Your name be glorified in all we think, do and say. In Jesus' precious name, we pray. Amen.

SEPTEMBER 17
KNOWING OUR FATHER

Luke 2:51-52: Then He went down to Nazareth with them and was obedient to them. But His mother treasured all these things in her heart. And Jesus grew in wisdom and stature, and in favor with God and men.

After the Feast of the Passover, Jesus stayed behind in Jerusalem. When His parents found Him, He was teaching the masters of the scriptures who were amazed at His wisdom at such a young age. When Mary asked Jesus why He had done this, He responded, "Didn't you know I had to be in my Father's house?" Other than this one episode, scripture does not elaborate on anything else in Jesus' childhood except that He then went with His parents and grew in wisdom and stature. The favor of God was upon Him, and we know that by the time He started his earthly ministry He walked so close to the Father that when He spoke it was with authority. It is amazing that we are God's creation, yet we know so very little about Him. He created us for His pleasure, but in our sinfulness our eyes have been clouded over. He loves us so much that He literally gave His only begotten Son so that whosoever believes in Him is saved from death and reconciled to Him. It is simple, yet we somehow make it difficult. It could be because we try so hard to be good on our own and want recognition for our efforts instead of the efforts of God through us.

Read Luke 2 & 3

Heavenly Father, thank You that each day is a new beginning. Yesterday is history, tomorrow is a mystery and today is a gift, that is why it is called the present. Help us to live in the present with You. Wrap Your loving arms around us, keep us close to Your heart and show us Your tender mercies. We ask this in Jesus' name. Amen.

SEPTEMBER 18
GOD'S WORD

Luke 4:13: When the devil had finished all this tempting, he left him (Jesus), until an opportune time. The King James Version says: And when the devil had ended all the temptation, he departed from Him for a season.

While Jesus was fasting, the devil tried to tempt Jesus into sinning. He thought he was so clever by twisting the word of God to his benefit. In what might be considered His weakest moment, after fasting for 40 days, Jesus used scripture in its proper meaning to rebuke Satan. This is an example of the importance of reading God's word. We are tempted and harassed by the devil, but when we have the Word of God hidden in our hearts and minds, we know how to rebuke him and turn our eyes to our Savior from whom comes our strength. Scripture also tells us to resist the devil and he will flee from us. What better way to resist him than to know God's word and use it.

Read Luke 4 & 5

Precious Jesus, we thank You for not only coming to earth to save all but that You gave us an example of how to live. Help us to be more like You each day. Fill our hearts and minds with the precious word of God. Holy Spirit, when the times come that we too are tempted and tried, bring scripture to our minds to speak with power and authority as Jesus did, knowing that it is the Word of God that is our sword and our shield. Thank You for another day. We love You, Jesus. In your precious name we pray. Amen.

SEPTEMBER 19
WHAT MEASURE YOU USE

Luke 6:37-38: Do not judge and you will not be judged. Do not condemn, and you will not be condemned. Forgive, and you will be forgiven. Give and it will be given to you. A good measure, pressed down, shaken together and running over, will be poured into your lap. For with the measure you use, it will be measured to you.

Jesus is telling us to be very careful in our thoughts and actions because the things we do at some point come back to us. If we sow seeds of righteousness, we reap the same. If we sow seeds of discord, if we gossip or treat someone unkind, that also comes back to us. Through His word, He teaches us how to live. When we pray, we need to talk to Him just like we would talk to our best friend. No, He is not here physically but He is closer to us than anyone physically can be for He lives within us. He is a constant companion. He wants to walk with us and talk with us and guide our every way. When we acknowledge Him in all we do, He is our partner in business and in life. We should make no decisions without Him. It takes time to hear His voice. Like any relationship, it doesn't happen overnight. When we seek Him with all our heart, we find Him and realize He has always been there, and we will do as He commands; that is, to do to others as we would like them to do to us.

Read Luke 6 & 7

Jesus, we come to You today praising You for Your goodness, for the wisdom of Your word that helps us to know what pleases You and how we should live. Cleanse our hearts and minds. Help us to sow love and righteousness so that we reap the same. Give us a greater understanding of Your love so we may love others with Your love, a holy and merciful love. We ask this in Your precious name. Amen.

SEPTEMBER 20
THE LIGHT OF JESUS

Luke 8:16-18: No one lights a lamp and hides it in a jar or puts it under a bed. Instead, he puts it on a stand, so that those who come in can see the light. For there is nothing hidden that will not be disclosed, and nothing concealed that will not be known or brought out into the open. Therefore, consider carefully how you listen. Whoever has will be given more; whoever does not have, even what he thinks he has will be taken from him.

Jesus' teachings sometimes seem harsh, but when we consider what He says, it is not harsh at all. He requires that we put Him first so that we know Him and serve Him. Then when the testing and trials come, we turn to Him instead of worrying. He wants us to be a light in our actions and words. That's what makes us different from the world. There can be no hidden sin in our lives. Jesus' sole purpose for coming was to sacrifice Himself on the cross for the forgiveness of our sins. When we live in sin, we live in spiritual darkness. When we confess our sin, He is faithful and just to forgive us. It takes faith to believe this. When we do, the light of Jesus illuminates our hearts.

Read Luke 8 & 9

Jesus, thank You so much for Your words, for teaching us how to live for You. Let us not be ashamed in any way of our walk with You but know that even when we are ridiculed, You are with us, always ready to pick us up when we are knocked down. Help us to follow the leading of the Holy Spirit so that Your word hits its mark and Your light shines brightly for all to see. We pray this in your precious name. Amen.

SEPTEMBER 21
KEEPING OUR EYES ON JESUS

Luke 11:34-36: Your eye is the lamp of your body. When your eyes are good, your whole body also is full of light. But when they are bad, your body also is full of darkness. See to it, then, that the light within you is not darkness. Therefore, if your whole body is full of light and no part of it dark, it will be completely lighted, as when the light of a lamp shines on you.

Our eyes enhance all of our senses because of what we see. This is why we must be so careful what we do with our time. When we see something that takes us away from the Word of God, we should not dwell on it but turn away. We must find time to read the Word and look to the Lord for guidance. This doesn't mean we have to spend all of our waking hours reading the Bible but we must keep our thoughts pure and holy before Him. We can only do that when our eyes see only that which is good and pleases Him. If there is any question about what we are reading, doing or looking at, the Holy Spirit lets us know whether it is darkness or light. He loves us and wants what is good for us, but we must keep our eyes upon Him or the spiritual darkness of this world overtakes us.

Read Luke 10 & 11

Lord, we praise You this day for Your goodness, for who You are. Thank You for so many blessings, too innumerable to even count. Keep us single-minded and our eyes fixed on things above so that we will honor You in all we think, do and say. Help us not to be tempted by the things we see in this world but be in continual prayer before You, to have discernment and wisdom and know light from darkness. We love You and thank You. In Jesus' precious name we pray. Amen.

SEPTEMBER 22
LIFE DOES NOT CONSIST OF ITS ABUNDANCE

Luke 12:15: Then He said to them, "Watch out! Be on your guard against all kinds of greed; a man's life does not consist in the abundance of his possessions."

Jesus tells the story of the man who had such an abundance of crop, he tore down the old barns in order to build new ones so he could take the fruit of his labors, sit back and relax for years to come. But the Lord said, "You fool! This very night your life will be demanded of you." This world is so temporary. We come into it with nothing and we leave the same way. As children, we are full of innocence and wonder. When we "come of age" so to speak, we strive to build a life on this earth. Unless it is built on the Solid Rock, with Jesus Christ as our foundation, if we gain the whole world but lose our souls, in the end we have nothing but an eternity of darkness. We are to store our treasures in Heaven because eternity is where everything is everlasting.

Read Luke 12

Jesus, thank You so much that we can open up the pages and read Your Holy Word. We can come to know You and learn how we are to live to the glory of God, our Father. Help us to take time each day to get to know You better. Faith comes by hearing and hearing by the Word of God. Thank You for a new and glorious day. In Your precious name we pray. Amen.

SEPTEMBER 23
BE HUMBLE

Luke 14:11: For everyone who exalts himself will be humbled, and he who humbles himself will be exalted.

In the preceding paragraph to this verse, Jesus says we are not to put ourselves above others. We are to be servants no matter what our position. He tells the story of a man who comes to a wedding feast. He admonishes him to not take the place of honor lest a person more distinguished comes and the person who so arrogantly took the place of honor is asked to give the place up and is so embarrassed when he has to go to the least important place. We are not to look for glory or recognition for ourselves. In all things, we should honor our Lord by doing our very best, in humility, not expecting praise from men for our efforts. The Lord alone is the One who honors us, which is the only honor we should be looking and longing for.

Read Luke 13 & 14

Heavenly Father, we thank You for this new day, for another new beginning. We pray for humbleness before You, to seek You and You alone, because You are the One we want to glorify. Let our light so shine before men that they will wonder, what is different about that person; why are they so happy and content in life? When the time comes, Lord, give us the words to speak, for Your honor and glory. In the precious name of Jesus we pray. Amen.

SEPTEMBER 24
WE CANNOT SERVE GOD AND MONEY

Luke 16:13: No servant can serve two masters. Either he will hate the one and love the other, or he will be devoted to the one and despise the other. You cannot serve both God and money.

Jesus teaches us to love the Lord our God with all of our heart, soul and mind, and to seek first the kingdom of God. We must work in order to provide for ourselves and our families. It is when we put our work first and foremost that interferes with our relationship with God. It's not wrong to pursue wealth but it is our attitude and desire towards doing so. Is this the reason we work so hard and want to get ahead in life, or is it our desire to please our Lord and know that He meets all of our needs? If we were to work hard and become wealthy or even very well off, if the Lord spoke to us to give it all away or to do something with it that we had not planned, we should gladly do so. The desires of our heart should be towards the kingdom of God because no matter how hard we try to get ahead in this world, it all amounts to nothing if we have not put our Lord first. At the hour of our death, we take nothing with us.

Read Luke 15 & 16

Heavenly Father, give us the desire to hide Your word in our hearts and follow the leading of the Holy Spirit and not be distracted by what this world has to offer. Give us wisdom so that we glorify You. Help each and every one of us throughout this day that we might be pleasing in Your sight. We love You and praise You. In Jesus' precious name. Amen.

SEPTEMBER 25
GOING BEYOND WHAT IS EXPECTED

Luke 17:10: So you also, when you have done everything you were told to do, should say, "We are unworthy servants; we have only done our duty."

Have we ever heard someone say, "That's not my job," which translates, "I'm not doing anything more than what is expected of me." If that is our attitude at work, that is most likely our attitude in life. Everything we do should be done as to the Lord. If He was physically standing next to us, we would go beyond what is expected of us and give it our all. If there are dirty dishes in the sink, wash them. Someone has to. If a co-worker is behind in their work and you can help, help them. Keep the door open for those behind you and smile as they pass through. We are to be the light in a spiritually dark world. We should excel and go above and beyond what is expected of us, not to an extreme but with a giving heart and attitude. We may not be rewarded for our efforts in this life, but when we do everything as unto the Lord our rewards are eternal.

Read Luke 17 & 18

Jesus, we thank You for the Word of God that tells us what the will of the Father is; that we should love Him with all our hearts, minds and souls and that we should love our neighbor as ourselves. Give us tender hearts, and as we go through the day let our lives touch those around us. We love You and thank You so much for who You are and what You have done for us. In Your precious name we pray. Amen.

SEPTEMBER 26
DO NOT BE CAUGHT UNAWARE

Luke 21:36: Be always on the watch, and pray that you may be able to escape all that is about to happen, and that you may be able to stand before the Son of Man.

In today's scripture, Jesus tells the signs of His coming and to be prepared for that day at all times because it will come as a thief in the night. When we go to bed at night, we assume we will wake up in the morning without incident, but what if something happens during the night that we are unprepared for. What if we wake up suddenly to an unusual noise like the rustling of papers, or we hear the tiptoeing of feet throughout the house. We remember we didn't put the alarm on or lock the door and it left us vulnerable to an unexpected intruder. Had we not forgotten, this may not have happened. Now it's too late to protect ourselves. We must not be caught unaware when the Lord returns, because He is coming back. We just don't know the day or the hour. Living as though He could return at any moment, being in an attitude of prayer and being thankful for each new day prepares us for the time when He will appear in the heavens coming to set up His kingdom on earth.

Read Luke 19-21

Jesus, we thank You for another new day. Teach us who You are and how we can best live for You and give glory and honor to our Father in Heaven. Help us prepare for Your return to this earth. As Your followers, that is what we look forward to, a time when there will be peace on this earth when You rule and reign from your throne in Jerusalem. Thank You for the promises we have in Your Holy Word. Help us to recognize and follow the leading of the Holy Spirit as we go along our day's journey. We ask this all in Your precious name. Amen.

SEPTEMBER 27
A TRANSFORMED LIFE

Luke 22:31-34: "Simon, Simon, Satan has asked to sift you as wheat. But I have prayed for you, Simon, that your faith may not fail. And when you have turned back, strengthen your brothers." But he replied, "Lord, I am ready to go with you to prison and to death." Jesus answered, "I tell you, Peter, before the rooster crows today, you will deny three times that you know me."

The disciples had been with Jesus for more than three years. He taught them about the Father. He sent them out two by two to heal the sick and proclaim the kingdom of God was here. Peter listened intently to His words but he was always trying to interpret what Jesus was saying. When Jesus was transfigured and Moses and Elijah spoke to Him, Peter wanted to build tabernacles for the three of them. He walked on water with Jesus. He proclaimed that Jesus was the Son of God. He did all of this with his mind but not his heart, and when his faith was tested he denied three times that he even knew Jesus. It wasn't until he was filed with the Holy Spirit that his heart was transformed and he became the rock upon which the church of Jesus Christ was built. We are a lot like Peter. We understand religion with our minds and either accept or reject it. It's not until we ask Jesus into our hearts that our lives are transformed into His likeness and image. It is then that we begin to understand all that He taught when He walked with His disciples.

Read Luke 22

Heavenly Father, take away our own intellect and replace it with the mind of Christ. When we build ourselves up, bring us down. It is only then that we are transformed into the people You desire us to be. Change our hearts on the inside so that outwardly we are the hands and feet of our Savior, Jesus Christ. Amen.

SEPTEMBER 28
TODAY YOU WILL BE WITH ME IN PARADISE

Luke 23:40-43: But the other criminal rebuked him, "Don't you fear God," he said, "since you are under the same sentence? We are punished justly, for we are getting what our deeds deserve. But this man has done nothing wrong." Then he said, "Jesus, remember me when you come into your kingdom." Jesus answered him, "I tell you the truth, today you will be with me in paradise."

As Jesus hung in agony on the cross, there were two criminals hanging on either side of Him. One of them asked Jesus to remember him when He came into His kingdom. He was an admitted criminal who was being crucified for his wrong deeds and yet even as he was drawing his last breath, when he asked Jesus to remember him Jesus immediately responded with love and told him he would be with Him in paradise that day. This is an example of God's unending love. He is not willing that any should perish but that all should have eternal life. If we live for Him while on this earth, we can experience His presence in everything we do. But even if we wait until the end, we can know Him. He said to ask and it shall be given to you. This criminal asked and he was given what he asked for. We should never give up on anyone because there is hope for their salvation even to their dying breath.

Read Luke 23 & 24

Heavenly Father, thank You for calling us to Your truths of who Jesus is and why He came. Forgive us our sins, we pray, that we may be worthy of You and Your goodness. Keep us ever mindful of the cross that we might be humble and know that it is not our works that get us to Heaven but our belief in the Savior who died for our sins that we might live eternally in Your glory when we too draw our final breath. In Jesus' precious name we pray. Amen.

SEPTEMBER 29
IN HIM IS LIFE

John 1:4: In Him was life, and that life was the light of men.

Solomon writes in Ecclesiastes: So I hated life because the work that is done under the sun was grievous to me. All of it is meaningless, a chasing after the wind. I hated all the things I had toiled for under the sun because I must leave them to the one who comes after me. This was written by the wisest man who ever lived. We do not find meaning in our lives until we know the purpose. We find the purpose when we ask Jesus Christ to come into our hearts and be our Savior. It's like walking into a dark room where we can see nothing, turning the light on and now we can see everything. Our eyes are open to the things of God. We find out what it means that in Jesus was life and that life was the light of men. Without Him, we walk in spiritual darkness. He illuminates the path He wants us to take and gives meaning and purpose to everything we do. There will be curves and rough spots in the road, but with His light shining ahead of us, we can safely pass over them all.

Read John 1

Heavenly Father, thank You for the light of Jesus in this dark and lonely world. In times of trouble, hold us close to Your side so we will not falter or be afraid. Watch over and protect all those who serve and love You and help those who do not know You to see the light of Jesus Christ. In His precious name we pray. Amen.

SEPTEMBER 30
REDEEMED

John 3:5: Jesus answered, "I tell you the truth, no one can enter the kingdom of God unless he is born of water and the Spirit."

When we are born into this world, we know nothing until we are taught. As time passes, we learn how to think, take care of ourselves and basically how to live, but that is only one aspect of life. That is the part we can now see and feel. There is another part of life that is much more important than that, and that is the spiritual life, that life which has no ending even when our earthly body dies. That is why we need Jesus, because we have no hope without Him. Man and woman were separated from God because of their sin. They were told not to eat from the tree of knowledge of good and evil, but they did. Because of Jesus' sacrifice on the cross, we are redeemed from that sin and joined once again to the Father in Heaven. When we give our hearts and lives to Jesus, when we truly believe and trust in Him, the Holy Spirit opens our eyes to the things of the spirit and we become like children. He reveals our Father to us and teaches us how to pray. When we read the Word of God, we begin to grow. Our spiritual eyes are open and we can understand and know the secrets of the eternal kingdom of God where there is no more sorrow, no more death and we will live forever with Him in His glory.

Read John 2 & 3

Dear Jesus, open our eyes to see You. By the power of the Holy Spirit, teach us more about who You are so we will daily grow in the things of the spirit. Thank You for the gift of the Holy Spirit, who teaches and guides us while You sit at the right hand of the Father in constant intercession for us. We love You and praise Your mighty and majestic name. Amen.

OCTOBER 1
JESUS, THE LIVING WATER

John 4:13-14: Jesus answered, "Everyone who drinks this water will be thirsty again, but whoever drinks the water I give him will never thirst. Indeed, the water I give him will become in him a spring of water welling up to eternal life."

When we are thirsty, we drink something. We are satisfied for a while but sooner or later we are thirsty again. If we don't drink, we become weak and dehydrated. Without water, we die. The drink that Jesus is offering is different from anything we can find to quench our thirst. It is a spring of living water that quenches our spiritual thirst. We are made to never be permanently full. Sometimes we eat and drink so much, we think we'll never want to do that again, but we do. When we drink from the spring of living water that Jesus offers us we will never thirst because it wells up within us to eternal life. He fills us with the knowledge of God and satisfies our spiritual longing. If we do not find Jesus Christ, we will seek to fill the longing and thirsting of our soul with alternatives. Just as water quenches the thirst temporarily, all other avenues to God do the same. It is only Jesus who satisfies the thirst permanently because He is the only way to a relationship with our Heavenly Father.

Read John 4

Heavenly Father, we thank You for the promise of eternal life. Help us to look heavenward and know that the things of this earth are only temporary. When we are filled with the Spirit, when we seek the things of Your Heavenly kingdom, then and only then will we know the fullness of who You are. Help us never to lose sight of that. Thank You for Jesus and His sacrifice on the cross. In Jesus' name we pray. Amen.

OCTOBER 2
COMMUNION

John 6:55-58: For my flesh is real food and my blood is real drink. Whoever eats my flesh and drinks my blood remains in me, and I in him. Just as the living Father sent me and I live because of the Father, so the one who feeds on me will live because of me. This is the bread that came down from heaven. Your forefathers ate manna and died, but he who feeds on this bread will live forever.

Communion is a symbol of the spiritual life we have in Jesus. When we partake in it, we do so in remembrance of Him. The bread is for His body which He gave for us on the cross and the blood is the sacrifice for the cleansing of our sins. This is how we are born into the spirit, when we believe that Jesus is the Son of God and by partaking in the sacraments as He commanded us to do. We are so blessed to have the Word of God. Its pages are full of the love and mercy of God. We learn who the Father, Son and Holy Spirit are. They are three, yet One. Jesus tells us that when we believe in Him we are also one with the Father. We do not lose our uniqueness or individuality when we become followers of Christ. It is through Him that we find our purpose. When we feed on His word, we grow in wisdom and power in the knowledge of God, which leads to eternal life. Jesus teaches us to labor for the Word of God, which feeds our souls, and not to labor for the things of this world. They are temporary; He is forever.

Read John 5 & 6

Heavenly Father, thank You for another new day. Help us to set our priorities straight, to always look to You, even in those areas that seem so inconsequential. We know You want to be a part of every aspect of our lives so we will come to know You more fully. Thank You for Your precious Word which fills our spirit and gives us the hope of eternal life. In Jesus' precious name we pray. Amen.

OCTOBER 3
STREAMS OF LIVING WATER

John 7:38: Whoever believes in me, as the Scripture has said, streams of living water will flow from within him.

These words were spoken by our Lord at a time when everything around Him seemed to be crumbling. His own brothers were mocking Him and there was much debate as to whether He truly was the Christ or a mere imposter. But Jesus knew where His strength came from and He did not have to rely upon man. There are times we are discouraged, feel isolated and all alone. It seems as though wherever we turn, there are problems that have no solutions. We can literally feel a darkness over us that wears us down. Jesus is always with us, especially in these times. If we do nothing but call upon His name and focus our thoughts and attention towards Him, He lifts our burdens and the darkness turns to light. It may not be instantaneous, but He is there. Streams of living water flow through us and fill us to overflowing.

Read John 7

Jesus, reach down and touch us with Your holy presence. As we read the Bible today, encourage us in Your strength that we might be filled with joy, knowing that even when we feel discouraged You lift us up. When we feel others have failed us, send the Holy Spirit in a special way so we might live in His presence and find peace. In Your precious name we pray. Amen.

OCTOBER 4
HE IS ALWAYS WITH US

John 8:29: The one who sent me is with me; he has not left me alone, for I always do what pleases him.

At almost every turn, Jesus was being questioned about who He was and asked who gave Him the authority to proclaim Himself the Messiah. Jesus knew who He was and that the Father in Heaven was with Him and loved Him. He was born without sin but He was still human and had the same desires in life as we do. He knew what His purpose in coming was and He never lost sight of that. He was in constant prayer. He gave us what is known as the Lord's Prayer in order to teach us how to pray. He had such love for people. There was even a time He wept for His dear friend Lazarus who had died. Life is full of pain and heartache, as well as joy. Sometimes it seems just when everything is starting to go well, wham, something else hits us right between the eyes and we might question whether Jesus is really present in our lives. We might wonder why all of this is happening. Jesus Himself was not without trials and persecutions. As we read through the scriptures, we see how much time He, who was the Son of God, spent in prayer. He teaches us how to pray, how to go to the Father and rest in the knowledge that no matter what our circumstances, in Him everything is going to be all right. As we draw closer to Him and trust in Him, we grow stronger in our faith.

Read John 8 & 9

Heavenly Father, we praise You for who You are and that You are with us, especially in our times of trial. Help us to know that all we need to do is call upon You and You answer. We thank You that Jesus came to not only die for our sins but to give us an example of how we should pray and how we should walk before You. You are there, walking with us, at times holding our hand and comforting us. We love You. In the precious name of Jesus we pray. Amen.

OCTOBER 5
THE GATE

John 10:9: I am the gate; whoever enters through me will be saved. He will come in and go out, and find pasture.

A gate allows free access to an area which is surrounded by walls or fencing. People can come and go through gates as long as they are open, but if the gate is closed it is another story. Without a key to open the gate, we might try and find some other way to enter, which probably isn't a good idea because if we are caught we can be arrested or at the very least thrown out. Chapter 10 tells us that the man who enters the sheep pen by the gate is the shepherd of His sheep. The watchman opens the gate for Him. He calls His sheep by name and His sheep follow Him because they know His voice. Anyone who tries to climb in by some other way is a thief and a robber. They try to steal the hearts and minds of people into believing there are many ways to Heaven, but they have no key to enter in except the one they have created. The only gate that opens the pathway to Heaven is Jesus Christ. He is the entrance into eternal life.

Read John10

Jesus, thank You for being the Good Shepherd and giving us the knowledge that You are our protector and we will never perish. Help us realize this and be quiet before You so we will know You better than we know anyone else on this earth. You are the Savior of the world. You answer all who call upon You. In You, we are given the promise of eternal life, which is something we all long for. Death brings great sorrow but knowing You brings great joy. Meet the needs of every one of us today and guide us with Your loving hand. In Your precious name we pray. Amen.

OCTOBER 6
HE WHO BELIEVES IN ME SHALL LIVE

John 11:25-26: Jesus said to her, "I am the resurrection and the life. He who believes in me will live, even though he dies; and whoever lives and believes in me will never die. Do you believe this?"

These verses are the crux of the Christian faith. Jesus Christ is the most unique individual on the face of the earth. The prophecies in the Old Testament that foretold His coming came to pass when He rose from the dead. He was a man who proclaimed to be the Son of the Living God. He said that if we have seen Him, we have seen the Father and that when He left this earth He would send the Holy Spirit to dwell within us. He never told a lie. He healed every person who asked. He raised from the dead at least two persons that we know of, Lazarus and the daughter of Jarius. He knew and knows the thoughts of every person. He bore the weight of a sinful world upon His shoulders. He died a horrific and painful death and shed every ounce of His blood to redeem mankind from the grips of sin and hell. He rose from the dead after three days. He walked among the people and there were many witnesses to His resurrection. He ascended into Heaven and now sits at the right hand of God. He intercedes for us day and night. He is coming back to earth just as He left but next time He will come as King of kings and Lord of lords. He will rule for a thousand years. He will judge the living and the dead when the Book of Life is opened. He will set up His everlasting kingdom, of which there will be no end. Those who believe in Him will be with Him forever. Those who do not will be cast into everlasting darkness where there is weeping and gnashing of teeth. If we believe this, we must live every day as if it is the last day of our lives, for we never know when we will draw our last breath.

Read John 11

Jesus, thank You for Your miracles that give testament to who You are. Thank You for Your words that ring with truth in our hearts. Thank You that you so loved us that You gave Your life so we do not have to suffer the consequences of our sin. Thank You for reconciling us to our Father, and thank You for giving us the hope of eternity where we will live with You in glory forever. Help us to look heaven-ward and call upon You through our triumphs and struggles. By the power of the Holy Spirit, teach us to pray continually. In Your precious name we pray. Amen.

OCTOBER 7
LOVE ONE ANOTHER

John 13:34-35: A new command I give you: Love one another. As I have loved you, so you must love one another. By this all men will know that you are my disciples, if you love one another."

If life doesn't go exactly the way we think it should, sometimes we pout and try to figure out how to make it go our way. In this process, we may not realize that we are not only hurting ourselves but those around us. But when we are in love with Jesus Christ, we give up our old ways. He has offered us love that is unconditional, and with His love it should be an easy thing to love one another. Jesus tells us that when we believe in Him, we are no longer in darkness. He is speaking of the spiritual darkness that blinds us from knowing the true love of God. Love conquers all things. When we tell someone we love them, how can they reject it except that they are so hurt they do not know how to receive it. In those times, Jesus tells us to love even more. True love does not stand in judgment of another. It just gives and gives and gives. We can do this through our faith in Jesus Christ.

Read John 12 & 13

Heavenly Father, when we go through times that overwhelm us, help us look to the cross of Jesus and see His love. Through it all, You guide, love and comfort us. We don't always understand, but in the end we are stronger and love You even more. Thank you for loving us so that we in return can love others. In Jesus precious name we pray. Amen.

OCTOBER 8
OBEYING JESUS

John 14:21: Whoever has my commands and obeys them, he is the one who loves me. He who loves me will be loved by my Father, and I too will love him and show myself to him.

There are only a few times Jesus commands us to do anything, and these should not be difficult tasks when He is Lord of our lives. There is no comparable love on this earth like the love of our Savior. When we serve Him, we realize it's not all about our wants and desires. Chapter 14 teaches us who Jesus is in the Father and who the Holy Spirit is and how they love and guide us. He teaches us that they are three in one, that one doesn't do anything without the other. When we follow the spirit, our body is taken care of as well. Even though it deteriorates with age and eventually dies, our spirit is what lives forever. It is important to pray and know Him so we feed our spirit. As we grow in our walk with the Lord, He teaches us and our spiritual eyes are open.

Read John 14

Heavenly Father, with all of our hearts we come before You. Teach us more about You and Your plan for our lives. Increase our faith so that we grow spiritually stronger and focus on our true purpose for being here. All the cares and battles of this world will one day pass away. Help us to know that as we go through life, You are by our side. We love You and praise you. We thank you for another day and ask that You be glorified in our lives. In Jesus' name we pray. Amen.

OCTOBER 9
NO BRANCH CAN BEAR FRUIT OF ITSELF

John 15:4: Remain in me, and I will remain in you. No branch can bear fruit by itself; it must remain in the vine. Neither can you bear fruit unless you remain in me.

A tree is not a tree without roots, a trunk, branches and leaves. All of these parts make it a whole unit. The roots represent the Father; the trunk, the Son; the branches, the Holy Spirit. It is all one unit and one could not exist without the other and be a tree, yet it has three individual functions. We are the leaves, the product of who they are. Jesus taught that He is the true vine of God, that in Him we grow in the love and knowledge of our Heavenly Father. He tells us this so that His joy will be in us and that our joy may be complete. The joy of God bubbles deep within us when we realize the powerful promise of this scripture. In Him, we are the sons and daughters of God Almighty, the Creator of the universe, the One who is the source of all wisdom and knowledge. When we remain in Him, He remains in us and we will never die.

Read John 15

Jesus, thank You for Your love for us. Open our eyes to Your word and its meaning that we might be full of Your love, and love one another. You are our Savior and we worship You. In Your precious name we pray. Amen.

OCTOBER 10
THE HOLY SPIRIT

John 16:14-15: He will bring glory to me by taking from what is mine and making it known to you. All that belongs to the Father is mine. That is why I said the Spirit will take from what is mine and make it known to you.

The Holy Spirit is referred to only three times in the Old Testament. Once in prayer by David when the Lord convicted him of murder, He asked the Lord not to take His Holy Spirit from Him. The other two times are in Isaiah where it talks about the kindnesses of the Lord towards His chosen people, yet they rebelled and grieved His Holy Spirit; so He turned and became their enemy and He Himself fought against them. Then His people recalled the days of old and asked, "Where is He who set His Holy Spirit among us?" In the New Testament He is referred to close to a hundred times. He overshadowed Mary with His presence and she became the mother of the Son of God. He filled Elizabeth with His power when she was pregnant with John the Baptist. He appeared in the form of a dove when Jesus was baptized. By His power, Jesus rose from the dead. Jesus told the disciples that whenever they were arrested and brought to trial not to worry about what they were going to say because the Holy Spirit would give them the words to speak. After Jesus' ascension into Heaven, the Holy Spirit was sent to dwell within our hearts to teach us about the things of God. He is so precious, so subtle yet so powerful, and we are told that every sin and blasphemy will be forgiven men, but blasphemy against the Spirit will not be forgiven; anyone who speaks against the Holy Spirit will not be forgiven. He is guilty of an eternal sin.

Read John 16

Holy Spirit of God, we thank You for dwelling within us. Fill us with Your power and might, and show us how to pray. Anoint each and every one of us with Your presence and reveal Yourself so that we may walk humbly before our God, yet boldly, with love for all, proclaiming the knowledge that Jesus is the life and the resurrection and that by Him all can be saved if they only believe. In Jesus' name we pray. Amen.

OCTOBER 11
ONE WITH THE FATHER

John 17:11: I will remain in the world no longer, but they are still in the world, and I am coming to you. Holy Father, protect them by the power of your name—the name you gave me—so that they may be one as we are one.

Right before Jesus was handed over for His crucifixion He prayed for not only His disciples but also for all those who were to come after them, who believe in Him and His message. It is a powerful prayer of love. He asked that the Father protect us by the power of His name so that as They are one we may be one with Them. He prayed not that we be taken out of the world but that we be protected from the evil one. He asked that we be brought into complete unity to let the world know that the Father sent Him and loves us as He loves Jesus. We are covered with God's protection by the words of this prayer and there is no reason to get bogged down with the affairs of this world. Our hope is in Jesus Christ. When we raise Him up, He raises us up. He is so wonderful. He loves us with a holy love, a righteous and unconditional love. He freely gives us this love and tells us to love one another.

Read John 17 & 18

Precious Jesus, Your prayer for us reached the throne of God. We thank You that by faith we can become one with You. By the power of the Holy Spirit, may we continually draw closer to You and become the children of God that we are meant to be. Amen.

OCTOBER 12
CONDEMNED

John 19:11: Jesus answered, "You would have no power over me if it were not given to you from above. Therefore the one who handed me over to you is guilty of a greater sin."

After Jesus was arrested, the Jews led Him from Caiaphas to the palace of the Roman governor. They brought Him before Pilate to be condemned to death, but Pilate wasn't too keen on their scheme. He asked Jesus several questions and then came out to the crowd and said, "Look, I am bringing him out to you to let you know I find no basis for a charge against him." There were shouts of, "Crucify! Crucify!" The Jews insisted that according to their law they could not crucify Him because he claimed to be the Son of God. This frightened Pilate and He went back inside the palace to question Jesus again. Jesus' response is our verse for today. He knew why He had come and even though Pilate thought he had the power to release Jesus, he actually had no power at all. The plan of the Father would come to pass, for Jesus came to die. The soldiers twisted together a crown of thorns and put it on his head and clothed Him in a purple robe. He was lead to Golgotha, the place of the skull, and crucified between two thieves. The scripture in Psalm 22:18 came to pass: They divided my garments among them and cast lots for my clothing. Not a bone of His body was broken, for He was the Passover lamb, and this prophecy was also fulfilled in Numbers 9:12 and Psalm 34:20. In Zechariah 12:10, another prophecy came to pass: They will look on me, the One they have pierced. After He rose from the dead, He appeared to Mary and the disciples. John tells us that Jesus did many other miraculous signs in the presence of His disciples which are not recorded in this book, but these are written that we may believe that Jesus is the Christ, the Son of God, and that by believing we may have life in His Name.

Read John 19-21

Heavenly Father, we thank You for Your eternal love. Sometimes there are not enough words to proclaim our love for You. We know that You sent Your Son to shed His blood on the cross for our sins so that we may be reconciled to You. We thank You for Jesus' resurrection which now gives us hope of eternal life. Give us wisdom and increase our faith daily so we will run the good race in Your strength and endure until the end. In the precious name of Jesus we pray. Amen.

OCTOBER 13
JESUS, SON OF THE LIVING GOD

Acts 2:24: But God raised him from the dead, freeing him from the agony of death because it was impossible for death to keep its hold on him.

The Book of Acts begins with an account of Jesus' followers being filled with the Holy Spirit and preaching so effectively that in one day 3,000 people came to Christ. There are stories of the life of the church in Jerusalem, the spread of the Good News of Jesus to Samaria, the activities of Peter and the persecution of believers. The focus then shifts to Paul and his mission to extend the life and teachings of Jesus to non-Jews. Paul's three missionary journeys are shared in detail, ending with his trip to Rome. The power of God was great in the days after Jesus' resurrection. His followers were instructed to stay in the upper room until they were filled with the Holy Spirit. They saw what appeared to be tongues of fire that separated and came to rest on each of them and they were filled with the Holy Spirit and began to speak in tongues. What a sight that must have been! That same power exists today. When we become believers in Christ, we are filled with His Holy Spirit. Jesus was not some great teacher or prophet who taught men how to live good lives. He is the Son of the Living God who came and dwelled among us and showed us how to receive eternal life. It was impossible for death to hold Him. When He rose from the grave, he conquered death forevermore.

Read Acts 1 & 2

Father, thank You for this new day. As we begin our journey through the Book of Acts, reveal the Holy Spirit to us in a new and glorious way. Search our hearts. If there is any sin, cleanse us anew by the blood of Jesus Christ. Fill us with the power of the Holy Spirit and help us to grow each day in the knowledge of who You are. Fill us with Your love so we have endless capacity to serve and love others, until that glorious day when our Savior returns to this earth. In Jesus' precious name we pray. Amen.

OCTOBER 14
SALVATION IN JESUS ALONE

Acts 4:12: Salvation is found in no one else, for there is no other name under heaven given to men by which we must be saved.

God so loved the world that He gave His only begotten Son that whosoever should believe on Him will be saved. Saved from what, some might ask? From death; from eternal separation from God. It is so easy, yet the world makes it so difficult. The world wants to figure it out on their own, find their own way by their own good works and deeds, but scripture tells us that man cannot earn his way to Heaven lest any man should boast, and surely they would. The only One we want to boast about is our Lord and Savior Jesus Christ. He has made it simple to become one of His children. After Jesus' ascension into Heaven, and being filled with the Holy Spirit, the apostles were on fire for God. They were like a fast-moving freight train that could not be stopped. Miracles were performed, yet they took no glory for themselves. They gave Jesus all the glory. We are to live this way, to be excited about our salvation and look upon each day as an opportunity to live for Him. Each morning when we pray, we should ask the Father to reveal His will for the day. He hears and answers in ways that surprise and delight us.

Read Acts 3 & 4

Heavenly Father, thank You for Your plan of salvation. It came at a high cost for Jesus, but now He is sitting in glory on Your right hand and is our intercessor. He is the only One worthy to be there. Thank You for Your incomparable love and for giving us the ability to accept and believe in faith that all You say is true. Help us to continually be a light for Jesus, in whose precious name we pray. Amen.

OCTOBER 15
HIS WITNESSES

Acts 5:31-32: God exalted Him to His own right hand as Prince and Savior that he might give repentance and forgiveness of sins to Israel. We are witnesses of these things, and so is the Holy Spirit, whom God has given to those who obey Him.

When a person takes the stand in court and raises their right hand to swear to tell the truth, they are proclaiming knowledge of something relating to a person or fact about which he or she will testify. The Holy Spirit is present in the world and reveals that Jesus Christ is the Son of God. He gives witness to the truth of God's Word, which enables us to be witnesses for Jesus. The Spirit descended as a dove on Jesus when He was baptized. By the power of the Spirit, temptation was overcome and Jesus Christ rose from the dead. The disciples were so filled with the Holy Spirit that they preached without fear of retribution. Even when they were flogged and instructed not to speak in the name of Jesus, they rejoiced that they were worthy to be punished for His Name, and they continued to preach and heal in the name of Jesus. Those who walked with Jesus witnessed all that He said and did. We are blessed to have all of this written down so we can read and reread the words that lead to eternal life with Him.

Read Acts 5 & 6

Heavenly Father, give us boldness, with love and compassion, to be witnesses for our faith in Jesus Christ, to be as the apostles of old who proclaimed Jesus and did mighty and wonderful works in His name, without fear, because they knew whom they served. In Jesus' name we pray. Amen.

OCTOBER 16
CONSEQUENCES

Acts 7:57: At this they covered their ears and, yelling at the top of their voices, they all rushed at him, dragged him out of the city and began to stone him.

Stephen was a man full of God's grace and power. He performed great wonders and miraculous signs among the people. Because of their jealousy, members of the Synagogue of Freedman seized Stephen and brought him to the Sanhedrin, which would be equivalent to our Congress. When they accused Stephen, he spoke of the history of God's chosen people and how they rejected God's ways then and do so this very day. Stephen then looked upward and the heavens opened. He beheld the Father on the throne with Jesus seated on His right hand. When Stephen declared this truth, what happened is found in today's scripture. Stephen was stoned to death for his faith. Although stoning for our faith in this country does not happen, at this very moment there are many in other lands who are persecuted and killed because they proclaim the Gospel. The world does not want to hear about it, but He will be proclaimed until the day He appears in the clouds and every eye beholds Him. When we are ridiculed, called Jesus freaks, holier than thou or judgmental, with our eyes firmly fixed on Jesus we must pray and ask for His love and strength. The enemy comes in like a flood and tries to cause us to doubt, but we know whom we believe. It is our responsibility to speak the word when the Holy Spirit guides us to do so, just as Stephen did, regardless of the consequences.

Read Acts 7

Heavenly Father, illuminate our hearts and fill them to overflowing with the power of the Holy Spirit so that we will have boldness to proclaim Your word, not in damnation to others but in love. We ask that You give us greater measures of faith so there is no doubt in our hearts and minds who we belong to. Eternity is our goal and we want all who will listen to know about it as well. We praise and honor You. In Jesus' precious name, we pray. Amen.

OCTOBER 17
PERSECUTION

Acts 9:16: "I will show him how much he must suffer for my name."

These words were spoken to Ananias, who was told to go to Saul (later Paul), and lay hands on him to receive his sight. At first, Ananias balked at going because he knew who Saul was but He obeyed the Lord and went. After Stephen was stoned, the church was persecuted and Saul was the main person who carried out the persecutions. His reputation among Christians was well known and they feared him. But on the road to Damascus, there was a transformation of Saul from persecutor to believer in the Lord Jesus Christ. From that point on, He never once doubted that Jesus is the Son of the Living God. Most of us do not have a road to Damascus experience where the Lord actually appears and speaks to us, but when we ask Jesus into our hearts our lives are changed. It is by faith that we receive and believe this. Jesus promised to never leave nor forsake us. He does this through the Holy Spirit. This does not mean we will not be tempted and that life will be a bowl of cherries with no trials. We will have joyous and happy times but troubles will also come. We are like gold that is being refined. When the refining process is finished, it shines for all to see and desire.

Read Acts 8 & 9

Heavenly Father, thank You for being with us through good times and bad. When we cry out to You, we know You hear and answer. Increase our faith so that we grow every day in our knowledge of You. Help us to be the witnesses for You that You want us to be. In the precious name of Jesus, we pray. Amen.

OCTOBER 18
NO FAVORITISM WITH THE LORD

Acts 10:34-35, 42-43: Then Peter began to speak, "I now realize how true it is that God does not show favoritism but accepts men from every nation who fear him and do what is right. . .He (Jesus) commanded us to preach to the people and to testify that He is the one whom God appointed as judge of the living and the dead. All the prophets testify about Him that everyone who believes in Him receives forgiveness of sins through His name."

Peter is given a vision of unclean animals and is told by the Lord to go to the house of a Gentile to preach the good news of Jesus Christ. He does so without hesitation. Our verses today are some of the words that Peter spoke to the Gentiles who accepted Christ as their Savior. As believers, it may be difficult to share with those who do not believe because they seem so sure of who they are or they seemingly have their act together, but we all need a Savior. We all have a desire for something beyond ourselves. The Lord has instilled that in us whether we realize it or not. When Peter went to the house of Cornelius, he had no idea why he was going or what he was to say but he trusted God, and when he opened his mouth the words of salvation were proclaimed. Most people who want to know about God ask. As Christians, we are to be loving and kind to everyone. We are also to be blameless before the Lord, to be witnesses to His miraculous gift of salvation and to speak when He guides us to speak.

Read Acts 10 & 11

Heavenly Father, we love You. Thank You for Your presence in our lives. We lift up Your Holy Name and pray for wisdom. Give us a heart to lovingly share the Gospel with those who do not know You. Continually fill us with the Holy Spirit so we are not only witnesses for Jesus by our words but by the way we live, so that others who do not know You will see something different in us and yearn to know You as well. In Jesus' precious name we pray. Amen.

OCTOBER 19
POWER OVER DEATH

Acts 13:30-31: But God raised Him (Jesus) from the dead, and for many days He was seen by those who had traveled with him from Galilee to Jerusalem. They are now His witnesses to our people.

There are only two people in the Bible who did not die. Enoch walked with God and was no more because God took him away (Genesis 5:24). Elijah and Elisha were walking together and suddenly a chariot of fire and horses of fire appeared and Elijah went up to heaven in a whirlwind (2 Kings 2:11). What a sight that must have been! And then there is Jesus, who even though He died, He rose again. It happened this way because there was no other way to save mankind from their sins, from death, and from an eternity without God. We all have a date when our physical bodies will die, but when we believe in the resurrection of Jesus Christ our spirits live forever and we will be with the Lord in His Heavenly Kingdom for eternity.

Read Acts 12-14

Heavenly Father, we know we are not Enoch or Elijah. So thank You for Your plan of redemption; for everyone who believes on the name of Jesus Christ will be saved. What a glorious promise, to know that when we leave this earth we will be with you in glory. Thank You for Your love, for Your gifts and for opening our eyes to receive Jesus as our Savior. We love you, and pray this in His precious name. Amen.

OCTOBER 20
WHAT MUST WE DO TO BE SAVED

Acts 16:30-31: He then brought them out and asked, "Sirs, what must I do to be saved?" They replied, Believe in the Lord Jesus, and you will be saved—you and your household."

Paul had been preaching the Gospel to the Jews and to the Gentiles, traveling to many cities. At times he was accompanied by Barnabas and Silas. At one point, Paul and Silas were being followed by a slave girl who had a spirit by which she could predict the future and she kept following them saying, "These men are servants of the Most High God." Paul was troubled by this. He turned around and rebuked the spirit and it came out of her. The owners of the slave girl saw she would no longer benefit them and immediately had Paul and Silas arrested and flogged. In prison, they began singing hymns to the Lord and an angel came to set them free. When the guard thought that all the prisoners had fled, he started to kill himself but Paul called out saying they were all still there. The guard then asked Paul what must he do to be saved. We may never be imprisoned, but these chapters show us that even during times of trouble we should sing praises and hymns to the Most High God and He will deliver us.

Read Acts 15 & 16

Heavenly Father, help us grow in our faith, to love Jesus more and more each day and to know that no matter what we are going through, no matter what our struggles, You are our deliverer. You know all things and You are with us to uphold us and strengthen us. Help us to not look at our circumstances but know that all things work together for good to those who love the Lord. We ask this in Jesus' name. Amen.

OCTOBER 21
THE UNKNOWN GOD

Acts 17:23: For as I walked around and looked carefully at your objects of worship, I even found an altar with this inscription: To an unknown god. Now what you worship as something unknown I am going to proclaim to you.

The unknown can be frightening. A dark alley is a place we wouldn't want to walk down because we don't know what might be lurking there. The future is unknown and there are those who consult mediums in hopes of finding out what lies ahead so they can prepare for it. There are many unknowns in life, yet we cannot hide from them in fear. Paul was in Athens and greatly distressed to see that the city was full of idols. He tried reasoning with the Jews and God-fearing Greeks but they thought he was advocating foreign gods when they heard him preaching the good news about Jesus and the resurrection. So they brought him to a meeting where they wanted to know what he was talking about. He revealed to them that their unknown god was the God who made the world and everything in it; that He is the Lord of heaven and earth and does not live in temples built by hands. After hearing these things, a few of them became followers of Paul and believed what he taught. He also preached in Thessalonica. If we have any doubts about the unknown God, we should be like those in Thessalonica who received Paul's message with great eagerness and examined the Scriptures every day to see if what he said is true. The Word of God reveals the unknown God of all creation and we receive the promise of eternal life by knowing Him.

Read Acts 17 & 18

Heavenly Father, we know that with You there are no mistakes and that everything in Heaven and on this earth is in perfect order. It is by choice that men serve You or do not serve You. We thank You for calling us and opening our eyes to who You are. Guide and keep us. Show us how to love others as You love us. Help us to live by example as well as words and deeds so those in the world will see the love of Jesus Christ through us. We pray this in His precious name. Amen.

OCTOBER 22
THE TASK BEFORE US

Acts 20:24: However, I consider my life worth nothing to me, if only I may finish the race and complete the task the Lord Jesus has given me—the task of testifying to the gospel of God's grace.

Paul was focused on his calling to the Lord Jesus Christ to preach and teach the gospel wherever he went. After his conversion, he was no longer known as the one who persecuted Christians. He was now persecuted for his faith. It grieved him greatly when he preached the gospel, left that place and returned only to find that those who had believed had turned away to worshiping other gods. He admonished those who first believed but now had fallen away, in order to bring them back to the faith. Although we may not be like Paul, we have the same calling in the sense that we are to live dedicated to the Lord, to be available to Him and do as He directs. It is an adventure to serve Him. He leads us in ways that we do not always know the outcome but we know we can trust Him. Paul was told by the Holy Spirit that he would be beaten and imprisoned for his preaching but he went boldly, knowing that if only one person came to the faith it was worth it all. Paul's responsibility was to be obedient to his calling, just as we are to be obedient. We are to stand firm in the truth of God in hopes that all will come to repentance and have faith in the Lord Jesus Christ.

Read Acts 19 & 20

Heavenly Father, draw us closer to You. Teach us how to live dedicated lives of faith; to love You with all of our hearts, minds and souls and to not lean to our own understanding. Your ways are higher than our ways. At times we struggle with the difficulties of this life, but we ask that You lift us up in the palm of Your strong hand and encourage us daily as we read Your word and get to know You more and more. Thank You for loving us and giving us Your precious Son Jesus, in whose name we pray. Amen.

OCTOBER 23
UNWAVERING FAITH

Acts 26:16: Now get up and stand on your feet. I have appeared to you to appoint you as a servant and as a witness of what you have seen of me and what I will show you.

These are the words of Jesus spoken to Paul on the road to Damascus. The next few chapters tell of Paul's journeys as he traveled from place to place, spreading the gospel with faith and conviction. He preached everywhere he went. He taught that God has given us the Spirit as a deposit guaranteeing what is to come and that we live by faith and not by sight. He spent his final days in Rome. Tradition has it that he was martyred, perhaps beheaded. By faith, we become followers of Jesus Christ and desire the things that are eternal. The world does not understand who He is or why He came because they do not know Him. They would rather live their own lives, fumbling along the way, trying to fix what is broken and also enjoying the blessings that they don't even realize come from Him. The only way to have true peace is to know Jesus. Without knowledge of His Word we starve because we need nourishment, and the Word of God is nourishment for our souls and spirits. We keep the faith by reading God's word daily and learning of Him.

Read Acts 21-28

Heavenly Father, help us to be in an attitude of prayer throughout the day. May we be faithful followers of Jesus, just as Paul was. Help us not wander away from our faith in directions that You have not called us to go. Thank You for opening our eyes to who Jesus is so we may believe His promises and look forward to the day when He returns to this earth. We love You and thank You, in Jesus' precious name. Amen.

OCTOBER 24
EVIL

Romans 1:28-32: Furthermore, since they did not think it worthwhile to retain the knowledge of God, he gave them over to a depraved mind, to do what ought not to be done. They have become filled with every kind of wickedness, evil, greed, and depravity. They are full of envy, murder, strife, deceit and malice. They are gossips, slanderers, God-haters, insolent, arrogant and boastful; they invent ways of doing evil; they disobey their parents; they are senseless, faithless, heartless, ruthless. Although, they know God's righteous decree that those who do such things deserve death, they not only continue to do these very things but also approve of those who practice them.

If we ever wondered how people can be so cruel to another, the answer lies in this scripture. When there is no knowledge of God, people do not believe that there is a judgment, or a God who is full of righteousness and love. Without God, our inner desire is self-gratification. When we search and find something that we think will fill that desire, we realize it doesn't and so we search some more. It's all about "me." To the extreme, this results in murder, school shootings, teen suicide, infidelity, and the list goes on. The good news is that through the power of Jesus Christ, our hearts and minds are changed from self-centeredness and our eyes are turned to Him. God moves mountains for those who love Him. He is a God of miracles and nothing is impossible for Him. Though there will always be those who are described in the above scripture until the day that Jesus returns, to those who love Him all His promises are true and they will reap the rewards of their service to Him in eternity.

Read Romans 1

Heavenly Father, we lift up Your name on high and glorify You. Your ways are higher than our ways and Your thoughts higher than our thoughts. There are many hurting people in this world who have been touched by sorrow and tragedy. Comfort them that they might experience the presence and power of Your transforming love. In their time of need, draw them to you and wrap Your loving arms around them. In Jesus' name we pray. Amen.

OCTOBER 25
MAN JUSTIFIED BEFORE GOD

Romans 3:21-26: But now righteousness from God, apart from law, has been made known, to which the Law and the Prophets testify. This righteousness from God comes through faith in Jesus Christ to all who believe. There is no difference, for all have sinned and fall short of the glory of God and are justified freely by his grace through the redemption that came by Christ Jesus. God presented him as a sacrifice of atonement, through faith in his blood. He did this to demonstrate his justice, because in his forbearance he had left the sins committed beforehand unpunished. He did it to demonstrate his justice at the present time, so as to be just and the one who justifies those who have faith in Jesus.

Paul was writing to the Romans explaining the difference between living by the law and living by faith, and how man is now justified before God by the blood of Jesus Christ that saves all from sin if they believe in Him. In the Old Testament, the chosen of God were required to offer sacrifices on the altar for their sins. They had a high priest who would go into what was known as the Holy of Holies to intercede for God's people and they would literally shed the blood of animals for cleansing of their sin. But now, through the sacrifice of Jesus Christ, all men are justified before God. Jesus accomplished this once and for all, so that all are free to receive. As followers of Jesus Christ, we are called to righteousness and to be an example of what it means to be a sinner saved by grace. We cannot do this in our own strength. We have to rely on the power of the Holy Spirit. We now live by faith, not by sight.

Read Romans 2 & 3

Jesus, we thank You so much for Your sacrifice. Help us to live the lives that you intend for us. Amidst the turmoil in the world these days, help us find comfort in the knowledge that You are who You say You are and no matter what we see with our eyes and hear with our ears, we can stand strong knowing that You are in control and nothing we do can change that. In Your precious name we pray. Amen.

OCTOBER 26
FAITH IN CHRIST

Romans 4:25-5:2: He was delivered over to death for our sins and was raised to life for our justification. Therefore, since we have been justified through faith, we have peace with God through our Lord Jesus Christ, through whom we have gained access by faith into this grace in which we now stand. And we rejoice in the hope of the glory of God.

Faith comes by hearing and hearing by the Word of God. Faith is being sure of what we hope for and certain of what we do not see. By faith, we understand that the universe was formed at God's command, so that what is seen was not made out of what is visible. Without faith, it is impossible to please God. Faith is something we have without visible proof that it exists. We cannot prove that God exists by sight because no man has seen His face. But if we look around us, we can see evidence of His existence. He spoke the world into existence and made the greater light for daylight and the lesser for the night. He created the animals, the land, the sea, and the clouds that produce rain. Faith is trusting that our Father is in Heaven; that He sent His Son to die for our sins; and that He sent the Holy Spirit to reveal the Son. We believe in Christ by faith. We know there's a heaven and hell by reading God's Word and believing by faith that it is the truth. It doesn't take faith to know that we will die one day. We see it happen every single day. Just open the paper to the obituary page. We are justified by faith in Jesus Christ, and we do not fear death because we know by faith we will enter His everlasting kingdom.

Read Romans 4 & 5

Heavenly Father, we thank You that we were born at this time in history and that we have Your word to read so we know Your purpose for our lives. Put within us a desire to grow in the knowledge of who we are in You that we might spread the love and message of Jesus Christ to all who want to receive it. Guide us by Your Holy Spirit and help us to walk humbly before You. In the precious name of Jesus we pray. Amen.

OCTOBER 27
WAGES OF SIN ARE DEATH

Romans 6:23: For the wages of sin is death, but the gift of God is eternal life in Christ Jesus our Lord.

After 70 years of exile in Babylon, a remnant of God's people returned to Jerusalem. After only 18 years, they became discouraged and destitute, until the Lord spoke by the prophet Haggai about their situation. Now this is what the Lord Almighty says, "Give careful thought to your ways. You have planted much but have harvested little. You eat but never have enough. You drink but never have your fill. You put on clothes but are not warm. You earn wages only to put them in a purse with holes in it" (Haggai 1:5-6). The people had put their own needs before the Lord's, which is why they were suffering. The wages they worked for were to build their own houses and not the temple of the Lord (Haggai 1:9). Once they realized this, they began rebuilding the temple and their situation changed dramatically. It didn't matter that the temple was small compared to the one Solomon had built (Haggai 2:6-9). So how does this relate to our own walk with the Lord? Too often we work to meet our own needs first and give to God what is left over, when it should be the other way around. The wages we work for should be those which lead to the gift of eternal life (Proverbs 10:16 & 11:18). We do that by putting the Lord first in our lives.

Read Romans 6

Jesus, help us to put You first and foremost in our lives. Forgive us for forgetting that when we seek first the kingdom of God all of the other things we need will be added to us. Thank you for willingly coming to this earth to set everyone free from the grip of sin. You know the trials and temptations we face. We ask that You shower us daily with the power of the Holy Spirit so that we do not succumb to our sinful natures any longer but look to You for strength and guidance. We pray this in Your precious name. Amen.

OCTOBER 28
THE LAW OF THE SPIRIT

Romans 7:4: So, my brothers, you also died to the law through the body of Christ, that you might belong to another, to him who was raised from the dead, in order that we might bear fruit to God.

Unless we are born again, we cannot see the kingdom of God. Flesh gives birth to flesh but the Spirit gives birth to spirit. Therefore we should not be surprised when Jesus says we must be born again. The wind blows wherever it pleases. We hear its sound but we cannot tell where it comes from or where it is going, and so it is with everyone born of the Spirit. Paul writes about the law that pertains to our natural body and the law of the Spirit. Though we cannot see our Heavenly Father, by faith in Jesus Christ we can know Him. One day we will be changed in a moment, in the twinkling of an eye, from flesh to spirit. The things of this world will no longer exist, such as lying, stealing, cheating, crying, sickness, to mention only a few. As we grow in our spiritual lives, the things we cannot see become as real as the things we see.

Read Romans 7

Holy Spirit, thank You for guiding us in the ways of our Heavenly Father. We pray You would open our eyes to see what You are doing in our lives each day. Illuminate our minds so our thoughts are the thoughts of our Lord and the fruits we produce are spiritual fruits. Increase our faith, knowledge and understanding so that we might die daily to self. We ask this all in the precious name of Jesus. Amen.

OCTOBER 29
NO CONDEMNATION IN CHRIST JESUS

Romans 8:1-2: Therefore, there is now no condemnation for those who are in Christ Jesus because through Christ Jesus the law of the Spirit of life set me free from the law of sin and death.

If someone commits murder or does some other heinous act, they will most likely go to prison and be condemned to die. What we don't realize is that the minute we are born, we are all condemned to die because we are born under the curse of sin and death. But thank God for Jesus Christ, for God did not send Him into the world to condemn it but to save it through Him. As He hung on the cross, the chief priests, the teachers of the law and the elders mocked Him saying, "He saved others but He can't save Himself. If He's the King of Israel, let Him come down now from the cross and we will believe in Him. He trusts in God so let God rescue Him now." They did not understand that this is why He came and that it was not time for Him to set up His earthly kingdom. If He did not first die, He would never have risen and given us the hope of eternal life through Him.

Read Romans 8 & 9

Heavenly Father, we thank You for the Apostle Paul who changed from the one that persecuted believers to the one who became a staunch believer. You used him in many ways, to write Your words and to teach us the ways of Christ. Thank You for Your faithfulness in giving us Your Holy Word. Give us a hunger and desire to study and absorb it so that we are filled to overflowing with who You are, and when the enemy of our souls comes against us we are prepared to fight the spiritual battles that are taking place. We love You and praise You. In the precious name of Jesus, we pray. Amen.

OCTOBER 30
ATTITUDES OF THE HEART

Romans 10:9-10: That if you confess with your mouth, "Jesus is Lord," and believe in your heart that God raised him from the dead, you will be saved. For it is with your heart that you believe and are justified, and it is with your mouth that you confess and are saved.

When we believe with our heart that Jesus is Lord, we are saved. This doesn't happen by the words that we speak or the things we do. It's what's in the heart. The Lord searches every heart and understands every motive behind the thoughts (1Chronicles 28:9). That is why He is the only righteous judge. The sacrifices of God are a broken spirit and a broken and contrite heart He will not despise (Psalm 51:17). A happy heart makes the face cheerful, but heartache crushes the spirit (Proverbs 15:13). What we see on the outside of someone is a reflection of the inward heart. Are we sad, happy, spiteful, gracious, greedy, generous, mean, kind? All of these come out of the heart. The word of God is living and active, sharper than any double-edged sword. It penetrates even to dividing soul and spirit, joints and marrow. It judges the thoughts and attitudes of the heart (Hebrews 4:12). We build walls around our heart when we are hurt. Instead of turning to the Lord, we allow our hearts to harden. We miss so much when we do this because life is a cascade of hurts in one form or another. We end up all alone when we allow our hearts to become closed off to God, because He has the power to heal and set us free.

Read Romans 10 & 11

Heavenly Father, we thank You that You know us so well that You even know the thoughts and attitudes of our heart. Help us to be completely open and honest with You because as hard as we might try we cannot hide from You. Teach us to pray with fervency and give us a burning desire to study Your word so the walls we have built around our hearts come tumbling down and we are set free. In Jesus' precious name, we pray. Amen.

OCTOBER 31
DO NOT CONFORM TO THIS WORLD

Romans 12:2: Do not conform any longer to the pattern of this world, but be transformed by the renewing of your mind. Then you will be able to test and approve what God's will is—his good, pleasing and perfect will.

Jesus told His disciples that the Counselor, the Holy Spirit, whom the Father will send in His name, will teach them all things and will remind them of everything He said to them (John 14:26). This is the same Holy Spirit that reveals the hidden secrets of our hearts, the things that we need to confess and ask forgiveness for. When we begin this journey with Him, we see things differently. The movies we used to watch don't appeal to us anymore. The jokes we used to laugh at aren't funny. This is just the tip of the iceberg when it comes to transformation. It is a process that takes a lifetime. As long as we live, there will be a battle with our flesh and spirit. The spirit is willing but the flesh is weak. When the Holy Spirit resides in our hearts, we overcome, and at the last trumpet sound we will be changed. The perishable must clothe itself with the imperishable and the mortal with immortality. Then the saying that is written will come true: Death has been swallowed up in victory (1 Corinthians 15:51-54).

Read Romans 12

Heavenly Father, we praise You. Your holiness is overwhelming at times but by faith we know You love us and have redeemed us. Transform us by the power of the Holy Spirit and give us an unquenchable desire to fill our hearts and minds with the truth of Your Word. In Jesus' precious name we pray. Amen.

NOVEMBER 1
NONE LIVES TO HIMSELF ALONE

Romans 14:7: For none of us lives to himself alone and none of us dies to himself alone.

If we were left alone as babies, we would soon die, for we need someone to feed and clothe us, to hold us and give us love. Those who live without human companionship become eccentric and lonely. They are unable to live in society because they don't know how to interact with others. We are not an island that is stuck out in the middle of the ocean somewhere, all alone with nowhere else to go. We might think we can do everything by ourselves, but when we try we soon become irritated and exhausted. Taking a trip is much more enjoyable when we do it with someone else. Family and friends make life interesting, especially with all the drama that's involved; but we love each other anyway! God did not give us life to be alone. When we come to know Jesus, we are never alone. The Lord promised Joshua that He Himself went before him and was with him. He said He would never leave nor forsake him. He told him not be afraid and not be discouraged. That promise is ours as well. If we live, we live to the Lord; and if we die, we die to the Lord. So whether we live or die, we belong to the Lord. He was with us when we were born and He is with us when we die

Read Romans 13 & 14

Heavenly Father, help us realize we are not our own but that we were bought with a price, the precious blood of Jesus Christ. Give us the desire to serve You with all of our hearts, minds and souls and lean not to our own understanding. May we be quiet before You; listen and follow when You speak. We ask this in Jesus' precious name. Amen.

NOVEMBER 2
OVERFLOWING WITH HOPE

Romans 15:13: May the God of hope fill you with all joy and peace as you trust in Him, so that you may overflow with hope by the power of the Holy Spirit.

Hope is desire accompanied with expectation of obtaining what is desired, or belief that it is obtainable. It is something in which we can place confidence or trust. We obtain hope by the power of the Holy Spirit. Without hope, life has no purpose. Christianity is different from any other religion on earth. We do not find hope in ourselves or in an inanimate statue that cannot see or hear. We do not find hope in dead prophets or in a god who requires its people to become martyrs by killing others who do not believe the way they do. None of those things bring hope. They cannot save us from the death that awaits us. The hope we have is that we have been changed into the image of Christ because we have been invaded by the Spirit of the Living God, who promises an eternity with Him.

Read Romans 15 & 16

Heavenly Father, thank You for the hope we have in You. When we pray and seem not to receive an answer, help us realize that You know why that is, and that we need to trust that You will answer. Our hope is eternal. We may not always understand Your ways or why we are even alive, but You know. Thank You for life and for the plans that You have for us. We pray in Jesus' name. Amen.

NOVEMBER 3
THE POWER OF THE CROSS

1 Corinthians 1:18: For the message of the cross is foolishness to those who are perishing, but to us who are being saved it is the power of God.

The cross is a powerful reminder that Jesus Christ died for the sins of the world. For those who do not believe this, they have worked long and hard to have crosses removed from the public domain. Even though they have been somewhat successful in doing this, it does not change what Christ did on the cross. In the first two chapters of 1 Corinthians, Paul talks about the foolishness of man and the wisdom of God, how God uses the foolish things of this world to confound the so-called wise. An unbeliever cannot comprehend what the cross of Jesus is all about unless they have the Holy Spirit. They have no understanding of the Spirit that is drawing them to the love of God. We all struggle for something or someone beyond ourselves. If that were not true, there would be no such thing as American Idol or the myriad of television shows that make idols out of people. God is the only reality that fills that void. The cross represents not only the death of Jesus Christ but His resurrection and it gives purpose and meaning to our lives. For God, through Jesus, reconciled to Himself all things, whether things on earth or things in Heaven, by making peace through the blood of Jesus that was shed on the cross (Colossians 1:20).

Read 1 Corinthians 1 & 2

Thank You, Jesus, for everything You have done for us. Our hope is in You, the One who shed Your blood on the cross; the One who rose from the dead and now sits at the right hand of the Father. Open our eyes to see and ears to hear the Holy Spirit who resides within us and reveals Your resurrection power. In Your precious name we pray, Amen.

NOVEMBER 4
WE ARE GOD'S TEMPLE

1 Corinthians 3:16-17: Don't you know that you yourselves are God's temple and that God's Spirit lives in you? If anyone destroys God's temple, God will destroy him; for God's temple is sacred, and you are that temple.

In the days of animal sacrifice, the temple was the place where the Jews came to offer a perfect lamb or dove on the altar for their sins. But the temple was not only the outer building, it also contained the Holy of Holies, the inner sanctum where only the high priest could go. At the moment of Jesus death, the veil of the temple was torn and that inner sanctum was exposed. The law of God was fulfilled and animal sacrifice was replaced by the blood of Jesus. It is now possible to live a righteousness life because we don't have to depend on ourselves to do it. We depend on the Spirit of God. When the Holy Spirit dwells within us, we become God's Holy Temple.

Read 1 Corinthians 3 & 4

Heavenly Father, we thank You for the life You have given to each and every one of us. Help us to use that life to give glory and honor to You. Teach us to pray and to be filled with the power and presence of the precious Holy Spirit so that our bodies, the temple of God, give honor to You. We love you, Lord, and pray this in Jesus' precious name. Amen.

NOVEMBER 5
BEING A CHRISTIAN

1 Corinthians 5:9-11: I have written you in my letter not to associate with sexually immoral people—not at all meaning the people of this world who are immoral, or the greedy and swindlers, or idolaters. In that case you would have to leave this world. But now I am writing you that you must not associate with anyone who calls himself a brother but is sexually immoral or greedy, an idolater or a slanderer, a drunkard or a swindler. With such a man do not even eat.

Paul is writing a letter to the Corinthians because they have gone astray from their love for Jesus Christ and they have allowed sin to come into their congregation without reproving it. In chapters 5 and 6, he explains how important it is to live a pure life in our bodies. These people had gone so far away from the Lord they were allowing an incestuous relationship to exist within their church and Paul was admonishing them that this is absolutely not allowed. He told them to hand this man over to Satan so that the sinful nature may be destroyed and his spirit saved on the day of the Lord. Paul was adamant that they were to stay away from those who call themselves Christians and do such things—immorality, greedy, swindlers or idolaters. When someone says they are a Christian, they are to live the way of Christ and not the way of the world. By associating in any way with them it is like saying it is really all right. But Paul did not admonish us to stay away from those in the world who do such things. Perhaps because by the way we live and love others, we may persuade them to become followers of Christ by our actions, deeds, and words. There is a fine line for each of us to walk as Christians. The temptations of this world are very great and the enemy of our soul works overtime when we become followers of Christ to try and make us look like fools, to dishearten us and make us think we are unworthy. But that is all a lie of the devil, who is not even worthy of our consideration. We must pray continually that the Lord guide and keep us in His way so we do not fall for the tricks of the enemy and we are an example to the world of who and what a Christian is.

Read 1 Corinthians 5 & 6

Jesus, we come humbly into Your presence this day, thanking You for a new and glorious morning. We lift up Your mighty and majestic name. We ask forgiveness for our sins before You in action and in thought. We are all sinners but we know and believe that You came to die for our sins so that we may come before the Father knowing that we are cleansed by Your blood. Help us keep our eyes on the Cross of Calvary and to know that we are bought with a price. Help us also to be witnesses for You as long as we walk upon this earth. Check our spirits when we are prone to wander. In Your precious name we pray. Amen.

NOVEMBER 6
THE EVERLASTING CROWN

1 Corinthians 9:24-25: Do you not know that in a race all the runners run, but only one gets the prize? Run in such a way as to get the prize. Everyone who competes in the games goes into strict training. They do it to get a crown that will not last; but we do it to get a crown that will last forever.

When Paul wrote this passage, he was talking about himself and his calling to preach the gospel and how he became all things to all people in order to possibly win them to the Lord. This applies to us as well in our walk with the Lord. When a runner trains to win a race, he does it with fervor and single-mindedness. He has a single focus in order to win that race. He learns how to use every muscle in his body to gain the most speed. We too are running a race, the race of life. Our goal should be to train fervently, to read and know the Word, to pray and be prepared when the time comes to share the Gospel with those who want to hear. Our race does not end until the day we leave this earth so we need to train continually. The reward for our training is the crown that lasts forever.

Read 1 Corinthians 7-9

Heavenly Father, help us to train with all our hearts for this race called life. Give us a fervent desire to read Your word and bind it to our hearts, to pray and draw closer to You so that when You give us the opportunity to share Your word with others, we are prepared to do so. There are so many needs in the lives of each of us. You know them all. Please meet those needs. Give us strength to carry on until the end for we know what awaits us. In Jesus' precious name. Amen.

NOVEMBER 7
NO TEMPTATION BEYOND WHAT WE CAN BEAR

1 Corinthians 10:13: No temptation has seized you except what is common to man. And God is faithful; he will not let you be tempted beyond what you can bear. But when you are tempted, he will also provide a way out so that you can stand up under it.

Our Lord is so merciful that when temptations come our way, He provides a way of escape. We are all tempted. The problem is not the temptation but what we do with it when it comes. Do we look to ourselves and ponder it and let it take hold of our hearts and our minds so that we are powerless over it and take the wrong path, or do we look temptation squarely in the eye and cry out to our Father for strength to show us the way out of it so that we can please Him. The devil searches for ways to tempt us away from our walk with Jesus, even as he did when Jesus was in the desert fasting and praying. He was so brazen, he told Jesus that if He would bow down and worship him all these kingdoms would be His. How ludicrous. Everything already belonged to Jesus. It wasn't Satan's to give away but yet he tried to deceive even our Lord, and he tries to deceive us that much more. When temptation comes our way, we should not let it take hold in our minds and hearts, lest the seeds be planted and it grows uncontrollably. Our Father will not tempt us beyond what we can bear. He always provides a way of escape.

Read 1 Corinthians 10 & 11

Father, thank You for the prayer Jesus taught us: Lord, lead us not into temptation but deliver us. Your Word is true and full of the knowledge of who You are. Continually fill our hearts and minds with Your truth so that when the tempter comes, we are ready for the battle. In Jesus' precious name we pray. Amen.

NOVEMBER 8
DIFFERENT CALLINGS, THE SAME LORD

1 Corinthians 12:4-6: There are different kinds of gifts, but the same Spirit. There are different kinds of service, but the same Lord. There are different kinds of working, but the same God works all of them in all men.

We are all special to the Lord. When He gave us life, He had a purpose in mind. The Bible says He knows the very count of hairs on our head. Even if we spent an entire week, we couldn't figure that one out. By the time we finished counting, new ones would have grown in and who knows how many would have fallen out. Chapter 12 teaches us about how we are one body but with different functions. If we are a hand, a foot, an eye, or any other part, we serve a particular function. All parts make up the body. When one part is missing, the entire body suffers. Because we are not preachers or teachers of the Word does not mean we cannot lead someone to Christ or share our faith. The Psalms give us insight into who the Father is. The Gospels teach us about Jesus. We learn from the apostles how to follow our Lord and discover our calling. We are to follow the innermost desire of our heart because that is where the Spirit resides. He gives all of us gifts and a desire to use them like no one else, not for our own glory but for His. If it is to be a mother or father, we should do it with all our heart as unto the Lord. If it is to be a teller at a bank, a clerk at a store, a doctor, a soldier, yes, even a politician, we should do it to the best of our ability, all the while praying for God to show us how we can use our calling to best serve Him. This life is not a game to play, to just pass the time mindlessly trying to figure out what we can do next to satisfy our own desires. Our calling is to love the Lord our God with all our mind, soul and spirit.

Read 1 Corinthians 12

Heavenly Father, whatever our calling in life, may we never forget that we are a part of the body of Christ and we each fulfill a purpose. By the power of Your Spirit, give us wisdom and teach us to pray with a whole heart, to seek Your face and to know Your will. We love You and want our lives to please You. Give us each a task to do this day that brings honor and glory to Your kingdom. In Jesus' name we pray. Amen.

NOVEMBER 9
LOVE

1 Corinthians 13:4-7: Love is patient, love is kind. It does not envy, it does not boast, it is not proud. It is not rude, it is not self-seeking, it is not easily angered, it keeps no record of wrongs. Love does not delight in evil but rejoices with the truth. It always protects, always trusts, always hopes, always perseveres.

Love can be described as the benevolence attributed to God as being like a father's affection for his children; also, men's adoration of God in gratitude and devotion. This is love: not that we loved God but that He loved us and sent His Son as an atoning sacrifice for our sins (1 John 4:10). In our human way of love, we often put conditions. Sometimes we want to be loved more than we can give love. Love is God's greatest attribute. He is not a God of condemnation. He has shown us how much He loves us. When we accept and believe this, it is not difficult to return love. God's love is an everlasting love, not one that comes and goes with circumstances. It is an enduring love that we can count on. His love never leaves us, even when we go astray. He watches over and keeps us. In times of trials and hardships, we should grow stronger in Him because we see His love at work in our lives.

Read 1 Corinthians 13 & 14

Jesus, we know You gave the ultimate sacrifice of love on the cross. You told us that greater love has no man than to lay down his life for His friends. By the power and wisdom of the Holy Spirit, reveal Your love in our lives so we may also love others unconditionally. Thank You so much. In Your precious name we pray. Amen.

NOVEMBER 10
RESURRECTION POWER

1 Corinthians 15:42-46: So will it be with the resurrection of the dead. The body that is sown is perishable, it is raised imperishable; it is sown in dishonor, it is raised in glory; it is sown in weakness, it is raised in power; it is sown a natural body, it is raised a spiritual body. If there is a natural body there is also a spiritual body. So it is written: The first man Adam became a living being; and the last Adam a life-giving spirit. The spiritual did not come first, but the natural, and after that the spiritual.

If there is no resurrection of the dead, as some proclaim, then not even Christ has been raised. And if Christ has not been raised, preaching is useless and so is faith. We are false witnesses about God because we say that He raised Christ from the dead. Our faith, therefore, is futile and we are still in our sins. If only for this life we have hope in Christ, we are to be pitied more than all men. Paul says that if the dead are not raised, we should eat and drink for tomorrow we die. But this is a lie, for there was a resurrection. The early Christians would not have died for their faith if this was not so. The Bible would not have been written if there was no God who had a master plan. There would be no controversy about Jesus and who He was and is if there was no resurrection. Paul asked the question: "Why do we endanger ourselves every hour?" He also said, "If I fought wild beasts in Ephesus for merely human reasons, what have I gained?" These are good questions. We might as well live to eat, drink and be merry if there is no hope of eternity with Christ. The sting of death is sin, but thanks be to God He gives us the victory over death through our Lord Jesus Christ. We should always give ourselves fully to the work of the Lord because we know that our labor is not in vain.

Read 1 Corinthians 15 & 16

Jesus, we cannot thank You enough for Your sacrifice on the cross. By the power of the Holy Spirit, may we live a life that seeks the kingdom of God, knowing that You meet our every need. Thank You for the hope we have in You. As scripture says, our minds are at perfect peace if they are stayed upon You. Help us each day to serve You with a willing heart and mind so that You and You alone will be glorified. In Your precious name we pray. Amen.

NOVEMBER 11
WALKING WITH JESUS

2 Corinthians 4:10-11: We always carry around in our body the death of Jesus, so that the life of Jesus may also be revealed in our body. For we who are alive are always being given over to death for Jesus' sake, so that His life may be revealed in our mortal body.

A daily walking regime has many benefits. It helps strengthen our bones and may even help prevent or manage heart disease, high blood pressure and Type II diabetes. It can also improve balance and coordination as well as lift our mood. The more we walk, the more benefit we derive from this form of exercise. Walking takes us places that driving is unable to. We can venture into the mountains and forests and discover unknown trails that take us to places of solace and beauty. Deep into a forest we might come across a waterfall that would have been impossible to see from a car. When we walk with Jesus, it is a similar type of journey.

Walking with Him leads to life everlasting. Each step we take with Him draws us closer to the things of God. We go places with Him that no one else can take us. He reveals the truth of God, and He has no greater joy than knowing His children are walking in the truth.

Read 2 Corinthians 1-4

We lift up Your name, Lord, and glorify You. Reveal the impurities that we have allowed to take up residence in our hearts. Sometimes we don't even know they are there. Thank you for loving us despite our failings. Help us to pray and seek Your will. In Your precious name we pray. Amen.

NOVEMBER 12
UNEQUALLY YOKED

2 Corinthians 6:14-16: Do not be yoked together with unbelievers. For what do righteousness and wickedness have in common? Or what fellowship can light have with darkness? What harmony is there between Christ and Belial? What does a believer have in common with an unbeliever? What agreement is there between the temple of God and idols? For we are the temple of the living God. As God has said, "I will live with them and walk among them, and I will be their God and they will be my people."

Before there were tractors, farmers used oxen to plow the fields. If they were not equally yoked, they could not perform properly. They would pull against each other and it would be impossible to plow the field. They needed to be of equal stature and weight so they could pull the plow in harmony and complete the task at hand. If we are yoked with an unbeliever in marriage, there is friction in the relationship. There is no understanding of spiritual things and eventually communication breaks down. When yoked with another believer, God works in harmony with the husband and wife. He accomplishes His purposes for bringing them together. Jesus said that a house divided against itself falls. So do relationships that are not bound together by faith in Jesus Christ.

Read 2 Corinthians 5 & 6

Heavenly Father, guide us in any relationship we are involved in. Help us to know when to stay and when to leave. We pray in advance for the life partner that you have chosen for us so that together we are in Your perfect will and draw ever closer to You. In Jesus' precious name we pray. Amen.

NOVEMBER 13
WE REAP WHAT WE SOW

2 Corinthians 9:6-7: Remember this: Whoever sows sparingly will also reap sparingly, and whoever sows generously will also reap generously. Each man should give what he has decided in his heart to give, not reluctantly or under compulsion, for God loves a cheerful giver.

The character of a person is revealed by how they respond to a situation. If they sow seeds of pity and depression, they reap the same and drag others down with them. If they sow seeds of encouragement, then something good can come out of something bad. In 2013, Polly Klaas would have turned 32 years old had she not been abducted and killed. As tragic as this was for the family, they took something horrible and began an organization to help prevent the same thing from happening to others. Hundreds have been helped because of their efforts. The organization MADD, Mothers Against Drunk Drivers, began after their children were killed by drunk drivers. We don't even know how many lives have been saved because of their efforts. These examples tell a story about the seeds that were planted and the harvest that has been reaped. With God's strength, we overcome any crisis. We don't always understand why bad things happen but we live in a fallen world and so they do. The seeds we sow in response are the fruits we reap.

Read 2 Corinthians 7-9

Heavenly Father, we ask for generous hearts so that not only will we be blessed by giving freely but we will bless others. Help us to sow seeds of love, trust and encouragement and do our very best no matter the circumstances that confront us. In Jesus' name we pray. Amen.

NOVEMBER 14
OUR BATTLES ARE WON

2 Corinthians 10:3-5: For though we live in the world, we do not wage war as the world does. The weapons we fight with are not the weapons of the world. On the contrary, they have divine power to demolish strongholds. We demolish arguments and every pretension that sets itself up against the knowledge of God, and we take captive every thought to make it obedient to Christ.

We have power and authority in the name of Jesus Christ. He is our ever-present strength in time of trouble. The world fights its battles with that which it sees, but we fight our battles with the help of God Almighty.

In the Old Testament, there are examples of how God fought battles for His people. When it seemed there was no way of escape, they humbled themselves and prayed and He made their enemies turn on themselves by blinding them with polished shields. The Lord stopped the sun in the middle of the sky and delayed its going down about a full day when Joshua was in a fierce battle with the Amorites. He saved Elijah from King Ahab. The Lord gave David, the shepherd, strength enough to kill a lion and a bear. These are a handful of examples of the mighty working power of our God. When we place our thoughts upon Him, even if our eyes tell us otherwise He hears and answers our prayers. We must believe His word and trust that the real war has already been won, that of victory over death, hell and the grave.

Read 2 Corinthians 10 & 11

Jesus, we come before you in humility, knowing that we are nothing, but in You we are everything. Lift us up with Your strong arm and help us keep our minds continually upon You no matter what our circumstance. Help us to know and realize that You are our warrior, our protector and that our battles are already won when we call upon You. We may not see everything that is happening, but we know we can trust You. In Your precious name we pray. Amen.

NOVEMBER 15
A THORN IN THE FLESH

2 Corinthians 12:20: For I am afraid that when I come I may not find you as I want you to be, and you may not find me as you want me to be. I fear that there may be quarreling, jealousy, outbursts of anger, factions, slander, gossip, arrogance and disorder..

Paul is admonishing the church in Corinth to repent of the impurity and debauchery in which they were indulging. The church had become but the shell of a building. The outside was beautiful but the inside was dirty, almost uninhabitable, because of sin. He was hopeful that by the time he arrived in Corinth, the people would have returned to their first love. The church is made up of sinners who have been redeemed by the blood of the Lamb, but unless we change from what we once were we lose any witness for Christ that we may have. Paul, who was highly educated, a Jew, a Roman, and who had been chosen by Jesus to reveal the truth, had every reason to be proud, but he knew that to boast took away from the glory of Jesus. To keep him from becoming conceited because of these surpassing great revelations, there was given him a thorn in his flesh, a messenger of Satan, to torment him. He pleaded with the Lord three times for it to be taken away from him but the Lord said to him, "My grace is sufficient for you, for my power is made perfect in weakness." We are to set an example of what Christ does for us when we ask Him to be our Savior. If we continue to sin, we are no different than the world around us. In our weakness, He is made strong, and the light of His presence shines through us.

Read 2 Corinthians 12 & 13

Jesus, our Savior, the Rose of Sharon, the Alpha and the Omega, Your grace is sufficient. We come asking forgiveness for our sins and humble ourselves in Your presence. Thank You for Your faithfulness. Thank You for showing us the love of our Heavenly Father, who reigns in the Heavens above, and thank You for sending the Holy Spirit to live and dwell within us so that we have fellowship with You. We pray for Your strength in time of adversity and Your tender mercies in times of joy. In Your precious name we pray. Amen.

NOVEMBER 16
CRUCIFIED WITH CHRIST

Galatians 2:20-21: I have been crucified with Christ and I no longer live, but Christ lives in me. The life I live in the body, I live by faith in the Son of God, who loved me and gave himself for me. I do not set aside the grace of God, for if righteousness could be gained through the law, Christ died for nothing.

What good is it for man if he gains the whole world yet forfeits his soul, or what can a man give in exchange for his soul? (Mark 8:36-37). Acquiring fame and fortune is not worth an eternity without God. If we obtain all the world's wealth, none of it goes with us when we die. When we are crucified with Christ, we lay our sins at His cross. Everything we have is His. Whatever we have accomplished without Him amounts to nothing because at the end of our lives we lose it all. Jesus gives us a different perspective on life and changes us. We no longer desire the things we once did. We are free not to sin any longer, and we focus on the eternal glory of God. If we died with Him, we also live with Him (2 Timothy 2:11). If we have been united with Him in His death, we will certainly be united with Him in His resurrection (Romans 6:5).

Read Galatians 1-3

Heavenly Father, thank You for the gift of life. Bring us into Your holy presence. Help us look to You and not to ourselves for the answers to life's persistent questions. May we die daily to ourselves so that the light of Christ shines through us. Keep us faithful and help us to grow in Your word so that we may be more like our Savior, in whose name we pray. Amen.

NOVEMBER 17
FRUITS OF THE SPIRIT

Galatians 6:22-23: But the fruit of the Spirit is love, joy, peace, patience, kindness, goodness, faithfulness, gentleness and self-control. Against such things there is no law.

Paul is warning the Galatians to beware of falling back into the trap of legalism. The people in the church had faith in Christ but then began requiring circumcision and keeping the law in order to go to Heaven. Paul tells them if this is the case then we are not free from sin; that if we cannot keep all of the laws, then we can't keep any of them. We are now covered by the blood of Jesus and set free from the law and are now free not to sin. Christianity is the religion that gives total freedom to be who we are intended to be, in Christ. In days gone by, sermons were full of hell, fire and brimstone. If we didn't do this, that or the other, or if we did this, that or the other, the wrath of God would condemn us to hell. This is not freedom in Christ. It is legalism; we have to do something in order to receive something. We are not required to do anything except repent and believe that Jesus is the Son of God. We should no longer desire fulfillment in the sin that once bound us but be filled with the fruit of the Spirit. Love, joy and peace bring us into perfect harmony with God. Patience, kindness and goodness bring us into harmony with other people. Faithfulness, meekness and self-control bring us into a good relationship with ourselves. What delectable fruits to partake in!

Read Galatians 4-6

Heavenly Father, by the power of Your Spirit, teach us to pray more effectively. Fill us with the fruits of love, joy, peace, patience, kindness, goodness, faithfulness, meekness and self-control. Against these, there are no laws. Help us to walk close with You so we are sensitive to the Holy Spirit and discern the difference between the flesh and the spirit and are whole and holy before You. In the precious name of Jesus we pray. Amen.

NOVEMBER 18
GOD'S POWER

Ephesians 1:18-21: I pray also that the eyes of your heart may be enlightened in order that you may know the hope to which he has called you, the riches of his glorious inheritance in the saints, and his incomparable great power for us who believe. That power is like the working of his mighty strength, which he exerted in Christ when He raised Him from the dead and seated Him at His right hand in the heavenly realms, far above all rule and authority, power and dominion and every title that can be given, not only in the present age but also in the one to come.

We know that Jesus is seated on the right hand of the Father in the heavenly realms and He has all authority, power and dominion. What we see with our natural eyes is the opposite of what this scripture proclaims. It looks like people are in control of their own destiny. We are not to look at these things and believe that this is all there is. We are to keep our eyes lifted up toward the heavens. Jesus is coming back to this earth. He has been given power on high. When the heavens open, He who is Faithful and True will appear riding on a white horse. The armies of heaven will follow Him, also riding on white horses and dressed in white linen. Out of His mouth comes a sharp sword with which to strike down the nations, and He will rule them with an iron scepter (Revelation 19:11-15).

Read Ephesians 1 & 2

Lord, may our focus be only on You and not what we see with our natural eyes. We pray to desire none of the things of this world, for the world serves itself and the one who is at war against our very souls to try and turn us away from You. One day You will appear in Your glory and of Your kingdom there will be no end. Glory to God in the Highest. Amen.

NOVEMBER 19
RECONCILED TO OUR FATHER

Ephesians 3:12: In Him and through faith in Him, we may approach God with freedom and confidence.

Christ came so we are reconciled to our Heavenly Father. Through this reconciliation, we can approach our Father with freedom and confidence. We can be in the presence of the One who created the entire universe by speaking it into existence; the One who hangs the moon, the sun and the stars upon nothing. He is a mighty and awesome God. He loves us so much and He wants us to come to Him, to love Him, to learn of Him and serve Him. He sets boundaries for our lives because He wants us not to go into the enemy's territory and suffer the consequences. There are a lot of questions we need answers to, especially during times of heartache and pain, but that is where trust comes in. We cannot ever compare our pain to that which Christ endured on the cross. We can only trust Him and know that whatever the reason, we can learn from it and come out stronger.

Read Ephesians 3 & 4

Heavenly and gracious Father, thank You for Your plan of salvation. We sometimes forget that we were once sinners and we become arrogant and proud. Give us a spirit of kindness and gentleness so that we are examples of the love of Christ in us, the hope of glory. In Jesus' name we pray. Amen.

NOVEMBER 20
IMITATORS OF GOD

Ephesians 5:1-2: Be imitators of God, therefore, as dearly loved children and live a life of love, just as Christ loved us and gave himself up for us as a fragrant offering and sacrifice to God.

The last two chapters of Ephesians are full of God's love for us. Paul tells us to be full of thanksgiving, and as children of light we are to consist of all goodness, righteousness and truth. When we come to know Christ, the old things of this world are taken away from us and we are not to return to them. He instructs us to refrain from obscenity, foolish talk and coarse joking. We are free from the darkness that once surrounded us and now the love of Christ fills our souls. To imitate God is to do what is good and not what is evil. Anyone who does good is from God, but anyone who does evil has not seen God (3 John 11).

Read Ephesians 5 & 6

Precious Jesus, thank You for Paul, who wrote such wonderful letters to those in need of understanding and encouragement. We are thankful that he gave instruction not only to those at the time but to all those who come after, for there is nothing new under the sun and the human heart and soul is still the same. We praise You for Your faithfulness. Help each of us to grow in our love for You. Give us the ability to walk in Your light. Take all the dark places away from us so that we may be truly free. In Your precious name we pray. Amen.

NOVEMBER 21
HUMILITY

Philippians 2:3: Do nothing out of selfish ambition or vain conceit, but in humility consider others better than yourselves.

It's difficult to be humble at times. We've all been proud of something we've accomplished in life. There's no shame to that. It's when we let pride reside in our heart that we become conceited and think of ourselves first and foremost. The Lord detests all the proud of heart. Be sure of this, they will not go unpunished (Proverbs 16:5). When we lift ourselves up, we are sure to fall down. Serving others and putting them above ourselves brings greater joy than having everything be about "me." When it's me, me, me, it doesn't take long before we find ourselves all alone. Most of us don't want to be with someone who thinks only of themselves and no one else. We are to clothe ourselves with humility toward one another because God opposes the proud but gives grace to the humble. When we humble ourselves under God's mighty hand, He lifts us up in due time (1 Peter 5:5-6).

Read Philippians 1 & 2

Heavenly Father, humble us. Help us to put others above ourselves. There are many who are in need of Your presence in their lives. There is sickness, financial needs, depression. We lift these things up to Your throne. We pray You would meet every need and bring everyone who cries out to You closer to You so they see Your hand in their lives. Give us strength and wisdom as we go through the day. Help us to honor and bless You in all we think, say and do. In Jesus precious name we pray. Amen.

NOVEMBER 22
DO NOT BE ANXIOUS

Philippians 4:6-9: Do not be anxious about anything, but in everything, by prayer and petition, with thanksgiving, present your requests to God. And the peace of God, which transcends all understanding, will guard your hearts and your minds in Christ Jesus. Finally, brothers, whatever is true, whatever is noble, whatever is right, whatever is pure, whatever is lovely, whatever is admirable—if anything is excellent or praiseworthy—think about such things.

The book of Judges in the Old Testament tells of a time when the Israelites were so impoverished by the Midianites that they cried out to the Lord for help. The angel of the Lord came and sat down under an oak where Gideon, the son of Joash, was threshing wheat in a winepress to keep it from the Midianites. The angel appeared to Gideon and said, "The Lord is with you, mighty warrior." "But, sir," he replied, "if the Lord is with us why has all this happened to us? And how can I save Israel? My clan is the weakest in Manasseh, and I am the least in my family." Talk about being anxious! Gideon was so unsure about what the angel had said to him that he placed a wool fleece on the threshing floor. He said that if there was dew only on the fleece and all the ground was dry, he knew that the Lord would save Israel by his hand. The next day, it happened as he requested of the Lord. Still unsure of himself, he asked the Lord to allow him one more test and this time he asked that the fleece be dry and the ground be covered with dew. That night God did so. Gideon started out to the battle with 32,000 men and ended up with only 300. This was God's plan to show that the battle would be won because of His mighty hand. When the Lord speaks to us, we have no reason to be anxious. We can be like Gideon and ask for a sign and perhaps in the Lord's graciousness He will answer that way, but He asks us not to be anxious but by prayer and petition, with thanksgiving, to present our requests to Him.

Read Philippians 3 & 4

Heavenly Father, we come before You with praise and thanksgiving for who You are. Help us keep our minds on those things that give praise and honor to You. Comfort us in our times of need and wrap Your loving arms around us. Forgive us when we don't completely trust in You and try to take matters into our own hands because we don't think You are answering our prayers. We know that You love us and we pray for a greater measure of faith to trust You more and more. In Jesus' precious name we pray. Amen.

NOVEMBER 23
JESUS, THE CREATOR

Colossians 1:15-17: He (Jesus) is the image of the invisible God, the firstborn over all creation. For by Him all things were created: things in heaven and on earth, visible and invisible, whether thrones or powers or rulers or authorities; all things were created by Him and for Him. He is before all things, and in Him all things hold together.

Epaphras was a man from Colosse who had converted to Christianity through Paul's teachings. He was concerned about what was happening in the church and went to visit Paul in prison. Paul himself never visited the Colossians but through Epaphras he knew there were a lot of cultural influences against the teachings of Jesus such as superstition, astrology, serving Greek and Roman gods and a liberal form of Judaism. And so he wrote this letter to the Colossians, seemingly arguing against all of the ideologies of their culture. As he had written to the Corinthians, he reminded them that the god of this age has blinded the minds of unbelievers so that they cannot see the light of the Gospel of the glory of Christ, who is the image of God. The church had allowed "religion" to form their beliefs and Paul was reminding them that there was only one way to the only true God and that was through faith in Jesus Christ. We know the God of the universe, and He asks only that we love and trust Him.

Read Colossians 1

Today's prayer is from Colossians 1:9-12. Heavenly Father, we love Your word and thank You that it gives us insight into who You are. As Paul wrote, we follow this prayer: We ask God to fill us with the knowledge of His will through all spiritual wisdom and understanding. And we pray this in order that we may live a life worthy of the Lord and please Him in every way, bearing fruit in every good work, growing in the knowledge of God, being strengthened with all power according to His glorious might so that we may have great endurance and patience, and joyfully giving thanks to the Father, who has qualified us to share in the inheritance of the saints in the kingdom of light. In Jesus' precious name we pray. Amen.

NOVEMBER 24
TREASURES OF WISDOM AND KNOWLEDGE

Colossians 2:2-4: My purpose is that they may be encouraged in heart and united in love, so that they may have the full riches of complete understanding, in order that they may know the mystery of God, namely, Christ, in whom are hidden all the treasures of wisdom and knowledge. I tell you this so that no one may deceive you by fine-sounding arguments.

The world has a myriad of arguments against Jesus Christ. We hear His name used as a byword or a curse word. There is no understanding of what they are doing by using the most precious, holy name there is, the one in whom is hidden all the treasures of wisdom and knowledge. Once we come to Christ, we should love the Lord our God with all our hearts, minds and souls, so that His Spirit permeates our lives and we so know and love Him that the arguments and philosophies of this world cannot lead us astray. Most "religions" believe in Jesus Christ as some great teacher or prophet but they deny that He is the Son of God. It is a lie of Satan. He knows who Jesus is and he wants to deceive all he can and take them with him when judgment comes. Treasures are something we search for because they have great value. With the Lord, we can have the full riches of complete understanding in order that we may know the mystery of God.

He doesn't reveal all of it because we would be overwhelmed. But He said to ask anything in His name and it shall be given to us. If we want to know more about the things of God, we must ask, pray and seek His face. He knows all the answers.

Read Colossians 2

Precious Jesus, Giver of Life, our Savior and Redeemer, we praise You and thank You for Your wisdom, knowledge and understanding. Keep us humble before You and let us not get puffed up in our own knowledge. Fill us anew with the Holy Spirit so we walk closer to You. Thank You for being our healer, deliverer and redeemer. May we never forget that in You are hidden all the treasures of wisdom and knowledge. We ask this in Your precious name. Amen.

NOVEMBER 25
FORGIVE AS THE LORD FORGAVE

Colossians 3:12-14: Therefore, as God's chosen people, holy and dearly loved, clothe yourselves with compassion, kindness, humility, gentleness and patience. Bear with each other and forgive whatever grievances you may have against one another. Forgive as the Lord forgave you. And over all these virtues put on love, which binds them all together in perfect unity.

We are not to hold grudges against anyone. The Lord's Prayer says to forgive us our debts as we forgive our debtors. If we forgive men when they sin against us, our Heavenly Father also forgives us. But if we do not forgive others their sins, our Father will not forgive our sins (Matthew 6:14). When we do not forgive, our hearts become bitter and our minds clouded. There is freedom in forgiveness. It opens our eyes and our hearts to receive God's blessings. When we forgive, we clothe ourselves in compassion, kindness, humility, gentleness and patience. These are all things that Jesus taught us as He walked upon this earth. There was nothing unkind about Him. At times, He told it like it was but He always had compassion and was not willing that any should be lost. When we love with Christ's love, it is simple and pure. We expect nothing in return. In the heart of every man, there is a desire to be loved and to love in return. Only through Jesus Christ, do we find that true love.

Read Colossians 3 & 4

Heavenly Father, search our hearts. If we harbor any unforgiveness, reveal it so that we can be set free. Fill our hearts with Your love so that we can love others. Heal our hurts. In Jesus' precious name we pray. Amen.

NOVEMBER 26
AVOID SEXUAL IMMORALITY

1 Thessalonians 4:3-5: It is God's will that you should be sanctified; that you should avoid sexual immorality; that each of you should learn to control his own body in a way that is holy and honorable, not in passionate lust like the heathen who do not know God.

The Church of the Thessalonians were imitators of the Lord and in spite of severe suffering, they welcomed with joy the gospel message given by the Holy Spirit. Paul was pleased with their service to God but he also knew human nature, so he not only praised them but also admonished them. He knew what was happening in the church and wanted to remind them to remain holy and honorable and not revert back to their former ways. This verse is the opposite of what the world believes. Its motto is: If it feels good, do it. Each time we are intimate with someone that is not our husband or wife, we give a part of our soul away. Our physical desires are met but our spirit dies. Marriage should be honored by all, and the marriage bed kept pure, for God will judge the adulterer and all the sexually immoral (Hebrews 13:4). It is a lifelong commitment intended for one man and one woman. In a faithful marriage, there is trust and no fear of infidelity or sexually-transmitted disease. All other sins a man commits are outside the body but those who sin sexually sin against their own body. Our body is the temple of the Holy Spirit, who is in us. We are not our own. We were bought with a price. Therefore, we are to honor God with our bodies (1Corinthians 6:18-20).

Read 1 Thessalonians 1-5

Holy Spirit, You have been sent to us by Jesus to guide us in all things. Give us power to overcome our sinful nature so that we remain faithful. We are weak but You are strong. Lead us away from temptation when we start to wander. In Jesus' name we pray. Amen.

NOVEMBER 27
OUR FATHER THE AVENGER

2 Thessalonians 1:6-10: God is just; He will pay back trouble to those who trouble you and give relief to you who are troubled, and to us as well. This will happen when the Lord Jesus is revealed from heaven in blazing fire with His powerful angels. He will punish those who do not know God and do not obey the gospel of our Lord Jesus. They will be punished with everlasting destruction and shut out from the presence of the Lord and from the majesty of His power on the day He comes to be glorified in His holy people and to be marveled at among all those who have believed...

Hear, O Israel, the Lord our God, the Lord is One. Love the Lord your God with all your heart, soul, mind and strength. The second is this: Love your neighbor as yourself. There is no commandment greater than these (Mark 12:30-31). All things work together for good to those who love Him, who are called according to His purpose. (Romans 8:28). The Lord tells us that He is the one who pays back trouble to those who trouble us. He tells us that if our enemy is hungry, feed him; if he is thirsty, give him something to drink. In doing this, we heap burning coals on his head. Do not be overcome with evil but overcome evil with good (Romans 12:20-21). God brings every deed into judgment, including every hidden thing, whether good or evil (Ecclesiastes 12:14). If we give everything over to Him, He takes care of it in His timing and we don't have to worry about it.

Read 2 Thessalonians 1-3

Heavenly Father, we put our trust in You, knowing that You are the judge of all mankind. Give us the ability to rest in You, even though things do not seem fair sometimes. Thank You so much for loving us. Help us to live in freedom, believing that You are in control of all things. In Jesus precious name we pray. Amen.

NOVEMBER 28
PRAY FOR THOSE IN AUTHORITY

1 Timothy 2:1-4: I urge, then, first of all, that requests, prayers, intercession and thanksgiving be made for everyone—for kings and all those in authority, that we may live peaceful and quiet lives in all godliness and holiness. This is good and pleases God our Savior, who wants all men to be saved and to come to knowledge of the truth.

No matter our feelings or beliefs about those in authority, it is our duty as Christians to pray for them. In the Old Testament, many kings forsook the ways of the God of Israel and went their own way. They taxed the people until they were in poverty and put them into slavery. There were always those who cried out to God and knew He would answer and there were righteous leaders that brought peace to God's people for a time. The Lord says, "If my people, who are called by my name, will humble themselves and pray and seek my face and turn from their wicked ways, then will I hear from heaven and will forgive their sin and will heal their land" (11 Chronicles 7:14). The ultimate destiny of a nation is determined on who their leaders are. If the leaders are righteous, there is peace in the land. If the leaders are evil, iniquity abounds and the hearts of many become cold and complacent. Through prayer, things change. It may be that through our prayers, those who are not now serving Him will come to know Him. Whatever choices those in authority make, our Father is still on the throne and there is no man and nothing on this earth that will ever change that. Our prayers should be for our leaders and our nation to turn to God so that we are at peace. He gave us this land to be free to worship Him.

Read 1 Timothy 1 & 2

Heavenly Father, we lift up those who have been chosen to lead this great nation. We pray for righteousness so there will be peace in the land. We pray for wisdom in the decisions that are made, that they will be for our nation as a whole and not for selfish reasons. Thank You for this fabulous country that is established on Your foundation. Protect those who protect us by their service to our country. Bless them and their families and bring them safely home. Be with each and every one of them in a special way this day. Draw them close to You and help them know that they are all special in Your sight. In Jesus' precious name we pray. Amen.

NOVEMBER 29
EVERYTHING GOD CREATED IS GOOD

1 Timothy 4:1-5: The Spirit clearly says that in later times some will abandon the faith and follow deceiving spirits and things taught by demons. Such teachings come through hypocritical liars, whose consciences have been seared as with a hot iron. They forbid people to marry and order them to abstain from certain foods, which God created to be received with thanksgiving by those who believe and who know the truth. For everything God created is good, and nothing is to be rejected if it is received with thanksgiving, because it is consecrated by the word of God and prayer.

We are told by the experts on one day that caffeine is bad for us and the next thing we know we are told it is good for us. We are told what foods are good, what ones aren't; how to exercise, how not to exercise. There are a multitude of opinions about everything. Even when there are studies to back up an opinion, someone else comes along with different results. One thing we can be certain of, our Lord never changes. He is always the same. He doesn't change like shifting shadows. But if we are not grounded in the Word of God, we don't know what to believe and it can be very confusing. The Lord said, "My people are destroyed from lack of knowledge" (Hosea 4:6). Jesus taught that nothing that enters a man's stomach can make him unclean, for it doesn't go into his heart but into his stomach and then out of his body. In saying this, Jesus declared all foods are clean. It is from within, out of men's hearts, come evil thoughts, theft, murder, adultery, greed, malice, deceit, lewdness, envy, slander, arrogance and folly. All these evils come from inside and are what make a man unclean (Mark 7:17-23). But everything God created is good.

Read 1 Timothy 3 & 4

Precious Jesus, keep us in an attitude of prayer so we come to know You in a greater and deeper way and return the love that You have bestowed upon us. Put the desires of Your heart in our heart so that we will never be tempted to fall away from serving You. We pray this in Your precious name. Amen.

NOVEMBER 30
THE ROOT

1 Timothy 6:10: For the love of money is the root of all evil (KJV).

A root is the part of a plant that usually sprouts underground. It is an anchor that absorbs water and nutrients from the soil that allow the plant to flourish and produce flowers, food, or whatever the plant is good for. The longer it is in the ground, the deeper it grows. When we plant love for something in our heart, it takes root. It is difficult to dig up and get rid of after years of growth. Jesus said it is easier for a man to go through the eye of a needle than for a rich man to enter the kingdom of God. His disciples were amazed at this saying. He told them, though, that all things are possible with God. It is not money that is the root of all kinds of evil but the love of it. It is a love that goes deep down to the very soul that causes someone to live, think and breathe money. Everything they do revolves around money and there is never enough. It is an insatiable desire that is never filled. There is another root that Isaiah talks about that shoots up from the stump of Jesse and from His roots a Branch will bear fruit. That root is Jesus Christ. He is the Root of Jesse, and when we are rooted in Him, we grow in His love which leads to eternal life.

Read 1 Timothy 5 & 6

Heavenly Father, You own the cattle on a thousand hills. Your riches are endless and You desire to share them with us. Help us to look to You for our sustenance, to know that we can do nothing of ourselves that will store up riches in eternity except through Jesus Christ, through whom all things are possible. Guide us and keep us in all our ways. In Jesus' precious name we pray. Amen.

DECEMBER 1
BE KIND TO EVERYONE

2 Timothy 2:22-24: Flee the evil desires of youth, and pursue righteousness, faith, love and peace, along with those who call on the Lord out of a pure heart. Don't have anything to do with foolish and stupid arguments, because you know they produce quarrels. And the Lord's servant must not quarrel; instead, he must be kind to everyone, able to teach, not resentful.

Those whose lives have been changed by Jesus Christ are filled with the Holy Spirit and God's eternal love. Scripture says be kind to everyone, be able to teach and be not resentful. When an unbeliever tries to argue about the Bible, oh, it has contradictions in it, you can't believe everything that was written in it, it was written by men, those are a few of their unmerited arguments. The truth is the Bible cannot be understood without knowing the teacher who wrote it, and that is the Holy Spirit. It is the inspired Word of God, backed up by over 27,000 ancient manuscripts. It's a book of instruction, love and redemption. If we live the way it teaches, we are full of God's love and mercy, and are kind to everyone.

Read 2 Timothy 1 & 2

Heavenly Father, fill us with Your presence. Renew us by Your Spirit and fill us full of Your glory and love, that as we set out upon our journey today we will touch those we come in contact with; that without our even saying anything they see something that is different in us and will want to know what it is. By the power of Your Spirit, bring them to the knowledge of who You are. Use us as Your instruments. In Jesus' precious name we pray. Amen.

DECEMBER 2
LISTEN

2 Timothy 4:3-4: For the time will come when men will not put up with sound doctrine. Instead, to suit their own desires, they will gather around them a great number of teachers to say what their itching ears want to hear. They will turn their ears away from the truth and turn aside to myths.

In 1 Kings 22, there is the story about the King of Israel, who asks the King of Judea to join him in battle against their enemy. The King of Judah agrees and says, "I am as you are, my people as your people, my horses as your horses. First, let's seek the counsel of the Lord." The king of Israel called about 400 of the prophets together and asked them, "Shall I go to war or shall I refrain?" They all answered, "Go, for the Lord will give it into the king's hand." The King of Judea was not convinced and asked, "Is there not a prophet of the Lord here who we can inquire of?" The King of Israel said, "There is still one man through whom we can inquire of the Lord, but I hate him because he never prophesies anything good about me, but always bad." So they brought the prophet before them. When he arrived, the kings were dressed in their royal robes and sitting on their thrones at the threshing floor by the entrance gate of Samaria. The king asked him, "Shall we go to war or refrain?" The prophet answered, "Attack and be victorious, for the Lord will give it into the king's hand." The king said to him, "How many times must I make you swear to tell me nothing but the truth in the name of the Lord," to which the prophet responded, "I saw all Israel scattered on the hills like sheep without a shepherd. These people have no master. Let each one go home in peace." The kings went into battle anyway and the King of Israel was killed, as the prophet had foretold. What we can learn from this story is that sometimes we hear what we want to hear and not what the Lord is telling us. When we consult others, sometimes they tell us what we want to hear, or even if they don't we still hear what we want to hear. The Lord knows what lies ahead in our battles of life. It is imperative to listen when He speaks, for He never leads us astray.

Read 2 Timothy 3 & 4

Holy Spirit, thank You that You only reveal to us the truth of God, which brings peace, comfort and joy to our lives. Help us to not only listen but to hear the Lord's direction for our lives. Draw us to You and let us not be deceived by the things of the world. Keep us focused on the Father and lead us to that which gives glory and honor to Him. In the name of Jesus we pray. Amen.

DECEMBER 3
JESUS WALKS WITH US

Titus 2:11-14: For the grace of God that brings salvation has appeared to all men. It teaches us to say "No" to ungodliness and worldly passions, and to live self-controlled, upright and godly lives in this present age, while we wait for the blessed hope—the glorious appearing of our great God and Savior, Jesus Christ, who gave himself for us to redeem us from all wickedness and to purify for himself a people that are his very own, eager to do what is good.

There's a hymn that says, "I come to the garden alone while the dew is still on the roses and the voice I hear falling on my ear, the Son of God discloses. And He walks with me and He talks with me and He tells me I am His own, and the joy we share as we tarry there none other has ever known." Imagine walking in a garden with Jesus. We are in perfect unison, sharing with each other the joys and heartaches of life. The time we spend with Him is invigorating and exciting. He imparts wisdom to us and shares the secrets of His kingdom. He is the Son of God and He is also our friend who loves us unconditionally. Therefore, we can pour our hearts out to Him without fear of rejection or judgment. Proverbs 18:24 says, A man of many companions may come to ruin, but there is a friend who sticks closer than a brother. Perhaps this passage can be interpreted several ways, but the one that seems most fitting is that it refers to Jesus. Before we even knew Him, He was with us. Now that we know Him, we walk together side by side.

Read Titus 1-3

Jesus, there is no one like You. You have made us Your brothers and sisters by becoming man and grafting us into the kingdom of God. Thank You for Your love and for sending the Holy Spirit to be a constant companion and reminder of You. We can have no better friend than You. You are trustworthy, kind, loving and giving. We ask that You impart these qualities into our lives so that we become more like You. In Your precious name we pray. Amen.

DECEMBER 4
RESTORATION AND LOVE

Philemon 8:9: Therefore, although in Christ I could be bold and order you to do what you ought to do, yet I appeal to you on the basis of love. . .

Paul is writing to Philemon about Onesimus, Philemon's slave who ran away, asking him to accept Onesimus back not only as his slave but as his brother in Christ. We are not told what the outcome of Paul's request was, but our assumption can be that it was granted. In our Lord's eyes, we are all equal. Master or servant makes no difference. When Jesus came to this earth, He was servant of all. He showed us how to serve our Father in Heaven and how to humble ourselves so that we would be pleasing to Him. The greatest thing we can do in this life is show God's love to all we come in contact with. By living this way, we represent Him. We have all been around those who are negative, angry, depressed, unforgiving, who complain about almost anything and everyone. If we're honest, we don't want to be around them, or at least we want to be around them as little as possible. But when we are with someone who is full of kindness, joy, speaks highly of others, who is excited when others do well, we want to be with them. Our spirits are lifted when we are around them. Our lives should be so full of God's love that we give that love to everyone we encounter and treat them as He would.

Read Philemon

Jesus, we lift up Your mighty and magnificent name above all names. You gave so much for us. You showed us what real love is and that that love can conquer all things, even death itself. Thank You that You love each and every one of us, that you care about all aspects of our lives and that because of Your love for us, we can give that love to others. We ask that You draw us closer to You so that Your love continually flows through us. In Your precious name we pray. Amen.

DECEMBER 5
TEMPTATIONS

Hebrews 2:14-15: Since the children have flesh and blood, He shared in their humanity so that by his death He might destroy him who holds the power of death—that is, the devil—and free those who all their lives were held in slavery by their fear of death.

We are tempted not only by lust but we are tempted to lie, steal, and cheat. Temptations surround us everywhere we look. Turn the television on, it's there. Spend hours on the Internet, it's there. Open up a magazine or newspaper, it's there. At work, while traveling, at parties, even among friends and family, it is there. Our natural desire may be to give into it, but that is not what we should do. We do not have a high priest who is unable to sympathize with our weaknesses but we have one who has been tempted in every way, just as we are, yet without sin (Hebrews 4:15). Because of His humanness, He knows our suffering and He knows what tempts us. When we are tempted, we should not say that God is tempting us, for God cannot be tempted by evil, nor does He tempt anyone, but each one of us is tempted when by his own evil desire he is dragged away and enticed. Then after desire has conceived, it gives birth to sin; and sin, when it is full grown, gives birth to death (James 1:13-15). Blessed are those who persevere under trial, because when they have stood the test, they will receive the crown of life that God has promised to those who love Him (James 1:12). We do not have to give into our temptations but trust Him who has overcome to make a way of escape.

Read Hebrews 1 & 2

Jesus, we lift up Your holy name. We thank You for Your love and that You gave of Yourself so freely that we might have the hope of eternal life with You. Guide us daily and reveal Yourself to us so we walk confidently in faith and trust You in all aspects of our lives. We pray that You would meet the needs of each and every one of us this day, in Your precious name. Amen.

DECEMBER 6
NOTHING IS HIDDEN FROM GOD

Hebrews 4:12-13: For the word of God is living and active. Sharper than any double-edged sword, it penetrates even to dividing soul and spirit, joints and marrow; it judges the thoughts and attitudes of the heart. Nothing in all creation is hidden from God's sight. Everything is uncovered and laid bare before the eyes of him to whom we must give account.

Hide and go seek is a fun game that kids play. While one person counts, everyone else runs to find a secret hiding place. Sometimes there's such a great place, the one who is looking never discovers it. With God, He always finds us. There is no place we can go that He is not there. Jonah is a case in point. The Lord instructed him to go to Nineveh and preach against it because its wickedness had come before Him. But Jonah ran away from the Lord and headed in the opposite direction. He found a ship and after paying the fare he went aboard to flee from the Lord. The Lord sent a great wind on the sea and such a violent storm arose that the ship threatened to break up. The sailors threw Jonah overboard because they knew he was the cause of the storm, and the raging sea grew calm. The Lord provided a great fish to swallow Jonah and he was in the belly of the fish for three days. It wasn't until Jonah called out in his distress that the Lord commanded the fish to vomit Jonah on dry land. There was no way he could hide from the Lord. He spoke to Jonah a second time to proclaim the message to Nineveh and Jonah obeyed. Jonah had gone so far as to take a ship which was going in the opposite direction of where God wanted him to go, but the Lord knew exactly where he was and His will was accomplished despite what Jonah did. It's good to obey the Lord and not hide anything from Him because He knows the direction we are headed in.

Read Hebrews 3 & 4

Holy Spirit, we can hide nothing from You. The Word of God is sharper than a double-edged sword. It penetrates so deep, even to the dividing of the soul and spirit, joints and marrow. It judges the thoughts and attitudes of the heart. Change us by the power of the Word so that our thoughts and actions are transformed into the image of Jesus Christ, in whose name we pray. Amen.

DECEMBER 7
JESUS LIVES FOREVER

Hebrews 7:24-25: But because Jesus lives forever, He has a permanent priesthood. Therefore He is able to save completely those who come to God through Him, because He always lives to intercede for them.

No other religion lays claim to a risen savior. That is why the name of Jesus is different from all others, because He is alive. Not only is He alive but he is able to save us from our sins. His priesthood has been established by the Father, and He now intercedes for us. In the Old Testament, Job proclaimed: I know my Redeemer lives, and that in the end He will stand upon the earth (Job 19:25). Isaiah 57:15 tells us that this is what the high and lofty One says, He who lives forever, whose name is holy: I live in a high and holy place, but also with him who is contrite and lowly in spirit. Many times, Jesus was referred to as the Son of David, and once He responded, "How is it then that David, speaking by the Spirit, calls Him Lord? For he says, the Lord said to my Lord, 'Sit at my right hand until I put your enemies under your feet. If then David calls him Lord, how can he be his son?'" No one could say a word in reply to Him (Matthew 22:43-45). In the beginning was the Word and the Word was with God and the Word was God. He was with God in the beginning (John 1:1). Because we know the One who lives forever, we have no fear of death. When we leave this earth, He is waiting for us on the other side to usher us into His eternal kingdom.

Read Hebrews 5-7

Precious Jesus, by the power of the Holy Spirit, draw us closer to You. Teach us Your ways so that we will never doubt or be uncertain of the God whom we serve. Keep us in a continual attitude of prayer so that we may please You and follow the plan You have for our lives. When we go through trials, remind us that those are the times we draw closer to You. When we trust in You, we can know that everything is going to work out. In Your Holy name we pray. Amen.

DECEMBER 8
NEW COVENANT

Hebrews 8:10: This is the covenant I will make with the house of Israel after that time, declares the Lord. I will put my laws in their minds and write them on their hearts. I will be their God, and they will be my people.

In Genesis 3:15, God pronounced His judgment on the serpent after enticing Eve into eating the forbidden fruit: "And I will put enmity between you and the woman, and between your offspring and hers; he will crush your head and you will strike his heel." This was in reference to the coming of the Messiah. Abraham was chosen by God to be the father of a nation which would serve God with all of their hearts, but they never did. Moses was given the Ten Commandments to guide God's people, but they continually chose to serve other gods not known to them. The rituals and laws of the covenant under the Old Testament were replaced when Jesus came. God said, "The time is coming when I will make a new covenant with the house of Israel and with the house of Judah. It will not be like the covenant I made with their forefathers when I took them by the hand to lead them out of Egypt because they did not remain faithful to my covenant and I turned away from them." If there had been nothing wrong with the first covenant, no place would have been sought for another. By calling this covenant new, He has made the first one obsolete; and what is obsolete and aging will soon disappear. We have a new covenant in Jesus, who died as a ransom for all and cleanses us from sin by His blood.

Read Hebrews 8 & 9

Heavenly Father, thank You for Your plan of redemption. Thank You for opening our eyes and hearts to receive the gift of eternal life through our Savior, Jesus Christ. Thank You for His obedience. Through the power of the Holy Spirit, help us to live the life He taught us to live. Keep us pure before You, by the blood of Your Son, Jesus. Help us to bring others to the knowledge of who Jesus is, why He came and the promise of eternal life with You forever. In the precious name of Jesus we pray. Amen.

DECEMBER 9
NEVER DOUBTING

Hebrews 11:6: And without faith it is impossible to please God, because anyone who comes to Him must believe that He exists and that He rewards those who earnestly seek Him.

No man has seen the face of God. We cannot stand in His presence, for the light of His righteousness is so pure that we could not bear to look at it. But through faith in Jesus Christ, we can come boldly to the throne of grace with our petitions, but we must come believing. There is no one like our Lord, holy and majestic and worthy of all praise. He is our Father. He wants us to know Him and to serve Him, to come seeking Him. To do that, we must have faith. Faith comes by hearing and hearing by the Word of God. He has given us His word to learn His ways so that we can be His sons and daughters through Christ Jesus. A walk with Him that is blameless is a walk that takes us through life like we have never known. We must trust Him, without any doubt in our hearts.

Read Hebrews 10 & 11

Heavenly Father, thank You for the Book of Hebrews, especially chapter 11, which is known as the faith chapter. You are an awesome God and we love You. Help us to not go our own way, because by ourselves we are nothing. With You, we are confident in our salvation. Thank You for being with us and never leaving nor forsaking us. Thank You for Your many promises. In Jesus' holy name we pray. Amen.

DECEMBER 10
ENDURE TO THE END

Hebrews 12:1-3: Therefore, since we are surrounded by such a great cloud of witnesses, let us throw off everything that hinders and the sin that so easily entangles; let us run with perseverance the race marked out for us. Let us fix our eyes on Jesus, the author and perfecter of our faith, who for the joy set before him endured the cross, scorning its shame, and sat down at the right hand of the throne of God. Consider Him who endured such opposition from sinful men, so that you will not grow weary and lose heart.

We fill our lives with many things and at times lose focus because we are so busy. Those who are in ministry, doing good deeds, preaching the word, traveling the world with the message of salvation, get burned out. We become weary in well doing. We must seek first the kingdom of God. Then all of these things will be added unto us (Matthew 6:33). Jesus opens our eyes to our frailty and how temporary life is. We cannot put our full faith and trust in another human being because at some point they either fail us or are taken away. We cannot put our full trust in ourselves because we are not capable of knowing all the answers, solving all problems and fulfilling all needs. The only One who can do that is Jesus Christ. During His darkest hour, hanging upon the cross, He could see the entire picture, and He knew it was worth it. If we hold on to these truths and do not lose faith, our eternal rewards are more than this world could ever offer. If we do not lose heart, eternity awaits us and we will see Him face to face.

Read Hebrews 12 & 13

Jesus, fill our hearts with a desire to serve You, to seek You and love You as You love us. Your yoke is easy and Your burden light. You care about the minutest details. Help us not to fill our lives with so many things that we lose sight of our purpose. We ask also that You watch over and keep our loved ones. Reach down from Your throne and touch them with Your healing presence, Your love and mercy, and draw them to You. In Your holy name we pray. Amen.

DECEMBER 11
THE POWER OF THE TONGUE

James 3:9-10: With the tongue we praise our Lord and Father, and with it we curse men, who have been made in God's likeness. Out of the same mouth come praise and cursing. My brothers, this should not be.

The tongue is a small part of our body, yet it has the ability to make great boasts. It is a fire, a world of evil among the parts of the body. It corrupts the whole person, sets the whole course of life on fire and is itself set on fire by hell (James 3:6). When we think before we speak, it can make a difference in the outcome of a situation. Once the words are spoken, they can never be taken back. In the heat of the moment, words can flow out of our mouths fast and furious, but when that moment is over the words can linger like a dark cloud. Words can pierce our very hearts and sometimes stay with us for a lifetime. They can make us bitter but they can also make us happy. If we find ourselves in a situation where we are angry, we should remove ourselves, if at all possible, and find a quiet place to pray. This can be a very difficult thing to do, especially if we feel we are being wronged. There was no one who was more wrongly accused than our Savior. Beaten almost beyond recognition, ridiculed, spit upon, yet He said not a word. By His silence, those who did such things were convicted. Philippians 4:8 says, whatever is true, whatever is noble, whatever is right, whatever is pure, whatever is lovely, whatever is admirable, if anything is excellent or praiseworthy, think about such things. If we do that, we will speak words of love.

Read James 1-3

Heavenly Father, teach us to earnestly pray, to seek You and know You and love You with all of our hearts so that within our innermost being we will have joy and peace and the words that flow from our mouth will be words of encouragement to all those we come in contact with. Help us to think before we speak, even when we are wrongly accused or spoken to unkindly. We thank You for Your grace and Your wisdom. We pray and ask this in Jesus' precious name. Amen.

DECEMBER 12
PATIENCE

James 5:7-8: Be patient, then brothers, until the Lord's coming. See how the farmer waits for the land to yield its valuable crop and how patient he is for the autumn and spring rains. You too, be patient and stand firm, because the Lord's coming is near.

Oh, patience, a virtue all of us crave but have very little of. How many times have we prayed: Lord, give me patience but I want it right now! Our Lord is longsuffering and very patient. He never hurries and yet everything He desires is accomplished. Patience is bearing or enduring pains, trials or the like, without complaint or equanimity; having, exercising or manifesting the power to endure physical or mental affliction. In our verse this morning, the farmer is given as an example. He prepares the soil, plants the seed and then he waits for his crop to grow. When it does, there is a great harvest. The difficult part is knowing he has done the work but not knowing what the yield will be. Because of our faith in Jesus Christ, when we prepare our soil (ourselves) and plant our seed (faith), we know what the yield is and we must be patient to receive it. As we go through life, sometimes it seems impossible to be patient, to wait for whatever it is the Lord is trying to teach us. If we are patient, the end results are always worth the wait. He knows us, He knows what He desires for us, and when we serve Him with all of our hearts it is no sacrifice to wait patiently for His answers.

Read James 4 & 5

Holy Spirit, fill us with Your presence this day and give us the ability to be patient. Help us not to be anxious. Instead, keep us in an attitude of prayer. Help our unbelief and give us the ability to trust completely in our Father, who knows all things and who only wants good for those who serve Him. We ask this in the precious name of Jesus. Amen.

DECEMBER 13
BE HOLY BECAUSE I AM HOLY

1 Peter 1:14-16: As obedient children, do not conform to the evil desires you had when you lived in ignorance. But just as He who called you is holy, so be holy in all you do; for it is written: Be holy because I am holy.

The first two chapters of 1 Peter give us a lot of instruction on how we are to live as Christians. If we read and reread them, fill our hearts and minds with their meaning, we will have a greater understanding of the God we serve and the purpose for our lives. Before we knew Christ, we lived however we thought was best. We based our decisions on our own experience or the guidance of others, but we were ignorant of the spiritual side of life. We lived for the moment perhaps, or however we felt we should. Holiness was not in our thoughts because we didn't know the Holy One. That all changed the day we asked Jesus into our hearts. We are to be holy as He is holy. We become that way by spending time with Him. As our relationship grows, we experience His holiness and we know that He is worthy of our adoration and praise. He is pure and there never has been nor ever will be any sin found in Him. We become holy when we are spiritually whole, sound or perfect, pure in heart and acceptable to God. The only way we can do this is through a relationship with Jesus Christ.

Read 1 Peter 1 & 2

Heavenly Father, we pray that You would impart Your holiness into us so we might be perfect in Your sight; not as the world defines perfection but as You define it, through the sacrifice of Jesus Christ. Thank You for Your precious word that was given for instruction and edification so that we may know You more fully. Give us a longing and desire to read it so that as we go through this journey called life, we have it in our hearts and minds. When we come to the end of our journey, we know that we will be with You, in Your kingdom, forever and ever. Thank You for loving us that much. In Jesus' precious name we pray. Amen.

DECEMBER 14
THE REASON FOR OUR HOPE

1 Peter 3:13-16: Who is going to harm you if you are eager to do good? But even if you should suffer for what is right, you are blessed. Do not fear what they fear; do not be frightened. But in your hearts set apart Christ as Lord. Always be prepared to give an answer to everyone who asks you to give the reason for the hope that you have. But do this with gentleness and respect, keeping a clear conscience, so that those who speak maliciously against your good behavior in Christ may be ashamed of their slander.

The apostles suffered at the hands of those in authority because they proclaimed the salvation of the Lord. They were imprisoned, tortured, beheaded, and hung upside down on a cross. John was the only one who died a natural death. He was banished to the Isle of Patmos where he penned the Book of Revelation. The Spirit of God gives us boldness to proclaim our faith as well. We may be unjustly accused, ridiculed and mocked but even if we suffer for the kingdom, we are blessed. Some are called to be missionaries, others preachers or prophets. No matter our calling, each of us should retain the place in life that the Lord assigned to us and to which God has called us (1 Corinthians 7:17). We are to be humble and gentle; patient, bearing with one another in love. We are to make every effort to keep the unity of the Spirit through the bond of peace. There is one body and one Spirit, just as we were called to one hope when we were called, one Lord, one faith, one baptism, one God and Father of all, who is over all and through all and in all (Ephesians 4:2-5). No matter our calling, our hearts should be full of hope, full of joy unspeakable and glory, for we know Jesus Christ, in whom is hidden all the treasures of wisdom and knowledge.

Read 1 Peter 3-5

Heavenly Father, help us to yield daily to the guidance of the Holy Spirit so that we may be Your witnesses. You are a God of love and of mercy and You want everyone to come to eternal life through Your Son, Jesus Christ. Use us as your instruments of love to show the world that there is a better way than what they have chosen and that the rewards are better than anything this world can offer. We pray this in the precious name of Jesus. Amen.

DECEMBER 15
THE QUALITIES OF FAITH IN CHRIST

2 Peter 1:5-8: For this very reason, make every effort to add to your faith goodness; and to goodness, knowledge; and to knowledge, self-control; and to self-control, perseverance; and to perseverance, godliness; and to godliness, brotherly kindness; and to brotherly kindness, love. For if you possess these qualities in increasing measure, they will keep you from being ineffective and unproductive in your knowledge of our Lord Jesus Christ.

Therefore, my brothers, be all the more eager to make your calling and election sure. For if you do these things, you will never fall, and you will receive a rich welcome into the eternal kingdom of our Lord and Savior Jesus Christ. There is not a lot that can be added to the scripture today. In these verses, we are told that if we do the things as described we will never fall and we will receive a rich welcome into the eternal kingdom of our Lord and Savior Jesus Christ. The Spirit within awakens us, and these are the things that we long to do. Jesus is full of goodness, knowledge, self-control, perseverance, godliness, brotherly kindness and love. Not only did He talk about them, He lived them and gave us an example to follow. His resurrection is what makes Him King of kings and Lord of lords. This should give us boldness in our walk with Him. We know whom we serve and we should never be fearful of standing on our faith, but do it in love towards others so that they may see Him in us.

Read 2 Peter 1

Precious Jesus, thank You for giving us the example of who we should be in our daily lives upon this earth. We will have peace in our hearts when we do these things. We pray for wisdom so we are sensitive to the Holy Spirit and can pray with fervency and know that when we pray, You answer. We lift up Your Holy Name and praise You. In Your Holy Name we pray. Amen.

DECEMBER 16
WITH THE LORD, THERE IS NO TIME

2 Peter 3:8-9: But do not forget this one thing, dear friends: With the Lord a day is like a thousand years, and a thousand years are like a day. The Lord is not slow in keeping His promise, as some understand slowness. He is patient with you, not wanting anyone to perish, but everyone to come to repentance.

Time is something we are always running out of. There are never enough hours in the day to accomplish our tasks. We cannot live without a clock telling us what time it is, how much time we have to do something. Time, time, time, we are controlled by time. And then it's over, and for us there is no more time. It has run out. That could be why we think the Lord doesn't answer when we pray. We look at our watches, we count the days and nothing has happened. But with Him, there is no time. He doesn't sit looking at the clock, saying, "Oh, I think enough time has passed. They have learned their lesson or they have suffered enough." That may be how we think but it's not how He thinks. Trust in Him at all times, O people, pour out your hearts to Him, for God is our refuge (Psalm 62:8). As God's fellow workers, we are urged to not receive God's grace in vain, for He says in the time of my favor, I heard you and in the day of salvation I helped you (2 Corinthians 6:1-2). The time we spend with Him is the time that counts. Today is the time of God's favor. Now is the day of salvation.

Read 2 Peter 2 & 3

Jesus, our time with You is the most important time we can spend. Help us not to waste it. Though we get busy with the hubbub of the day, may we always be mindful of Your presence and know that You love and guide us. Keep us in tune with the direction of the Holy Spirit so that we don't use our time unwisely. In Your precious name we pray. Amen.

DECEMBER 17
LOVE NOT THE WORLD

1 John 2:15-17: Do not love the world or anything in the world. If anyone loves the world, the love of the Father is not in him. For everything in the world—the cravings of sinful man, the lust of his eyes and the boasting of what he has and does—comes not from the Father but from the world. The world and its desires pass away, but the man who does the will of God lives forever.

The last sentence of this verse sums it up: The man who does the will of God lives forever. His will is that we no longer conform to the pattern of this world but be transformed by the renewing of your mind. Then you will be able to test and approve what God's will is, His good, pleasing and perfect will (Romans 12:2). When we desire only Him, we do not want the temporary things of this world. Before Jesus ascended into heaven, He told His disciples that in His Father's house there are many mansions; if it were not so, He would tell us. We have a home in Heaven that is everlasting, that will not be corrupted or destroyed by the elements or broken into by thieves. It is something we don't have to work for; it is ours when we believe in Jesus. Our eyes can be deceitful. We look around us and see that the things of this world are not so bad; there are seemingly no consequences to the actions of those who do wrong. Oh, but there is, for we serve a just and holy God who is the judge of all the earth. We never know what is really going on in another person's life, but He does. Those who do not serve Him have very real problems whether they acknowledge it or not, and they are searching for something or someone to fill the void that is in their lives. He is the true light that came into this world and He gives light to everyone. Those who believe this become the children of God (John 1:9-13).

Read 1 John 1 & 2

Heavenly Father, we thank You for Your plan of salvation, for the precious blood of Your Son, Jesus Christ, and for the forgiveness of sins. Help us to draw close to You, to read Your word and learn of You, so that the things of this world will not overtake us. Thank You for the gift of eternal life with You, where moth does not corrupt and evil no longer exists. Help us to draw others to You by living lives that show Your love for us and them. In the precious name of Jesus we pray. Amen.

DECEMBER 18
WE ARE CHILDREN OF GOD

1 John 3:1-2: How great is the love the Father has lavished on us, that we should be called children of God! And that is what we are! The reason the world does not know us is that it did not know him. Dear friends, now we are children of God, and what we will be has not yet been made known. But we know that when He appears we shall be like Him, for we shall see Him as He is.

We are God's children, not because we chose Him but because He chose us. He chose us in Him before the creation of the world to be holy and blameless in His sight (Ephesians 1:4). But we ought always to thank God for you, brothers, loved by the Lord, because from the beginning God chose you to be saved through the sanctifying work of the Spirit and through belief in the truth (2 Thessalonians 2:13). But you are a chosen people, a royal priesthood, a holy nation, a people belonging to God, that you may declare the praises of Him who called you out of darkness into His wonderful light (1 Peter 2:9). Our bodies are the temple of the Living God. He said, "I will live with them and walk among them, and I will be their God and they will be my people. I will be a Father to you, and you will be my sons and daughters," says the Lord Almighty (2 Corinthians 6:16 & 18).

Read 1 John 3 & 4

Heavenly Father, keep us walking in the light of who You are so that we will not yield to the desires of this world and fall into temptation. Thank You for calling us out of darkness into Your wonderful light and making us Your sons and daughters. Help us to walk with Your power through all the trials that this life brings. You did not promise us a life free from hardships but You have promised life everlasting to those who trust in You and endure to the end. We pray this in the precious name of Jesus. Amen.

DECEMBER 19
BELIEF IN JESUS OVERCOMES THE WORLD

1 John 5:3-5: This is love for God: to obey His commands. And His commands are not burdensome, for everyone born of God overcomes the world. This is the victory that has overcome the world, even our faith. Who is it that overcomes the world? Only he who believes that Jesus is the Son of God.

There is no other way to heaven except by faith in Jesus Christ as the Son of God and the Savior of all mankind. Those who say otherwise do not know Him and have not been filled with His Holy Spirit. There is no other way to believe other than by faith. After Jesus was resurrected, He appeared to His disciples who were at first frightened upon seeing Him but then rejoiced when they realized that all He had told them was true. The only one who was not there was Thomas. When the disciples told him about Jesus' appearance, He did not believe. He said he would only believe if he could put his hands in Jesus' side and his finger in the nail prints. When Jesus appeared the second time, Thomas was present and He said to Thomas, "Put your finger here; see my hands. Reach out your hand and put it into my side." Then Thomas said, "My Lord and my God." Jesus replied, "Because you have seen me, you have believed; blessed are those who have not seen and yet have believed" (John 20:24-29). He gave this promise and said that we who believe have eternal life in Him. There should be nothing in this world that can stop us from believing His words are true. One day we will be with Him forever where there is no more lying, no more death, no more tears, no more sorrow.

Read 1 John 5

Lord, as the man who was looking for a miracle cried out to You, help my unbelief, we cry out to You as well that You would give us such a measure of faith in You so we have no doubts but would only believe. Thank You for the power and authority we have in You over all the powers of the enemy. Give us hearts to follow You with everything that is in us so that we are able to show Your love to all those we come in contact with. We love You and thank You for Your sacrifice upon the cross. It is in Your name we pray. Amen.

DECEMBER 20
DECEIVERS

2 John 7: Many deceivers, who do not acknowledge Jesus Christ as coming in the flesh, have gone out into the world. Any such person is a deceiver and the antichrist.

It's strange how people respond when the name of Jesus Christ is mentioned, especially by those who do not know Him. Some actually get quite agitated and annoyed; others, it's no big deal. Most everyone has heard of Jesus but most do not know Him. And if we don't know a person, we really cannot have an opinion about them. That is how deceit comes in. If we don't read the Word for ourselves, if we don't pray and seek the face of the Lord, then when deceivers come in talking up a good story, it is possible to be swayed by them. Jesus Christ was born in Bethlehem as the Savior of the world, a newborn baby born to a virgin. This was

A Daily Devotional of God's Unending Love

prophesied in the Old Testament and it came to pass hundreds of years later. He was a child just like we were. When He became a man, He taught the Word of God. He knew who He was, and He knew who His Father was. He also knew why He came to this earth, and that was to die on the cross for our sins. He had to shed His blood because there is no remission for sins without the shedding of blood. But then the most incredible thing happened, He rose from the dead. He appeared to many people, including his disciples, and taught them more about what the future would hold. He instructed them to go into the world and preach the good news to all creation (Mark 16:15). Then He ascended into Heaven. If anyone says otherwise, they do not know Him and they are a liar. We are to watch and not be deceived. For many will come in His name claiming they are Jesus and that the time is near. We are not to follow them (Luke 21:8). False Christs and false prophets will appear and perform great signs and miracles to deceive even the elect, if that were possible. He has told us this ahead of time so that if anyone says, "There he is, out in the desert," we are not to go out; or "Here he is, in the inner rooms," we are not to believe it. As lightning comes from the east and is visible even in the west, so will be the coming of the Son of Man (Matthew 24:24-27).

Read 2 John & 3 John

Heavenly Father, You are the only true God. We thank You for Your plan of salvation to bring us back to You. Keep us from being deceived. The world is full of greed, selfishness and hatred, all of which is the opposite of who You are. Help us to not be caught up so much in what is around us but keep us close to You and help us to keep our eyes on the prize, eternal life, knowing that the things of this world soon pass away. We pray this in the name of Your precious Son, Jesus Christ. Amen.

DECEMBER 21
EQUAL IN THE SIGHT OF GOD

Jude 20-23: But you, dear friends, build yourselves up in your most holy faith and pray in the Holy Spirit. Keep yourselves in God's love as you wait for the mercy of our Lord Jesus Christ to bring you to eternal life. Be merciful to those who doubt; snatch others from the fire and save them; to others show mercy, mixed with fear—hating even the clothing stained by corrupted flesh.

We have an awesome responsibility as believers in Christ. We know that Jesus is the way, the truth and the life and believing in Him leads to everlasting life in His kingdom. Our hearts' desire should be to share that good news but we mustn't do it by being judgmental or condemning another. We must always remember that we too are sinners; that it is by grace we are saved, through faith, and this is not from ourselves but it is the gift of God. And it is not by works so that no one can boast (Ephesians 2:8-9). Jesus tells the story of the landowner who goes out early in the morning and agrees to pay the workers a certain amount. Throughout the day, up to the eleventh hour, which would be the end of the day, he hires others to work. When it came time to pay everyone, he gave them all the same amount. Those who were hired early in the day grumbled but the man responded by saying, "Friend, I am not being unfair to you. I want to give the man who was hired last the same as I gave you. Don't I have the right to do what I want with my own money? Or are you envious because I am generous?" So the last will be first and the first will be last (Matthew 20:1-16). This parable tells us that we are all equal in the sight of God. It doesn't matter when we accept Jesus. It matters whether we believe and know Him. Only through the love of the Holy Spirit will anyone be drawn to Him, and we can share that love when we have Jesus in our heart.

Read Jude

Heavenly Father, the enemy of our soul is going to and fro seeking whom he may devour. He especially relishes it when he can deceive Your children. Help us to walk with the Holy Spirit so that He checks our spirits and we then know when we should or should not do something. Remind us often that we are saved by grace and that we have a responsibility to share Your grace and mercy with others. We pray this in the precious name of Your Son, Jesus. Amen.

DECEMBER 22
REPENTANCE

Revelation 1:4-6: John, to the seven churches in the province of Asia: Grace and peace to you from Him who is, and who was, and who is to come, and from the seven spirits before His throne, and from Jesus Christ, who is the faithful witness, the firstborn from the dead, and the ruler of the kings of the earth. To him who loves us and has freed us from our sins by his blood, and has made us to be a kingdom and priests to serve his God and Father—to Him be glory and power forever and ever! Amen.

Revelation 2:10:. . .Be faithful, even to the point of death and I will give you the crown of life.

Revelation 2:11:. . .He who overcomes will not be hurt at all by the second death.

The Apostle John had been sent to the Isle of Patmos as punishment for preaching the Word of God. While there, Jesus appeared to him in all His glory and told him to write the last book of the Bible, The Revelation. Jesus spoke to the seven churches of Asia which are represented by the seven golden lampstands that John sees. His instructions are given in love but they are also very harsh because they expose the complacency that is going on in the churches, and the consequences if they do not repent. Repentance is the crux of our relationship with Christ. If we claim we have not sinned, we make Him out to be a liar and His word has no place in our lives (1 John 1:10). If we confess our sin, He is faithful and just and forgives our sins and purifies us from all unrighteousness (1 John 1:9). Godly sorrow brings repentance that leads to salvation and leaves no regret, but worldly sorrow brings death (2 Corinthians 7:10). We were not only born into a sinful world, we are all sinners in need of a Savior. The first step towards salvation is repentance. The Lord says, "This is the One I esteem: He who is humble and contrite in spirit and trembles at my Word (Isaiah 66:2). Our Lord has laid His plan before us. It is ours for the taking.

Read Revelation 1 & 2

Jesus, thank You for the Book of Revelation. We pray that the Holy Spirit enlightens us as we read this book so that we gain a better understanding of You. We know that You are coming and of Your kingdom there will be no end. Help us to live like it might happen today so that we are prepared and not caught unawares. In Your precious name we pray. Amen.

DECEMBER 23
OVERCOMERS

Revelation 3:11-12: I am coming soon. Hold on to what you have, so that no one will take your crown. Him who overcomes I will make a pillar in the temple of my God. Never again will he leave it. I will write on him the name of my God and the name of the city of my God, the new Jerusalem, which is coming down out of heaven from my God; and I will also write on him my new name.

Revelation 3:21: To him who overcomes, I will give the right to sit with Me on My throne, just as I overcame and sat down with My Father on His throne.

These are the words of Jesus, the risen Christ. His instructions to John to give the seven churches in Asia apply to our lives today. When we keep focused on the end prize, serving Him should be a joy that thrills our hearts from the moment we wake up in the morning until the time we go to bed. There is nothing on this earth that compares to the glory that awaits those who are faithful to Jesus until the end of time. What awaits us in His kingdom are things our minds cannot even comprehend. He has in store for us everlasting riches, where moth and worm does not corrupt. When this earth passes away, there will be a new heaven and a new earth where Jesus will rule and reign forevermore. For those who overcome this world, He has written on them the name of His God.

Read Revelation 3 & 4

Precious Jesus, our Savior, our Redeemer, the Rose of Sharon, the Great I Am, may the words that You have spoken penetrate our hearts and minds so that we never lose focus of the ultimate prize, eternal life with You. Thank You for Your many blessings while on this earth. Teach us patience and wisdom as we go through life's trials. Guide us by Your precious Holy Spirit. In Your wondrous name we pray. Amen.

DECEMBER 24
THE LAST DAYS

Revelation 7:9-10: After this I looked and there before me was a great multitude that no one could count, from every nation, tribe, people and language, standing before the throne and in front of the Lamb. They were wearing white robes and were holding palm branches in their hands. And they cried out in a loud voice: Salvation belongs to our God, who sits on the throne, and to the Lamb.

John is given a vision of the last days by an angel of God. He is shown what is happening in the heavens as the beginning of the end days approach. He is also shown a scroll with writing on it and the angels are looking for one who is worthy enough to open the scroll. At first, no one is found, which causes John to weep, but then the angel tells him not to weep as there is one worthy to open the scroll, which is Jesus. Revelation 5:9 says, "You are worthy to take the scroll and to open its seals, because you were slain, and with your blood you purchased men for God from every tribe and language and people and nation. You have made them to be a kingdom and priests to serve our God, and they will reign on the earth." Before that time comes, every ear must hear of Jesus. "Then I saw an angel flying in midair, and he had the eternal gospel to proclaim to those who live on the earth, to every nation, tribe, language and people. He said, 'Fear God and give Him glory because the hour of His judgment has come. Worship Him who made the heavens, the earth, the sea, and the springs of water.'" (Revelation 14:6-7) The word of God will come to pass just as it is written.

Read Revelation 5-7

Jesus, as we read Your word and enter the last Book of the Bible that tells us about the things to come, show us what it means and how we should prepare ourselves for the time when You will be here to reign upon this earth. Sometimes it seems like a dream and so far away, but we know that You will come as a thief in the night and we should be prepared at all times. Help us to be diligent and have a heart for God so that we may be ready when the time comes and also be ready to share Your word with others. In Your precious name we pray. Amen.

DECEMBER 25
JESUS, ALL POWERFUL

Revelation 9:20: The rest of mankind that were not killed by these plagues still did not repent of the work of their hands; they did not stop worshiping demons, and idols of gold, silver, bronze, stone and wood idols that cannot see or hear or walk.

Revelation 10:7: But in the days when the seventh angel is about to sound his trumpet, the mystery of God will be accomplished, just as He announced to His servants the prophets.

Jesus said that in the last days if He did not cut short those days, no one would survive. But for the sake of the elect whom He has chosen, He has shortened them (Mark 13:20). It is going to be bad when the end is near; worse than our human minds can imagine. Those who trust in the Lord, who know Him, who serve Him, will be light in the darkness. Even amidst the horrors that lie ahead, in Revelation chapter 9:4, the angels were told not to harm the grass of the earth or any plant or tree, but only those people who did not have the seal of God on their foreheads. We are God's servants and He has sealed us with His seal. The harm that befalls unbelievers in those days will not befall His sealed ones. Revelation is a complex book that many have tried earnestly to understand and interpret. Some say that there will be a rapture of the church and we will not have to endure those times of utter darkness upon the earth. Others say the Bible does not support the teaching of a rapture. No matter, because when He returns, His throne will be established and everyone will bow down and worship Him.

Read Revelation 8-10

Heavenly Father, You have not given us a spirit of fear but of power and of love and of a sound mind. You are our Creator and our Strong

Deliverer. Thank You for Your everlasting love. Help us to grow in our faith and stay in an attitude of prayer so that we will be ready at any time to follow the leading of the Holy Spirit and do Your will. Go before us and behind us and keep us safe. We thank You and praise Your mighty and glorious name. Amen.

DECEMBER 26
JESUS REIGNS FOREVER

Revelation 11:15: The seventh angel sounded his trumpet and there were loud voices in heaven, which said: The kingdom of the world has become the kingdom of our Lord and of His Christ, and He will reign for ever and ever.

Jesus overcame death, hell and the grave. All that the prophets had proclaimed was fulfilled. The devil still prowls around like a roaring lion seeking whom he may devour so we must be self-controlled and alert, resisting him and standing firm in our faith (2 Peter 5:8-9). And those who stand firm to the end will be saved (Matthew 24:13). When the end comes, loud voices in heaven will proclaim that the kingdom of this world has become the kingdom of our Lord and of His Christ. Jesus Christ will return to this earth not as a newborn baby but as King of all creation. He will rule in love but with a rod of iron and of His kingdom there will be no end. This is the God whom we serve. He is a God of love and compassion, but there is coming a time when He will be the judge of all.

Read Revelation 11 & 12

Heavenly Father, open our minds and hearts to receive the meaning of Revelation. May we live every moment of our lives for You, being prepared always for the end to come. Help us to keep focused on You and know that no matter what, everything is going to be all right. We proclaim this in the precious and holy name of our Savior, Jesus. Amen.

DECEMBER 27
TIME OF JUDGMENT

Revelation 14:13: Then I heard a voice from heaven say, "Write: Blessed are the dead who die in the Lord from now on." "Yes," says the Spirit, "they will rest from their labor, for their deeds will follow them."

Chapters 13 through 15 speak again about the end days and how horrific that time will be, for God's judgment is sure and there will be no escape. Yet, amidst all of the turmoil, we are told that this calls for patience, endurance and faithfulness on the part of the saints. It is difficult to write about these chapters. We know that the God whom we serve is merciful, forgiving and full of love, but there is coming a time when the angels of heaven will be instructed to pour out His wrath because the end has come and He will wait no longer. His judgments are righteous and there is no doubt all these things will come to pass: the beast who was wounded and then healed; the fact that if anyone does not worship the beast they will be killed; that the beast will be given power to make war against the saints, to conquer them; he will be given authority over every tribe, people, language and nation; he will do great miracles such as causing fire to come down from heaven to earth in full view of men, yet at the same time use blasphemies and utter proud words. He will proclaim that he is God, and people will worship him. The One true God, though, resides in Heaven. He has only love and mercy for those who serve Him. He has given us a free will to choose who we will serve. Even to the end, those who call upon His name will be saved. When this time is over, Satan and his fallen angels will be put into a pit and Jesus Christ will return in glory and triumph. He will reign upon this earth for 1,000 years and we will know what it it's like to live on earth without sin.

Read Revelation 13-15

Heavenly Father, thank You that we can open the pages of Your Word and learn about You, the God whom we serve. Keep our hearts and minds focused on You, and continually remind us that no matter what we are going through, You are in control; You created the heavens and the earth and all that therein is, and You will do with it what pleases You. Thank You for calling us to serve You. Give us tender hearts full of Your love and mercy so that we are an example of who Christ is. In Jesus' precious name we pray. Amen.

DECEMBER 28
GOD'S WRATH COMPLETE

Revelation 17:14: They will make war against the Lamb, but the Lamb will overcome them because He is Lord of lords and King of kings—and with Him will be His called, chosen and faithful followers.

For then there will be great distress, unequaled from the beginning of the world until now, and never to be equaled again. If those days had not been cut short no one would survive, but for the sake of the elect those days will be shortened (Matthew 24:21-22). In the end days, there will be deception in the world that is unparalleled. We can thank God this is not possible for the ones who are grounded in His Word. Jesus foretold all of these things so that those who believe in Him are prepared when the time comes. God's wrath will be poured out of the seven bowls. Those with the mark of the beast will break out with ugly and painful sores. The sea will be turned into blood and every living thing in it will die. The rivers and springs of water will turn to blood. The sun will scorch the people with fire. They will be seared with intense heat. They will curse the name of God who has control over these plagues but they will refuse to repent and glorify God. The throne of the beast will be plunged into darkness. The great river Euphrates and its water will be dried up to prepare the way for the kings from the east. Then out of the temple will come a loud voice from the throne saying, "It is done!"

Read Revelation 16 & 17

Heavenly Father, open our eyes to what is happening around us. Help us to be faithful and ready for the day when Jesus appears in the clouds. Give us Your strength so that we will endure to the end. Help us to keep our eyes on the ultimate prize of eternal life. Thank you for Your faithfulness, for Your love and Your protection. Keep us always mindful of who You are and the love that You have for us. Lord, help our nation to turn back to You. We have drifted so far away. You are faithful and just to forgive us our sins when we repent. Help us as a nation to do this. In Jesus' name we pray. Amen.

DECEMBER 29
THE FALL OF BABYLON

Revelation 18:9-10: When the kings of the earth who committed adultery with her and shared her luxury see the smoke of her burning, they will weep and mourn over her. Terrified at her torment, they will stand far off and cry: "Woe! Woe! O great city. O Babylon, city of power! In one hour your doom has come!"

Babylon was a great ancient city in the Euphrates Valley, which about 2225 B.C. became the capital of Babylonia, whose empire reached into Asia Minor and Egypt. It was the center of the world's commerce and of the arts and sciences. It was marked by luxury and magnificence. Though Babylon does not exist today as it did in ancient times, its ways have come to represent a way of life, a philosophy and a religious view. Revelation 18:23 says that by her sorceries all nations have been deceived. Since shortly after Creation, the philosophy of its political system has been a means of control. Throughout history, Babylon has revived over and over again. With few exceptions, it has always been opposed to God. We don't know if Babylon represents a physical place in Chapter 18, but it clearly represents the things that this world has to offer. Our Lord tells us that all of those things will be destroyed in the matter of one hour; that the nations of the world will weep because of it. As Christians, we will rejoice because in Chapter 19:6, we are told: Then I heard what sounded like a great multitude, like the roar of rushing waters and like loud peals of thunder, shouting: Hallelujah! For our Lord God Almighty reigns. Let us rejoice and be glad and give Him glory! For the wedding of the Lamb has come and His bride has made herself ready.

Read Revelation 18 & 19

Heavenly Father, we know that Your words are faithful and true. Although we may not understand all the things that are spoken about in Revelation, we know that You will return to set up Your kingdom on this earth. Prepare our hearts and minds to receive what You have for us. Use us each day for Your glory, that Your will might be fulfilled until that great and glorious day that Jesus appears in the sky victorious, holy and righteous! In Jesus' name we pray. Amen.

DECEMBER 30
THE LAMB'S BOOK OF LIFE

Revelation 21:27: Nothing impure will ever enter it, nor will anyone who does what is shameful or deceitful, but only those whose names are written in the Lamb's book of life.

Chapters 20 and 21 describe life for those who endure to the end. Satan will be bound for 1,000 years. Those who have been martyred or who have died because of their faith will be resurrected and rule with Him for 1,000 years. Righteousness will prevail and there will be peace and tranquility on earth for that period of time. Thereafter, Satan will be released from the pit for a short time and amazingly there are those who will turn away from Jesus after knowing what it is like to live in His peace. They will quickly be consumed by fire and thrown into everlasting darkness along with Satan and his fallen angels. Then there is the final judgment, where the Book of Life is opened and each person will be judged according to what they have done. When the Son of Man comes in His glory, and all the angels with Him, He will sit on His throne in heavenly glory. He will say to those on His right, "Come, you who are blessed by my Father. Take your inheritance in the kingdom prepared for you since the creation of the world. Then He will say to those on His left, depart from me you who are cursed into the eternal fire prepared for the devil and his angels." (Matthew 25:31, 34, 41).

Read Revelation 20 & 21

Jesus, we ask for Your strength to help us not be sidetracked by the things this world has to offer. Life is short and all of these things we see will soon fade away, but You are forever. You are the Alpha and the Omega, the beginning and the end. We thank You for Your precious blood that washes away all of our sins. Amen.

DECEMBER 31
A NEW LIFE

Revelation 22:3: No longer will there be any curse. The throne of God and of the Lamb will be in the city, and his servants will serve him. They will see his face, and his name will be on their foreheads.

The last chapter of Revelation and of the Bible reveals what awaits those who are faithful and true to God's Word. The disciples thought Jesus would return in their lifetime, but time has gone on and now we are in the days where there are many signs that these are the end times, the days when Jesus will soon return. No matter the time, though, we are to always be prepared for that glorious day when He actually comes back. We are not to be like the servant who when His master went away he decided to do evil and when his lord returned unexpectedly he was cast into everlasting darkness. No. We are to watch and wait; be yielded to the Holy Spirit and follow His direction. The world can be very enticing, but our hope and our rewards are much greater if we stand faithful until the end. Eye has not seen nor ear heard the things that the Lord has prepared for those who love Him. The wolf will live with the lamb, the leopard will lie down with the goat, the calf and the lion and the yearling together; and a little child will lead them. They will neither harm nor destroy on His holy mountain, for the earth will be full of the knowledge of the Lord as the waters cover the sea (Isaiah 11:6-9).

Read Revelation 22

Jesus, we thank You for Your faithfulness. We thank You for Your precious Word that teaches us how we should live for You. We pray for power in the Holy Spirit in order to continue on life's journey as You guide and keep us. Help us to seek You and Your ways continually so that we do not fall into the deceitfulness of the world but stay faithful to You until the end. In Your precious name we pray. Amen.

A PERSONAL RELATIONSHIP WITH JESUS

Acts 16:31 says to believe in the Lord Jesus and you will be saved. What does that mean exactly? Jesus Christ is a real person who lived on this earth. He walked among the people and taught the truths of God, the Father. He died for the sins of all mankind so that we could be assured of eternal life. He rose from the dead and He is now seated at the right hand of God Almighty. He intercedes for us day and night. One day He will return to this earth to set up His kingdom. We can know Jesus in a real and personal way today, right now. We don't have to wait until He returns. He sent His Holy Spirit to guide us. Say this prayer: Lord Jesus, I am a sinner. I have lived my life for myself and not for You. Jesus, forgive me of my sins. Cleanse me by Your blood which was shed on the cross at Calvary. Teach me Your ways and from this day forward help me to live my life for You.

If you have said this prayer, begin reading the Bible. Find a church in your area that teaches the resurrection power of Jesus Christ and that the Father, Son and Holy Spirit are three-in-one. Get into a small group at your church and begin a journey with Jesus that will transform your life forever!

ABOUT THE AUTHOR

At the age of 20, Mindi surrendered her life to Jesus Christ, who not only changed her but filled her with an unquenchable desire to follow Him with all of her heart. She has read through the Bible several times and is always amazed at the unconditional love and mercy of God Almighty. His Holy Word is alive, and reflects God's nature and plan for redemption. By the power of His Holy Spirit, He reveals His heart to us. The Lord has taught her to put Him first and foremost in her life and she has never regretted the decision to follow Him. She lives in Palm Beach Gardens and worships at Christ Fellowship. She loves to travel, volunteer at Hannah's Home, play the piano and spend time with friends. She travels frequently to California to be with her family and worships at Calvary Temple when visiting them. If you wish to contact her, please send an email to mindi.colchico@gmail.com.

FURTHER READING

The Treasury of David by Charles H. Spurgeon
Unlocking the Bible by David Pawson

END NOTES

*The New Testament portion of this devotional was written 2 to 3 years prior to the Psalms and any scripture references are incorporated into the body of the text rather than denoted separately.

Any references to the male gender only, in scripture or text, is also meant to include women.

INDEX

TITLE	DATE
A Blameless Life	May 2
A Broken and Contrite Heart	March 5
A Cry for Justice	March 13
A Firm Foundation	May 6
A High Priest	May 19
A Lie	August 10
A New Life	Dec. 31
A Thorn in the Flesh	Nov. 15
A Time to Sing	July 7
A Transformed Life	Sept. 27
A Whole Heart	May 13
Abundance in Him	March 21
All-Knowing	April 25
Acknowledge the Lord in all Our Ways	July 25
Always Faithful	June 8
Always Present	February 8
Anger	February 6
Are We Who We Say We Are?	August 9
Asaph's Cry	April 12
Attitudes of the Heart	October 30
Avoid Sexual Immorality	Nov. 26
Be Careful Where We Walk	August 4
Be Holy Because I am Holy	Dec. 13
Be Humble1	Sept. 23
Be Kind to Everyone	Dec. 1
Be Not Ashamed of Our Faith	Sept. 11
Being a Christian	Nov. 5
Being a Servant	Sept. 12
Belief in Jesus Overcomes the World	Dec. 19
Blessings	June 28
Boast in the Lord	August 18

A Daily Devotional of God's Unending Love

TITLE	DATE
Burden Bearer	March 25
Calming The Storms of Life	August 27
Choices	April 15
Commitment	July 27
Communion	October 2
Condemned	October 12
Consequences	October 16
Corrupt Judges	April 11
Countless Wonders	February 19
Creator of All Things	January 8
Crucified with Christ	Nov. 16
Deceit of Riches	August 14
Deceivers	Dec. 20
Delight in the Lord	February 15
Deliverance	January 23
Deliverance From All Troubles	March 8
Denying Self	Sept. 1
Despair	January 27
Different Callings, the Same Lord	Nov. 8
Divided We Fall	Sept. 9
Do Not Be Anxious	Nov. 22
Do Not Be Caught Unaware	Sept. 26
Do Not Conform to this World	October 31
Do Not Forget	May 11
Do Not Turn Away	April 7
Drowning in Despair?	March 26
Each Man is but a Breath	February 18
Endure to the End	Dec. 10
Equal in the Sight of God	Dec. 21
Establishing the Throne	April 19
Eternal Hope in His Unfailing Love	July 19
Eternal Word of God	June 9
Eternity Awaits Us	April 24
Ever-Present Help in Trouble	February 26
Everything God Created is Good	Nov. 29
Evil	Oct. 24
Exalt the Lord	February 11
Extol Him	May 26
Eyes of the Lord	August 6
Faith	August 30
Faith in Christ	October 26
Faith in the Midst of Turmoil	May 21
Faithfulness	April 14

A Daily Devotional of God's Unending Love

TITLE	DATE
Faith as Small as a Mustard Seed	Sept. 2
False Hope in Riches	March 1
Fearfully and Wonderfully Made	July 10
Final Destiny	March 31
Fleeing from Adversity	March 9
Freedom	June 3
Fruits of the Spirit	Nov. 17
Forever and Ever	February 25
Forgive as the Lord Forgave	Nov. 25
Forgiveness Through the Blood	June 30
Fountain of Life	February 14
Fully Trusting the Lord	April 20
Glorious City of God	April 16
Glorious Splendor	July 16
God of Mercy	May 12
God Never Fails	March 10
God's Faithfulness	April 18
God's Great Works	April 23
God's Heavenly Throne	June 23
God's Perfect Plan	April 4
God's Power	Nov. 18
God's Righteousness	March 6
God's Silence	May 17
God's Word	Sept. 18
God's Wrath Complete	Dec. 28
Going Beyond What is Expected	Sept. 25
Great is the Lord	April 27
Guard my Mouth	July 12
Happiness and Joy	March 24
He Answers	January 19
He Delivers Us from Distress	May 14
He is Faithful	May 16
He Formed Us	June 7
He Heard My Cry	May 25
He Hears and Answers	June 20
He is Always with Us	October 4
He is the Light	April 28
He is Limitless	May 9
He is Worthy of Praise	July 8
He Never Fails	May 10
He Never Slumbers nor Sleeps	June 21
He Provides	January 21
He Restores My Soul	January 29

TITLE	DATE
He Walks with Us	May 15
He Who Believes in Me Shall Live	October 6
He Who Holds the Pillars Firm	April 3
He Who Wins Souls is Wise	August 2
Hear My Cry, Lord	January 6
Hear Me in My Distress, O Lord	April 17
Heartfelt Cry	March 20
Heaven	April 1
Heaven and Earth Will Praise Him	March 27
Help Us, O God	April 8
His Commandments	May 29
His Love Endures Forever	July 6
His Plan Stands Firm	February 10
His Path Lights the Way	June 11
His Presence	January 1
His Promise	June 4
His Statutes are Trustworthy	June 15
His Statutes Last Forever	June 16
His Witnesses	October 15
His Words Are True	June 17
His Words are Sweeter Than Honey	June 10
Hope	January 28
Hope in Desperation	May 3
Hope in His Word	June 12
How Great is Our God	April 5
Humility	Nov. 21
I Am Your Servant	June 13
I Will Give You Rest	August 29
Imitators of God	Nov. 20
In Him is Life	Sept. 29
In Times of Affliction	June 6
Jerusalem	June 22
Jesus, All-Powerful	Dec. 25
Jesus, Son of the Living God	October 13
Jesus, the Cornerstone	May 28
Jesus, the Creator	Nov. 23
Jesus, the Living Water	October 1
Jesus Lives Forever	Dec. 7
Jesus Said, Follow Me	August 25
Jesus Walks with Us	Dec. 3
Jesus Reigns Forever	Dec. 26
Joy	June 26
Judgment Belongs to God	Feb. 13

A Daily Devotional of God's Unending Love

TITLE	DATE
Keeping Our Eyes on Jesus	Sept. 21
Knowing Him	April 30
Knowing our Father	Sept. 17
Let Not Man Triumph	January 10
Let Our Light Shine	August 26
Life Does Not Consist of its Abundance	Sept. 22
Life Lifter	March 17
Life Quickly Passes	April 21
Lift Your Hands	July 4
Lip Service	August 31
Listen	Dec. 2
Living According to God's Word	May 30
Love	Nov. 9
Love the Lord Our God	Sept. 4
Love Not the World	Dec. 17
Love One Another	October 7
Love Your Enemy	August 16
Make Wisdom Our Sister	July 29
Man, Justified Before God	October 25
Never Doubting	Dec. 9
Never Forsaken	February 16
Never Put to Shame	January 31
New Covenant	Dec. 8
No Branch Can Bear Fruit of Itself	October 9
No Condemnation in Christ Jesus	October 29
No Favoritism with the Lord	October 18
No Fear in Trusting God	February 3
No Other God	January 20
No Hiding Place	March 4
No Temptation Beyond What We Can Bear	Nov. 7
None Lives to Himself Alone	Nov. 1
Nothing is Hidden from God	Dec. 6
Nothing Withheld	April 13
Obedience	Sept. 16
Obeying God's Law	June 2
Obeying Jesus	October 8
One with the Father	October 11
Open Eyes	May 31
Our Battles Are Won	Nov. 14
Our Choices	August 17
Our Days are Like Grass	May 5
Our Father, the Avenger	Nov. 27
Our Fortress in Times of Trouble	March 18

TITLE	DATE
Our Mighty God	May 27
Our God of Mercy	July 13
Our God Reigns	January 2
Our Gracious God	June 5
Our Help and Deliverer	March 28
Our Protector	January 25
Our Provider	May 8
Our Refuge	February 7
Our Righteous God	January 7
Our Strength and Shield	February 4
Overcomers	Dec. 23
Overflowing With Hope	Nov. 2
Patience	Dec. 12
Peace in Turmoil	June 18
Persecution	October 17
Power Over Death	October 19
Praise Him	March 22
Praise the Lord	July 22
Pray for Those in Authority	Nov. 28
Prayer and Fasting	Sept. 8
Preach the Good News	Sept. 15
Pride Brings Man Low	August 20
Prideful Man	March 15
Protector and Deliverer	January 3
Purification	August 8
Put Your Hope in God	February 22
Quiet Time	January 4
Rebuke Not a Mocker	July 31
Reconciled to Our Father	Nov. 19
Redeemed	Sept. 30
Refined and Tested	January 14
Repentance	Dec. 22
Rescue Us	July 15
Resurrection Power	Nov. 10
Restore Us	April 9
Restoration and Love	Dec. 4
Results of Our Actions	August 12
Rewards of Virtue	August 22
Riches without Understanding	March 2
Righteous Rulers	March 30
Righteousness Leads to Everlasting Life	August 3
Ruler of All	March 3
Salvation in Jesus Alone	October 14

A Daily Devotional of God's Unending Love

TITLE	DATE
Secure in the Lord	January 18
See What God Will Do	March 14
Seek Wisdom	July 24
Serving Jesus, and Others	Sept. 3
Set Apart	February 2
Shrewd as Snakes, Innocent as Doves	August 28
Signs of the End	Sept. 13
Sing to the Lord	April 29
Sons and Daughters	January 5
Straying Like Lost Sheep	June 19
Streams of Living Water	October 3
Strength in God	March 12
Sweet Smelling Aroma	August 1
Teaching the Next Generation	April 6
Teach Us Your Will	July 14
Temptations	Dec. 5
The Avenger	February 12
The Beginning	May 4
The Body and the Blood	Sept. 6
The Everlasting Crown	Nov. 6
The Fall of Babylon	Dec. 29
The Fear of the Lord	July 23
The Fool	March 7
The Fool's Heart	January 16
The Gate	October 5
The Glory of God	January 24
The God Who Rescues	April 22
The Good Shepherd	May 1
The Highest Heavens	May 24
The Holy Spirit	October 10
The King of Glory	January 30
The Lamb's Book of Life	Dec. 30
The Last Days	Dec. 24
The Law of the Spirit	October 28
The Light of Jesus	Sept. 20
The Living God	July 5
The Lord Confides	February 1
The Lord Hears Our Cry	January 12
The Lord is Our Refuge	January 9
The Lord is Righteous	June 29
The Lord Loves Those Who Love Him	July 30
The Lord Upholds the Fallen	July 17
The Lord Victorious	February 23

TITLE	DATE
The Lord Provides Our Needs	August 21
The Lord's Banner	March 16
The Lord's Chosen	July 21
The Love of God Brings Unity	July 3
The Name	June 24
The Only True One	January 22
The Power of the Cross	Nov. 3
The Power of the Tongue	Dec. 11
The Promises of God	April 10
The Qualities of Faith in Christ	Dec. 15
The Reason for Our Hope	Dec. 14
The Root	Nov. 30
The Savior of the World	August 24
The Solid Rock	March 29
The Sluggard Finds Nothing at Harvest Time	August 11
The Task Before Us	October 22
The Temple	July 2
The Throne of God	February 27
The Unknown God	October 21
The Vastness of our God	May 20
The Veil is Torn	Sept. 7
The Virtue of Wisdom	July 26
The Voice of the Lord	February 5
The Ways of the Lord are Righteousness	August 5
The Weight of Sin	February 9
The Wisdom of His Works	May 7
The Word of God	July 20
The Work of His Hands	April 26
The Yield of the Harvest	March 23
Things the Lord Hates	July 28
Thirsting of Our Souls	March 19
Through the Darkness	February 24
Through Love and Faithfulness	August 7
Time of Judgment	Dec. 27
To the End	February 28
Today You will be With Me in Paradise	Sept. 28
Train a Child	August 13
Treasures of Wisdom and Knowledge	Nov. 24
Tremble at His Presence	May 23
True Obedience	August 23
Trust in Him	March 11
Unclean	Sept 10
Understanding His Precepts	June 1

TITLE	DATE
Unequally Yoked	Nov. 12
Unfailing Love	January 15
Unfolding Your Word	June 14
Unless the Lord Builds the House	June 27
Unlimited Supply	May 18
Unreliability of Man	February 20
Unshakeable Trust	June 25
Unwavering Faith	October 23
Vengeance is Mine, Says the Lord	August 15
Victory	January 26
Vigilance	Sept. 5
Wages of Sin Are Death	October 27
Walk in Wisdom and Keep Safe	August 19
Walking With Jesus	Nov. 11
Watch and Pray	Sept. 14
We are Children of God	Dec. 18
We Are God's Temple	Nov. 4
We Cannot Hide From God	July 9
We Cannot Serve God and Money	Sept. 24
We Will See His Face	January 13
We Reap What We Sow	Nov. 13
What Measure You Use	Sept. 19
What Must we do to be Saved?	October 20
When the Spirit of Man Departs	July 18
When We Sin	February 17
When We Wander	April 2
Where Are You, Lord?	January 11
Where is Our God?	February 21
With the Lord, There is no Time	Dec. 16
Who is Like the Lord?	May 22
Who May live on Your Holy Hill?	January 17
Yielding to God	July 1
You Are My God	July 11

www.ingramcontent.com/pod-product-compliance
Lightning Source LLC
LaVergne TN
LVHW091532060526
838200LV00036B/574